ierra Liona at abt. 2 Leagues dist

om the Shoar

D. Tho.Will

Cape Jagrain at E¼.NE. about 8 Leagues

A. Here is a passage for Ships
B. Cape Jagrain . C. an Isl.d

Negros going abard Ships with Provisions in their Canoes

Captain Ino.Thomas's house

Mille

an Idol
or
Grigri

a Negro praying to ÿ Idol

Negros drinking and smoaking

Entry

CALUMET COLLEGE

EAST CHICAGO, INDIANA

Soldier in Paradise

Also by Louise Collis

Novels
WITHOUT A VOICE
A YEAR PASSED
AFTER THE HOLIDAY
THE ANGEL'S NAME

Historical Essays
SEVEN IN THE TOWER

Biography
THE APPRENTICE SAINT

Soldier in Paradise

The Life of
Captain John Stedman
1744—1797

Louise Collis

Harcourt, Brace & World, Inc.
New York

First American edition 1966
Library of Congress Catalog Card Number: 66–19484
Printed in the United States of America

ACKNOWLEDGEMENTS

My particular thanks are due to Mr Stanbury Thompson, for permission to quote from his edition of *The Journal of John Gabriel Stedman* (Mitre Press, 1962). Chapters I–V and XIX could not have been written without his generous co-operation.

I am indebted also to Miss Catherine Bull for quotations from John Newton's *Journal of a Slave Trader*, ed. Bernard Martin and Mark Spurrell (Epworth, 1962); to Yale University for quotations from *Boswell in Holland*, ed. Frederick A. Pottle (McGraw-Hill, 1952); and to Mr F. C. Heath Caldwell for quotations from Nicholas Owen's *Journal of a Slave-Dealer*, ed. Eveline Martin (Routledge, 1930).

In Chapters I to VI all quotations unless otherwise stated are from *The Journal of John Gabriel Stedman, 1744–1797*, ed. Stanbury Thompson, 1962. In Chapters VI to XIX all quotations unless otherwise stated are from Stedman's *Narrative of a Five Years' Expedition Against the Revolted Negroes of Surinam*, 1796.

CONTENTS

ILLUSTRATIONS

(Between pages 60 and 61)

All the illustrations were drawn by Stedman while in Surinam and are taken from his *Narrative of a Five Years' Expedition Against the Revolted Negroes of Surinam.* Nos. 2, 4, 5, 6, 8, 9, 13, 18 were engraved for the printers by William Blake. Nos. 1 and 3 by Bartolozzi. Endpapers: People and places on the Guinea coast of Africa, from Barbot's *Description of the Coasts of North and South Guinea.*

Soldier in Paradise

I

THE STEDMAN FAMILY

The Stedman family would scarcely be known to history were it not for the prodigious, if erratic, industry of John Gabriel Stedman, captain in the Scots Brigade of the Dutch army. From an early age, he made a habit of keeping a diary, a labour in which he persevered, despite a strongly gregarious nature that took him from his desk to dances, bars, bawdy houses; and an aggressive spirit necessitating many fights with persons by whom he supposed himself to have been insulted.

Like Boswell, his contemporary, he was immensely interested in his own activities and reactions to circumstance. Though sometimes silly, he had a passion for justice, humanity and truth. This extreme temperament led him into many adventures in different parts of the world, won him hosts of friends and enemies, and gave his writings a sharpness and an individuality that bring the eighteenth century to life in a manner hardly surpassed by more famous men of his age.

For his struggles to earn a decent living, and the shifts to which he was put to make ends meet, his protests against what seemed an immutable scheme of things render him more immediately comprehensible to us who have largely lost the calm and leisured views induced by ample private means. He had not time for the devotion to civilized elegance of a Lord Chesterfield, though he tried to practise the code of a gentleman in all situations. Boswell's pursuit of celebrity and literary evenings in coffee houses were beyond the reach of such as Stedman. He was as far from the high class gossip of a Horace Walpole as the average professional man, or soldier, of today.

His father, Robert Stedman, was a Scotsman, the son of a minister and vaguely related to Lord Elgin. As there was little money in the family, the sons were strongly advised to go into trade and make a fortune. Robert Stedman thought this prospect unattractive and felt that an army career would suit him much better. It was a wise decision. A handsome, dashing, active man, he had not the remotest aptitude for business. He therefore bought a commission in the Scots Brigade in Holland. This was a mercenary regiment, maintained by the Dutch since the sixteenth century, the time of their successful revolt against Spanish rule. By the eighteenth century, however, though still offering a possible career for gentlemen's sons, the Scots Brigade had become a sort of Foreign Legion. While the colonel was Scotch, the officers were not invariably so. The rank and file were open to all nationalities.

In 1735, Robert Stedman found himself posted to Bergen op Zoom, a garrison town near the frontier between Holland and the southern Netherlands, which belonged to Austria at that time, though the Dutch were allowed by treaty to occupy certain key fortresses.

Here he met and married a young woman 'descended of a very respectable family'*, having had the right to the title Count of the Holy Roman Empire since 1562, though without any particular fortune to sustain it. However, they were comfortably off and had connections that proved useful to Robert Stedman in his efforts to gain promotion in the army. He had no money to spare for the purchase of higher commissions and could not hope to rise unless there should be a war, giving him an opportunity of distinguishing himself in the field. The small property he owned in Scotland had almost vanished under careless management. He was also much incommoded by a rash generosity.

These things his wife gradually learned during the first years of her marriage, enduring continual miscarriages meanwhile. John Stedman was her ninth child and the first to be born alive. Under such circumstances, it is hardly surprising that her nerves suffered and a latent unbalance and ferocity of character began to develop.

For life was both boring and frustrating to persons of ambition in eighteenth-century Holland. It was a country in decline from a period of greatness, during which the Dutch had captured the carrying trade of the entire European coast from Lisbon to the

* *The Journal of John Gabriel Stedman* 1744–1797, ed. Stanbury Thompson, 1962. The manuscripts here first collected and published by Mr Thompson, consist of an autobiographical sketch of Stedman's early life and various other short diaries. Until Chapter VI, all quotations are from this source, unless otherwise stated.

Baltic. Their ships were to be seen in Indian waters, in Japan, off Guinea, Guiana, Brazil and the West Indies. The East and West India Companies had been formed to exploit the wealth of tropical lands: the spices of Java and the Moluccas; the luxurious silks, porcelains and lacquers of the empires of China and Japan; the sugar and coffee of the West Indies and Guiana; the slaves of Africa. They conquered Ceylon and Formosa. Their trading posts were scattered throughout the East. They sailed round Australia, discovered New Zealand and penetrated into the unknown South Pacific. Their East India Company was far richer and more formidably organized than that of their chief rivals, the English.

The entrepôt for this vast traffic was Amsterdam, a city of canals, like Venice, and similarly built on a foundation of innumerable wooden piles driven into the mud. Venice, too, had had the eastern trade and her galleys had coasted the Mediterranean with precious cargoes. Venetian merchants and bankers had been among the richest and most magnificent of the late Middle Ages. But, in 1498, Vasco da Gama rounded the Cape of Good Hope. From that time, the importance of the old trade routes across Asia to the Levant declined and, with them, Venice.

In the Dutch case, it was not new discovery, but a straight fight with a powerful nation which brought their halcyon period to an end. The English navy proved stronger and more skilful than the Dutch. Moreoever, they allied themselves with the French during the seventeenth century, whose army had no difficulty in invading Holland; for the country was too small to support a large army as well as a navy and huge merchant fleet. Laws were also enacted in England that had an extremely adverse effect on the carrying trade, much of which passed through English ports.

These reverses, together with a series of disastrous wars, had so reduced the Dutch power by the eighteenth century, that they were no longer a danger to anybody. The merchants of Amsterdam were still rich, for they had taken up international banking with success. Yet, it was a matter of individual fortune only. The country as a whole was impoverished and the armed forces practically non-existent.

In addition, the Dutch constitutional system was so antiquated

13

and cumbersome and decentralized that, unless the chief posts happened to be occupied by strong personalities, the government could scarcely be made to work effectively. The condition was the more aggravated in 1741 in that the office of stadholder, or head of the state, was in abeyance.

At this time war broke out in Europe between Prussia and England on the one hand, and France and Austria on the other. It was a period of continual struggle among the nations, some of whom were anxious to aggrandize themselves by conquering their neighbours and others, such as France and England, desired to become rich by expanding their trade from India to America, as the Dutch had done before them.

Holland was most anxious to remain neutral for as long as possible. Owing to corruption in the civil service, only eight ships in the navy were found to be seaworthy and the army was totally inadequate, even for the defence of fortified posts. A recruiting campaign was therefore started for the Scots Brigade. Robert Stedman was given a captain's commission on condition that he recruited a company in Scotland at his own expense. He was responsible for keeping the force up to full strength, no matter what the rate of death and desertion. This, combined with his open-handed way with money and his inability to prevent himself being cheated, completed the ruin of his fortunes. The little estate in Scotland had to be sold for what it would fetch after years of mismanagement.

The spring of 1744 found Robert Stedman at Dendermonde on the Scheldt, awaiting a French invasion. His wife was with him, pregnant for the ninth time, 'she praying heaven . . . that she might have one living child'. It seemed, on the face of it, an un-likely prayer to be granted to a delicate woman in these circum-stances of barrack life and impending battle. Yet, contrary to all expectation, John Stedman came safely into the world.

The war continued with a distressing sameness, the Dutch retreating after engagements which the French invariably won. Their commanders were superior and their forces better equipped and trained than the heterogeneous Dutch army. At the battle of Roucoux, for instance, in 1746, 'my father assisted most gallantly though the French gained the day', and Mrs Stedman devoted herself to the care of the wounded, who were daily brought into the camp on litters. There seemed to be no hope of preventing the French from taking the whole Netherlands, if they chose.

At the sack of Bergen op Zoom in 1747, Mrs Stedman's mother had such terrible experiences that she died shortly afterwards in Delft, to which she had fled. Mrs Stedman was obliged to attend her last illness, leaving her son in his father's care. A young soldier was appointed to guard him.

One day, as they were playing with a couple of loaded pistols in the kitchen, the youth carelessly fired at the child from a range of two feet, in order to demonstrate the use of arms. Several bullets grazed his head and passed through the cook's skirt before lodging in the chimney stack. He was also blinded by the explosion. It was thought he would die or, at least, lose his sight. However, such was the strength of his constitution, that he recovered in a month or so, though his face was scarred for life where grains of gunpowder had had to be picked out with a needle.

When Mrs Stedman was informed of the accident to her ninth and only child, she fell down in a fit on the deck of the boat on which she was returning from Delft. One feels Captain Stedman must have had a bad time all round. As for the young soldier, he disappeared into the countryside and was not seen again for a considerable period. But, at the earnest solicitation of a certain Miss Susan, he was eventually forgiven and, strange to say, received back into favour.

The next year, 1748, proved a landmark: Mrs Stedman bore a second son, her only other child to survive infancy. He was named William, after the Prince of Orange and George after the King of England. And the war came to an end with the treaty of Aix-la-Chapelle. The French had been defeated at sea and the English on land. As neither could subdue the other further, it was pointless to continue hostilities. This was the greatest possible relief to the Dutch, more helpless than ever since 1745, when the Duke of Cumberland had been obliged abandon his allies, on account of the Stuart rebellion.

Prince Charles had spent his boyhood dreaming of the moment when, to the acclamations of his grandfather's subjects, he would mount the throne of England and live happily ever after. It was a natural thing in one so young and proud and of such a romantic temperament. The French, seeing their chance to use him in the struggle with England, promised a fleet, an invasion, money, everything necessary. They did assemble a fleet of transports, but these were so badly damaged in a sudden storm off Brest, that the invasion had to be abandoned.

If the Young Pretender had been a man of common sense, he would have, at least, postponed the great adventure of his life to some more propitious occasion. But he could not. Carried away by excitement and false information, he landed, in the Hebrides without any troops at all. Many of his countrymen rallied to him, it was true. On the other hand, many did not. He found himself captain of a horde of wild clansmen, very different from the disciplined Scots Brigade that Robert Stedman knew. Brought up amongst the gloomy splendours of Albano, the prince must have found them very uncouth. However, he made efforts to reciprocate the overwhelming loyalty they offered by wearing a kilt, drinking whisky, eating porridge and learning suitable phrases in Gaelic.

The sequel was inevitable. The mass of his proposed subjects preferred George II and everything he stood for. Confronted by this brutal truth, the prince retreated. All his hopes and plans and aspirations had been reduced to mere theatricals, as though he acted scenes from some ridiculous opera. The defeat at Culloden in 1746 finished him.

Thereafter, he was a fugitive, a broken man, subject to chattering nightmares in which he would exclaim, 'O God, poor Scotland!' Or, mutter incomprehensibly in French, or in Italian, his companions were not sure which, their knowledge of either being extremely small. Yet still, he had sufficient faithful friends to save him from capture and death. Disguised as a lady's maid, under the name of Betty Bourke, he was rowed to Skye in an open boat by the indomitable Flora Macdonald. Several of the local people recognized him, though they kept quiet. He was too tall and strongly built to make a convincing servant girl. Besides, as he himself remarked, 'I have so odd a face that no man ever saw me but that he would know me again.'*

* See Boswell's *Journal of a Tour to the Hebrides with Samuel Johnson*, 1785. The tour took place in 1773 when many of the people connected with the prince's last adventures were still alive.

John Stedman had no sympathy at all for this sad figure of a prince, Scottish though he was. Echoing the sentiments of the vast majority of Englishmen, he notes severely in his *Journal* under 1746: 'This was the time when the glorious Duke of Cumberland put an end to the rebellion by beating the Highlanders at Culloden.'

II

THE DUTCH SCENE

Peace having descended on a more or less ruined Holland, the Stedman family settled down to the usual army routine of posting from one garrison to another, perhaps taking a *trek schuit*, or covered barge, drawn by a horse, unless the whole regiment was moving together. These vessels plied the canals like buses, keeping to a punctual timetable and providing an easy and comfortable method of travel, especially for a family with babies and luggage.

Everybody used them, rich and poor. Foreign visitors were especially struck by such democratic arrangements. One might sit down beside the burgomaster of one of the great cities, as happened to Mrs Calderwood, a Scotch lady who took a holiday in the Netherlands in 1756.* The burgomaster spoke English and was so polite and unassuming. His carriage met him at the quay.

As the Stedmans were quite grand, in their own way, they would certainly have hired the private cabin, as did Mrs Calderwood. It 'is like a little closet with seats round it,' she notes, 'and plenty of cushions; if you incline to sleep, you may lay yourself out on the bench at your ease.'

To face the common cabin, it was necessary to be a native of the country. This was not from any dirtiness on the part of the inhabitants – on the contrary, the Dutch were renowned for their washing, scrubbing and polishing. It was the smoke. 'To a stranger it is very odd to see . . . everybody smoking tobacco all day long – even the little boys of ten and eleven years old, as well as others, few people being long without a pipe in their mouths, let them do what they will.'† 'When a scoot passes,' adds Mrs Calderwood, having observed the phenomenon from the bank, 'you see the smoke stoving out at the windows.'

Once safely ensconced in the private cabin, however, reclining on the excellent cushions, one could admire the flat fields gliding

---

* See *A Journey in England, Holland and the Low Countries* by Margaret Calderwood, 1756.
† *A Tour Through Holland, Flanders and Part of France* by Cornelius Cayley, 1777.

past, the neat cultivation, villages in the distance, the little bridges. Sometimes the reeds were rather too high and shut off the prospect. That would be a moment to open a basket of nourishing Dutch provisions.

At intervals, one would meet another *trek schuit*, or a hay barge 'perhaps fifty or sixty foot long, and broad in proportion'* with all the haymakers asleep on the top. 'Then there were scoots loaded with peats as large, and others loaded with baskets full of herbs.'*

For those less interested in simple views, the slow progression through the countryside was apt to prove tedious: 'I travelled between Leyden and Utrecht nine hours in a sluggish *trek schuit* without any companion, so that I brooded over my own dismal imaginations,' Boswell noted peevishly in 1763.†

We don't know in what manner the Stedmans diverted themselves, but Captain Stedman had become sufficiently Dutch to enjoy his pipe. 'As to the women smoaking, there is no such thing,' Cornelius Cayley grudgingly remarks. 'I never saw or heard of one; but then they drink tea continually.'

A quicker, though more expensive, way of travelling was to hire 'what they call a ratted waggon, that being the genteelest conveyance'.* It was pulled by two horses and the road was on top of the dyke. Nothing could be neater, Mrs Calderwood exclaims, than the ferry arrangements at canals, or rivers, too wide for bridging. At such points, there were special flat boats, hauled across by ropes. The end let down and one drove on board. At the other side, one drove off similarly. 'This is an improvement may easily be transplanted into Scotland,' she remarks, the memory of many detours round lengthy sea lochs before her as she writes.

On arriving at the new place, by whatever method, the Stedman family liked to explore the neighbourhood on fine afternoons. There were everywhere plenty of coaches, carriages or phaetons for hire, very smart, well-kept equipages 'finely carved and gilt and lined with flowered velvet'.* In one of these, they sometimes went on outings to visit famous battlefields of the late war, Robert Stedman discoursing in a muddled way for, though

* Mrs Calderwood's *Journey.*
† *Boswell in Holland* 1763–4 ed. Frederick A. Pottle, 1952.

only 49, he was beginning to show symptoms of mental confusion.

Thus, while viewing the field of Fontenoy, the scene of a French victory in 1745, he suddenly saw, from the coach, 'a strong human jawbone with fine teeth'. Shouting to the driver to stop, he jumped out and picked up the grisly relic with the greatest enthusiasm, declaring that it must evidently, from the look of it, have belonged to an English soldier. No foreigner could have possessed such a splendid apparatus. Carrying it home with careful pride, he put it among his treasures, where it was found after his death, twenty years later. 'Such partiality had my poor father for the English nation.'

In 1750, a daughter was born for whom he developed an extraordinary fondness. His whole life centred on the little girl, extravagantly. But she was delicate and, in 1752, caught something and died. Nine children had now been lost to Robert Stedman. His patrimony had disappeared. His wife had conceived a contempt for him that was almost past words and which must have completed his humiliation since, though too easily deceived and imposed on, he had been a dashing soldier in his day. Whatever the exact reason, a crisis was precipitated. He went out of his mind and never entirely recovered, lingering on from year to year, a bewildered shadow of his former self.

All practical business in connection with the family therefore devolved on Mrs Stedman. Her husband did not retire from the army; he was even gradually promoted, thanks to her relatives' influence. But she had to see to every detail as they moved from town to town.

English visitors were always much struck by the principal Dutch cities. 'Amsterdam appears to me near half as big as London,' writes Cornelius Cayley, for the information of faraway readers in Leeds. The houses seemed to him like palaces, the food the best in the world, the huge crowd frequenting the Exchange, many of them Jews, quite miraculous. 'In general, money is the god that is worshipped at Amsterdam,' he notes disapprovingly.

The Venetian outlook pleased Mrs Calderwood most: in Rotterdam, 'ships of good burthen saill from canall to canall . . . so that the town is intirely a mixture of houses, trees and ship masts from the one end to the other, and this is the appearance and plan of every town in Holland'.

The extraordinary cleanliness was noted by all from foreign parts. 'Ah, Leeds!' cries Cayley, 'when wilt thou imitate it?' The servants did nothing but scrub clothes, saucepans, rooms and the pavement outside the door. As a result, 'their streets are keeped as clean as any parlour floor'.*

Though some people thought the Dutch a slow-witted nation, this was only a deceptive manner they had. 'They do not appear of quick, bright genius; far from it,' Cayley remarks. Yet, speak to them of money in any language and the lowest peasant understood you at once. But Robert Stedman could not even be trusted with his own pay. His wife kept the purse, brought up the two sons, ran the household and, as some relief to her nerves, bullied her husband unmercifully.

The most fashionable residential streets of the main cities were lined with gates containing large glass panes 'through which you see the gardens behind, full of flowers and statues, with walks and parterres, all laid with shells of various colours, or pieces of glass like birds' eggs ... which appear like a raree-show box, when seen through the glass gate'.*

This splendour was, to some extent, misleading. 'Luxury prevails much both at The Hague and among the rich merchants of Amsterdam,' Boswell noted in his diary in 1764. But let one get off the tourist track and things assumed a different face: 'Utrecht is remarkably ruined. There are whole lanes of wretches who have no other subsistence than potatoes, gin and stuff they call tea and coffee.' What seemed worse, they had lived so long in starving idleness as to be quite demoralized. They did not fancy the idea of work any more. 'Most of their principal towns'† had marks of this sad decay. For the Dutch were a nation past their glorious days, defeated in war and trade.

The Stedmans must therefore be imagined as inhabitants of a succession of melancholy cities. The floors might be marble and spotlessly clean, but was the roof sound? The beds, no doubt, were a marvel of comfort, compared with those of Scotland, but sometimes one fell downstairs because rotten boards gave way. Mrs

* Mrs Calderwood's *Journey*.
† *Boswell in Holland*.

Stedman's frontage may have been as immaculate as a parlour floor, but what of the streets round the corner where they drank gin all day for lack of anything more interesting to do?

Unfortunately, Mrs Stedman never possessed the least trace of the renowned Dutch placidity. Painful scenes continually occurred, for she was hasty and inclined to jump to conclusions from which it was impossible to move her by any process of reasoning, or logic.

She had a constant fear, for instance, that her boys, particularly John, would develop bad characters. Let them pick up, in childish curiosity, some object that did not belong to them – a handkerchief, thimble, or piece of rope – and Mrs Stedman was immediately convinced that they had started on a regular career of theft. They would disgrace the title, Count of the Holy Roman Empire. They were bound for the gallows, unless prompt measures were taken. 'A damnable flogging' was the only certain cure.

To us, this seems undue severity and a pessimistic view of human nature. But in her eighteenth-century context she appears as a well-meaning and anxious mother. Though some reaction against brutality was coming in, it was far from generally accepted. 'When Johnson saw some young ladies in Lincolnshire who were remarkably well behaved, owing to their mother's strict discipline and severe correction,' Boswell related, the great doctor exclaimed, in a burst of poetic feeling: 'Rod, I will honour thee for this thy duty.' He would have regarded Mrs Stedman as a most estimable woman.

Things having reached this impasse, the question of John's education became difficult to settle: whatever the father proposed, the mother would not hear of. However, it was finally agreed that he ought to learn French and he was sent to a convent for the purpose. All denominations were allowed perfect freedom in the running of their establishments. One could see Jews in their synagogues, foreigners noted, and catholics at mass, as if it were the most ordinary thing and quite to be expected in a protestant country.

Nothing could be more convenient. France was the centre of European civilization and no one with pretensions to gentility could possibly afford to be ignorant of the language and manners of that country. Earnest educationalists, such as Lord Chesterfield*, were adamant on this point. Study their pronunciation, dress, conversation, eating, drinking, gallantry, all their habits, if you wish to be acceptable in the best society, this overwhelming father exhorts his bastard son in letter after letter. 'The Graces, the Graces; remember the Graces!'

With high hopes and a proper sense of parental duty, therefore, Mrs Stedman left her son at the convent door. The nuns were very sweet to him, he found, pressing into his hand cakes, gingerbread and apples. They explained to him, in French perhaps, the terrible fate which awaited his parents in the next world, on account of their heretical religion. Soon, they had the child repeating 'the Popish prayers and catechism'. Worse was to follow. He became an acolyte at the mass, serving enthusiastically at the altar steps. But, being one day discovered there by his scandalized parents 'with a bell in one hand and the skirts of the priest's robe in the other, I was instantly taken out of their clutches and converted once more to be a protestant'.

It was decided that he had better learn English instead, for the time being, at least. He was placed, for this purpose, 'with one MacWilliams, a soldier and regimental schoolmaster'. But he did not get on too well with this person, who became so irritated at last that, 'for a very paltry offence (he) almost tore one of my ears from off my head'. Roused from his apathy and remembering that he was a captain, Robert Stedman made such a fierce demonstration that the poor schoolmaster, fearing arrest, imprisonment, ruin, execution, got down on his knees and begged for mercy. It was granted. Anxious discussion was renewed.

For his part, Robert Stedman maintained that john was a genius. His drawings and paintings showed that he would grow up at least the equal of Rembrandt, or, possibly, Rubens. What he needed was a really superior education to bring out his natural abilities. Who could be better to provide it than his brother, Dr John Stedman, then living at Dunfermline in Scotland? This eminent relative, besides his medical career, had studied philosophy to great advantage, 'having published *Lelias and Hortensia* on taste and genius, with other valuable works'.

Thus it was arranged. In 1755, John was started on his journey

* See *The Letters of the Earl of Chesterfield to His Son* ed. Charles Strachey, 1924.

to Scotland and the new life, in charge of 'one Clephen Malcolm, a Highlander, who had been a soldier and a gentleman's servant'. John was eager to go, for it seemed to him that nothing could be worse than his mother's methods of character training. He was sorry to leave his father and cried a little on saying goodbye, though not nearly in so heartfelt a manner as at parting from a small girl called 'Alida Paris, of whom I was desperately fond'.

He soon found, however, that Clephen Malcolm, though carefully selected and well paid to look after him, was totally unsuited to the job of escort to an unprotected boy. He was mostly drunk and of an extremely brutal temper. The slightest thing put him in a vile rage and he would knock the child about until he was bruised all over.

At last the boat from Scotland came and prepared to return to the Firth of Forth. John now thought he might be more protected from the savage into whose care he had been confided by a trustful father; for two officers of the regiment were also to take passage. In this he was mistaken. With the careless inhumanity which underlay the civilized glitter of eighteenth-century life, they would kick him down companionways whenever they felt he had made a nuisance of himself.

The ship was fully loaded with gin. Arriving at a secluded bay in Scotland, everyone set to work feverishly, in order to get as much ashore as possible before the customs officers turned up, which they did the next morning, and seized the considerable quantity still left in the hold. Fortunately, they did not proceed to sterner measures. 'After a deal of damning and sinking on one side and cringing and fanning on the other,' Stedman notes, 'we all went ashore together at West Wemyss.'

John's final destination was Dunfermline, where his uncle lived, and also several of his aunts, his father's sisters. A horse was hired and Clephen Malcolm walked beside it in a dignified silence, chewing tobacco. As they neared the town, his dourness lifted to a remarkable degree. He got out his whisky and some cake and pressed them on his charge. On arriving at the aunts' house, where John was to stay the first night, he hung about in an ingratiating manner, hoping for a tip. But, when the good ladies heard their nephew's account of his adventures, they were indignant. The man had been well paid for the job and this was how he had performed his duty. They dismissed him with ignominy at once.

Just before supper, Dr Stedman appeared. Here was inhumanity in a new form: remote, rapt in the higher reaches of the intellectual sphere, a tall, thin figure, dressed in white, a member of the philosophical set. 'How does your father, sir?' this personage enquired politely of his nephew and prospective pupil. These were the only words he spoke to him throughout the evening.

III

THE PHILOSOPHIC UNCLE

The eighteenth century was the great age of the philosopher. It was a time when received ideas were questioned and new theories of government, divinity, science, economics, and political practice eagerly discussed. With the expansion of trade and empire, the world began to appear in a different perspective. Christianity, for instance, was far from being the dominant religion. Was it reasonable to suppose that so many millions of Indians and Chinamen had been created by God simply in order that they might feed the fires and torture chambers of hell? But, once one began applying the test of reason to God's mysterious ways, his very existence became difficult to demonstrate. At best, he became a vague kind of Supreme Being, presiding with ethereal benevolence from some post beyond the stars.

Studies in astronomy and chemistry, also, revealed a state of things very different from what had hitherto been generally supposed. All sorts of phenomena were found to have laws which, once discovered, could be worked out in a logical manner, thus making it unnecessary to say that they were activated by supernatural agencies.

The liberation of the intellectual faculty extended also to politics. By what right had some men authority over others? Certainly not a divine right, as the Stuart kings had been accustomed to claim. If it was to be supposed that people were born free and equal and had voluntarily placed themselves under the direction of selected leaders, it followed that sovereignty ultimately resided amongst the populace and that governments which did not look after the happiness and best interest of the nations under their care were unworthy.

In this connection, could it be said that the Negro slaves had consented to their captivity? Or the American colonists agreed to taxes and trade restrictions laid down in a country beyond the ocean and clean contrary to what they believed to be necessary for their future prosperity?

Again, the omnipotence of God having been much diminished by the light of reason, it seemed clear that free-thinking and the whole multiplicity of sects had a right to toleration. And if it was wrong to oppress, whether politically or religiously, in the name of some divine sanction, ought not the inhumanities daily practised on soldiers, sailors, criminals, servants, children, slaves and others to cease forthwith? For these were all sentient beings, endowed with reason and certain inalienable rights that ought to be respected.

What was the nature of truth? How could miracles and the spiritual world be fitted scientifically into the new scheme of things? Was it possible to say that moral attitudes were innate in human beings? Equality and the rights of man, together with the perfectibility of human nature were avidly discussed. Was there really such a thing as the natural man, or noble savage, pure and uncorrupt simply because uncivilized?

The eighteenth century was a time of change and economic pressures, culminating in American independence and revolution in France. Society was moving towards the industrial age. What about the balance of trade, the wealth of nations, the flow of commerce and all the phenomena of the business world? The influence trade in some distant country might have on matters seemingly unconnected with it much nearer home, was beginning to be appreciated.

All this meant that ideas, which were not always new so much as received with a new excitement and interest, were widely disseminated among the educated class. They were particularly fascinating to persons who considered that the existing social and political system gave them small opportunity for the exercise of talents they were sure they possessed.

Such notions and many others more abstruse, eccentric, and of implications hardly realized by their authors were fermenting in the heads of thousands of philosophers scattered round the drawing rooms, societies and clubs of Europe. Of course, there were many, such as Johnson, who looked on the whole movement with suspicion, believing that it would lead to anarchy, if put into practice. Others, whose livelihood and position depended on the established order of things, were equally averse to innovation. The very principle of reason, so frequently invoked, proved easily enough that the new ideas could not be of much benefit to them. But they could not hold out against the siege indefinitely. By the end of the century, the French Revolution and the American War of Independence had occurred; the agitation for prison reform and the abolition of slavery were under way.

For the fact was that the philosophers were headed by an unusual number of persons of great ability, even genius in some cases. Montesquieu, Rousseau, Diderot, Voltaire and, in England, Hume were all publishing their books in the 1750's. Seldom has the status of the intellectual been so high. Emperors and empresses, kings and queens, felt it necessary to get in touch with the leaders of thought, to ask them into their palaces and treat them with honour. Frederick the Great of Prussia sent his poems to Voltaire for improvement. When Diderot, in later years, fell on hard times, Catherine of Russia bought his library and offered him the job of librarian. He went to St Petersburg and had many long conversations with his patroness; though heaven knows how much of what he said she understood. But reform was in the air and both these potentates were anxious to introduce a little to their subjects, if it could be done without too great upheaval.

The humbler ranks of the philosophers spread far and wide, even into Scotland. Hume was in the act of composing his famous works at Edinburgh while the young Stedman pursued his education at Dunfermline. Dr Stedman must have read them with excitement as they came out, one by one. Perhaps he had met the author, who was renowned for his kindness to learned aspirants.

We don't know the exact theses propagated by Dr Stedman, as his *Lelias and Hortensia* and other valuable essays on the subject of taste and genius have been lost to posterity. It was possible, of course, for extensive study to lead one into curious by-paths, not usually traversed by the main body of opinion. Such a fate befell poor Lord Monboddo. Reading widely, madly, happily all the philosophical books he could lay hands on from the time of the Greeks, he felt impelled to call Hume to order in six quartos of *Antient Metaphysics* and a similar number of octavos on the progress of language. Some of his remarks were sensible; others not so plainly actuated by the principles of reason he endeavoured to apply to the problems before him.

Being a firm believer in the inertness of matter, for instance, he could not accept that there was such a thing as the force of gravity. This was connected also with the proofs he wished to bring forward for the existence of the soul, not only in humans, but in animals and vegetables as well. Not wishing to reduce God to the vagueness of a Supreme Being, or Essence, he demonstrated the truth of the doctrine of the Trinity by means of quotations from Plato and Aristotle.

He persuaded himself that the highest knowledge had originated in Egypt, with the assistance of certain demon kings who whispered secrets to the people of those days. But perhaps his most original contribution concerns the noble savage, or natural man, on whom Rousseau expended so much eloquence: this personage was, he thought, none other than the orang-outang. Here, he exclaimed, one had a being endowed with all the potentialities of an intellectual life and merely lacking the ability to develop them. He supported his contention with passages from various authors.

It can be seen that the career of philosopher offered wide gradations and variations, sufficient to suit the most exacting student. No speculation was too far-fetched to be buttressed by some writer, somehow. It was only necessary to put the tests of reason to any proposition with sufficient ingenuity for miracles to be accomplished. One could live a satisfactory, and even respected, life dreaming and reading the years away, writing extraordinary books and finding readers for them.

It is not certain exactly what system Dr Stedman followed, or what individualities of his own he may have contributed, but he plainly had very definite ideas of child management. While, on the one hand, he never beat his nephew, on the other, he was equally averse to any sort of encouragement. Perhaps with some faint idea of the noble savage, or supposititious natural man, whose favourable development depended on his freedom from the restraints of civilization, he ordered that the boy was not to be supervised in any way, not even as to his cleanliness.

Here, he diverged from another contemporary school of thought. 'In your person,' the careful Earl of Chesterfield instructs his son, 'you must be accurately clean; and your teeth, hands and nails should be superlatively so.' Wash the teeth; have no wrinkles in the stockings; never pick the nose, or blow it, except into a handkerchief; look after the ears and the hair. 'I dare say I need not tell you how rude it is . . . to seize immediately upon what you like at table,' his lordship valiantly continues. Never pick the teeth with a fork, or help yourself with a spoon you have already licked.

Every one of these necessary precepts seemed to Dr Stedman absolutely superfluous and, it may be, even harmful. John, on the contrary, was anxious to receive the proper education of a gentleman's son which, at that time, consisted mainly of a close study of the Greek and Latin authors and a training in the composition of classical verse. The mind was thus disciplined, the memory improved and many essential virtues imperceptibly imbibed, in particular from the well-known events of Roman history: 'There is nothing so instructive, nor which furnishes so many examples of virtue, wisdom and courage,' in Lord Chesterfield's opinion. Not only that, but 'nothing forms so true a taste as the reading of the ancient authors with attention.'

Dr Stedman disagreed, for reasons he did not condescend to explain. He sent his pupil to a master twice a day to learn the psalms and catechisms by heart and, for the rest, attempted himself to inculcate a little geography and grammar. But, as his theories prevented him from insisting that John apply himself and prepare the lessons conscientiously, progress was imperceptible. 'I regularly knew nothing of my lesson,' Stedman notes, 'of which, after the Doctor had heard me repeat two lines, he regularly threw the book on the ground before my feet and then, turning round, marched out.'

One of the many benefits Captain Stedman fondly imagined his favourite receiving was the pleasure of participating in elevated philosophical discourse, somewhat in the manner of Plato's dialogues. His boy would return to Holland with his native genius blazing like a star of the first magnitude and a glorious career of some sort would be his for the asking. These proved the fancies of a doting father. Whether from indolence, disillusion, or tactics imposed on him by researches into the nature of God and humankind, Dr Stedman could not bring himself to converse with his nephew who, every day, appeared to him more verminous, uncouth and generally beastly.

He could not face it first thing in the morning, for instance. John's breakfast, consisting of porridge, 'was served me in the kitchen among the servants, the dish a round wooden cup and the spoon made of a cow's horn'. At dinner, Dr Stedman felt obliged, for some reason, to endure the unsympathetic youth's presence, but could not force himself to speak a word on any subject, even an improving monologue being beyond him, apparently. Supper was another helping of porridge in the kitchen. After that, he went to bed 'up three pair of stairs and on the way to it was a small open closet, with a human skull, ribs, arms, legs, etc., of a man who had some time before been hanged and which my uncle had begun with wire to joyn, intending to make a moving skeleton'. In this job, also, he had become discouraged and there the bones lay, horribly collecting dust.

Under these daily circumstances John, a vigorous strong boy, now nearly twelve, struck up undesirable friendships: 'One Jack Chalmers was my principal companion, who teached me everything wicked'. On occasion, he would be obliged to defend the honour of the Scots Brigade, of which he was a member, having been entered in his father's company as a cadet while still an infant. There were many fervent Jacobites among the Dunfermline youth, who jeered at him and threw things and beat him up for belonging to a government force, thus ranking as a traitor to his countrymen.

As a result of his activity, Stedman became notorious for miles around. 'I was call'd by some a good nut for the Devil to crack and by others a good fire-stick to light his furnace,' he notes. When Dr Stedman perceived the unexpected result of his carefully considered educational system, he was very put out. Instead of showing signs of mental and moral growth, of a developing apprehension of the higher wisdom with which his uncle's study overflowed, the disgusting boy presented himself, day after day, covered with blood and dirt and pursued by complaints of disreputable behaviour, the absolute negation of a gentleman as described by Lord Chesterfield, or anybody else with the faintest conception of what such a position in society implied. Far from seizing this great opportunity to cultivate his soul, improve his barrack-room manners and generally transform himself from a noble savage into a credit to his uncle's care, he went about disgracing the name of Stedman with low companions every day. It was like casting pearls before swine. But then, he was half Dutch. What could you do with a mixture like that? Young John had better return to those foreign parts from which he had unfortunately come. He would write immediately to his brother Robert to that effect.

'I have a letter, Sir, from your father,' he proclaimed one afternoon. 'Go upstairs and pack your trunk. You are going to return back to Holland.' 'No angel from heaven could have uttered a more welcome sound,' was John's reaction. 'Up I flew, pack'd all, and down again like lightning.' Within half an hour of reading his reprieve, Dr Stedman had taken his nephew and the luggage to his sister's house, 'where desiring me to give his compliments to my father and giving me a cool shake by the hand, he disappeared' with the utmost celerity. Once more, he could pursue his studies, uncontradicted by awkward practical demonstrations.

It was now 1756 and war had broken out again, the Seven Years' War, as it was called. The treaty of Aix-la-Chapelle at the end of the War of the Austrian Succession in 1748 had settled none of the vital questions outstanding between England and France. A renewal of the conflict was therefore inevitable. Indeed, hostilities had never altogether ceased in Canada and India, where each side endeavoured to manoeuvre into such a position as to squeeze the other out.

The Dutch wished to stand aside. Their southern towns were still in ruins from the French invasion of 1746/7. They had neither the heart, nor the money for another struggle. The French were ready to offer certain commercial privileges, in order to detach them from their English allies. Their possessions in the East and West Indies and along the Guiana coast of South America were not directly threatened. They settled for a strict neutrality and managed to preserve it.

Against the background of this wide battle, young John Stedman passed an agreeable fortnight with his Edinburgh aunt, waiting for a ship. They had to collect together and sail in convoy, as the seas were far from safe. It was known that the French were preparing for an invasion of England.

When the opportunity came, he went aboard a collier at Newhaven. The boat was crowded with 160 recruits for the Scots Brigade and four officers. These last were not inclined to put up with the tricks of a tiresome boy in the confined cabin space. They told him plainly to keep out of the way and shut up. 'I gave them all so much ado to manage me,' he afterwards recalled, 'that it was unanimously resolved to lock me in the mate's box-bed, day and night.'

'In this dark hole did I lay,' he continues, 'when I heard the most terrible noise of swearing, damning, trampling and hauling of ropes upon the quarter deck.' Fearing it was a French attack and that he would go to the bottom, enclosed in the detestable box-bed, he broke his way out by main force and rushed up the companion-way. The situation proved less alarming than he had thought. They were being pursued by the press-gang, armed to the teeth in a small boat. By means of a brisk fusillade, they obliged the collier to put into Yarmouth. There they 'came on board, sword in hand, threatening to sink us'. Every able sailor was needed to man the fleet against the expected invasion by France. The best of the crew were taken away and the captain invited to proceed on his voyage.

This was not easy, as the convoy had disappeared in the direction of Holland. In due course, however, they arrived in Zeeland, where Stedman and some of the recruits took a *trek schuit* for Bergen op Zoom. He had grown into such a powerful young ruffian and was so dirty and dishevelled that his family did not recognize him, although they were standing at the window, anxiously watching the street. He was obliged to introduce himself to them, rushing into 'the embraces of my enraptured parents, cover'd from head to foot with lice', and also a skin disease prevalent among the troops called the scots fiddle.

Mrs Stedman cried with joy and horror and set to work at once on her son, cutting off his hair and scrubbing him 'all over with butter and flower of brimstone'. Meanwhile the good captain brought out a special dish of strawberries and wine. He enquired at once whether John had been having regular painting lessons from the best masters of Dunfermline. On being informed that this side of things had been totally neglected, he was extremely angry and cursed his philosopher brother, using the considerable vocabulary available to a military man of that date.

IV

LOW LIFE

Holland remained poised precariously on the edge of peace, while Captain and Mrs Stedman debated the next move in their son's education. The important question was: how best to further John's career as a great painter; for neither his father nor those of his friends in whose judgement he trusted had the slightest doubt that the boy was a genius. With proper cultivation, he might well outdistance Rubens and Van Dyck, as well as Rembrandt. 'This was the real and general opinion,' Stedman notes in his *Journal*.

He was put under the most famous artists of Bergen op Zoom, but soon quarrelled with them on the ground, as he said, that they knew even less than he did about art. Couldn't he go to Italy and really learn the business at the fountainhead of painting, drawing, sculpture and every facet of the artistic life? But his mother rejected the idea, chiefly for the reason that he would certainly be seduced into the Roman religion. Also, as she very truly pointed out, though this was a secondary consideration, there were no funds for anything on this grand scale.

Stedman took the disappointment much to heart. With a temperamental revulsion equal to those habitually suffered by his mother, he refused absolutely to attend any art lessons whatever.

The question of his career had still to be settled. He himself had an inclination for the navy. The idea of voyages to strange countries on the other side of the world appealed to his romantic and adventurous nature. Seen from the flats of Holland and the depressing decay of Bergen op Zoom, the East and West Indies, Formosa, Japan and Guiana appeared magical places, hovering like a mirage at the end of the ocean.

His greatest dread was of being trapped in the army. Since he would have no money with which to buy promotion, he could not hope to rise much above lieutenant, unless by some unexpected stroke of fortune, no matter how efficiently he applied himself to military subjects. This was too dismal a prospect for a boy of spirit.

His parents were ready to be persuaded that a naval career would suit their son. A certain Dutch admiral was approached who agreed to take him on his cruise in the Mediterranean. But, of course, it was essential to be smartly fitted out for a ship of the line. The admiral sent a memorandum of all necessary payments. When Mrs Stedman read this, she put it on the fire. No comment, explanation, argument or judgement could have been more apt, or more succinct.

Unable to find satisfaction, or hope of improvement, in his life, John veered from one mood to another with bewildering intensity. Sometimes he would read all day. There were moments when he thought of becoming a presbyterian minister and he would devour improving tracts and books of sermons. Mrs Stedman must have had gleams of hope at such periods. But they did not last long.

Once, he packed a bag with the intention of running away to England and joining the navy there. But he was frustrated by his inability to leave home for ever, as he thought, without saying goodbye to his father. 'He took me by the hand and, with a look which pierced me to the soul, said, "My dear John, shall you thus leave me alone? Shall you leave alone your poor aged father to break his heart?" ' In such an atmosphere, the request was impossible to refuse. The old man hurriedly brought out a tumbler of claret and pressed it on his son.

There was nothing for it but to take a commission as ensign in the regiment. He did so in 1760. His father was immensely pleased to see his favourite boy following him into a military career. He had always believed him a genius. True, the new life did not, on the face of it, offer much encouragement to painting. But who could tell? Though a little confused in his reasoning here, the old man was not so inaccurate in his conclusions as might have been supposed at the time. John's gifts were indeed to be put to good use in subsequent adventures.

An ensign's pay was barely sufficient to exist on. He was abominably poor, but, by reducing his meals to one a day, found he could manage without getting into debt. There was even enough over for cutting a dash as a dandy. He modelled himself on a certain admired Dutch officer 'who not only wore colour'd shoes, crimson breeches and had his hair most elegantly frizzed, but actually painted his face'.

Yet, sometimes, he would have a revulsion and, on one occasion, engaged 'an elderly maid named Maria Esmonds, to teach me the thorough principles of the Protestant faith, which she did, though never to my full satisfaction'. His gay friends were much amazed by this sudden pious turn. But it wore off in due course and he again accompanied them to 'the balls, card assemblies and Play-house, which in this country are a very small expense, especially the last'. The public dances were held in what was called a *speelhuis*. 'These are a kind of taverns and halls where young people of the meaner sort, both men and women, meet two or three times a week for dancing. Here they only make their rendezvous, but the execution is done elsewhere.'* Everything was outwardly decorous. One should especially beware, the innocent visitor is warned, of offering 'familiarities to any girl that is engaged with another man . . . for the Dutch are very brutish in their quarrels'.*

He also enjoyed billiards and smoking in coffee houses. 'I now looked on myself as a compleat man of the fashion,' he notes, and had quite some success with local girls, being handsome and well grown.

His military duties were not arduous, consisting mainly of mounting guard at various points on the walls of Maestricht, to which town he had been posted, and a certain amount of drill. There were diversions available suited to boys of his age. Yet, every so often, he would be overcome with dissatisfaction and a feeling of emptiness, somewhat in the manner of his contemporary, James Boswell, though never with his modish self-pity: 'I have been melancholy in the most shocking and tormenting degree,' he wrote from Rotterdam in 1763. 'I have been at Leyden and from thence I went to Utrecht . . . I sunk altogether. My mind was filled with the blackest ideas and all my powers of reason forsook me. Would you believe it? . . . O my friend, how much was I to be pitied!'

'There are few or none of the English who are not troubled with low spirits and vapours, of which they speak very freely,' remarks sensible Mrs Calderwood. 'They will tell you they are

* Thomas Nugent, *The Grand Tour*, 1749.

36

quite overrun with the hip, or that they are quite hipacondryick; that is the name they give to low spirits or nervous.'

At such vaporous moments, Stedman would cure himself either by getting furiously drunk and smashing up the bar, or else by retirement to the solitude of his lodgings where he would play the flute and violin, make drawings and read. Sometimes his choice of authors was improving: Plutarch's *Lives*, Josephus' *History of the Jews*, Addison's essays in the *Spectator*. At other times, he felt more inclined for novels, taking up Fielding and Smollett. '*Roderick Random* I liked best.' The young officers of the regiment regarded these intellectual fits with the same amazement with which they had watched him regularly set off to his lessons in protestantism with elderly Maria Esmonds.

In 1763, Robert Stedman 'dislocated his hip-bone by a fall from his chair by the fireside, as he was slumbering after dinner'. Though only 62, he had become a frail old man. It was thought he might die from the complications that set in. As always a crisis brought out the best in Mrs Stedman. All the sterling qualities that had enabled her to keep the family going through every difficulty came to the fore: she sent for John, for the best doctor available and lavished on the invalid the care and skilful nursing learnt on the battlefields of the War of the Austrian Succession. He never completely recovered, however, and spent the few years he had left in a chair, on permanent furlough in Breda. But he did not become melancholy. On the contrary, 'he kept up his spirits amazingly without ever doing anything,' as his son remarked, except stare out of the window, sing little ditties, talk of the old days, and occasionally, read for a short time.

John could do nothing to help except scour the quays for English visitors. He would introduce himself and try his best to persuade them into the house for a chat with the captain 'who was so extremely fond of the English nation'. Once, without knowing it, he approached the Earl of Lonsdale in this manner, earnestly inviting him 'to go home with me and drink a glass of punch'. Concealing his surprise, the earl merely said that he had a pressing engagement and vanished with a polite smile.

Stedman was the more anxious to make his father happy in that he thought he saw a chance of foreign service, which might mean several years' absence. In 1763, news arrived in Holland that the slaves in Berbice, on the Guiana coast of South America, had risen in revolt. This was a small colony, consisting of plantations strung out along the banks of the River Berbice. There was a fort, but it had been allowed to fall into such disrepair that the cannon would not work, nor the walls impede the slightest assault. The militia hardly existed except on paper and the Europeans had been decimated by an epidemic the previous year.

Perceiving their masters to be in a state of weakness, the slaves seized their chance. 'To see a colony like Berbice totally ruined and deserted in nine days, more than forty whites . . . massacred in the most barbarous manner, the Fort burnt and abandoned,' wrote the governor of the neighbouring colony of Essequebo, 'these occurrences fill everyone with terror and amazement.'* Well they might, for Essequebo and Demerara were almost equally helpless: the houses were dilapidated, the same writer reports, 'the cannon without gun-carriages, the batteries out of repair, the beams of the redoubt already propped up, the great platform falling in – everything in a most pitiable state'.

Surinam, further east along the coast, though larger, and more prosperous, was scarcely more secure. Previous revolts had taken place there and had never been properly suppressed. Escaping into the forest, the slaves had preserved their freedom and become tribes, living the African life to which they had been accustomed before their captivity. These bush Negroes, as they were called, were a perpetual menace to the plantations which, as in Demerara, Essequebo and Berbice, were spread out along the main rivers. There were no roads through the impenetrable tropical forests and swamps by which the settlements were surrounded. No one quite knew where the bush Negroes had their camps and villages. They might suddenly appear from among the trees, bent on robbery and destruction. The only thing that could be done was to make treaties with their chiefs and try by bribery, presents and sweet words to keep them in a good temper.

If the Berbice slaves were to set up in this manner, it was feared that the colony could never be revived. The plantations were too few and newly founded to stand the strain and expense. Help

* See *Extracts from the Dispatches of Storm van's Gravesande*, ed. C. A. Harris and J. A. J. de Villiers. Hakluyt Society, 1911.

must be sent from Holland as quickly as possible. 'The Governor of Berbice is at his wits' end,' Gravesande of Essequebo reported in October 1763, 'and, according to his last letter, not able to hold out for more than another fortnight' in the position he had taken up after being driven from his fort. Everything had been done to obtain local help. A crowd of Caribs had been given arms. Some ships had come from Barbados. Surinam was going to send a detachment, but there was a sudden mutiny in the army which reduced the numbers that could be spared. Perhaps the whole of Guiana would be conquered by these terrible ex-slaves.

The authorities in Holland at once set about raising the necessary force. Everything took time. Letters had to sail the Atlantic, volunteers be called for and an expedition finally fitted out. Months passed while the hard-pressed governor of Berbice despaired. At this particular moment, Stedman was not sufficiently in touch with his regiment to hear the news immediately. Though he put in an application, it came too late. He was extremely disappointed. When could he hope for another chance of adventure, active service and promotion, should he acquit himself well, and also survive? Perhaps he had missed the only opportunity that would offer of escaping a life of garrison duty in decayed Dutch towns. The prospect of continued indigence also depressed him greatly.

It was with envy, therefore, that he watched the preparations of those of his comrades who had been quick enough to put their names down. Many were never seen again. Tropical diseases, rather than the enemy, carried them off apace. Yet, they accomplished their task. The rebels were exterminated, more or less. Prisoners were hung, broken on the wheel, or burnt alive. 'This seems to me a little too cruel,' Gravesande protested faintly. But it was not a moment to rouse humanitarian feelings in the ordinary Dutchman. Money was at stake. The plantations were in ruins, the stock destroyed. Berbice never fully recovered from the setback.

'I now having no other views than for a lifetime in the Scots Brigade, strove as much as possible to make the best of it,' Stedman notes. To this end, he took lessons in fancy riding from a famous cavalryman. It was considered a gentlemanly accomplishment, on the grounds that it improved deportment and enabled one the more easily to behave on all occasions with that efficient charm and moderation which was the mark of perfect breeding. 'I acknowledge myself at this time one of the completest flecks,' he sighs, 'and was very careless of what was to become of me.'

Hogarth and Rowlandson in caricature, Boswell, Defoe and Cleland in words, have described for us the underworld into which the young Stedman plunged, despite his aspirations to a life that could embrace music, the arts, books and humane treatment of inferiors. The gross brutality, profligacy and drunkenness of these haunts provided a perhaps necessary relief from the artificiality and restraint prescribed by Lord Chesterfield. One could not always be graceful, dainty, ready with the polite response, the apt quotation, observing the best rules of gallantry and becoming dress; dancing a sedate quadrille; listening to Mozart; posing for those portraits of dignified and studied informality at which Gainsborough and Reynolds excelled.

There were many of superior fortune to Stedman who, on a wild carousal, full of gin, burst into some filthy tenement where the girls were so poor, or improvident, that there was not even a bed to lie down on. 'Tables and chairs have often been broke by our manoeuvres in such sad places,' he writes.

Sometimes the women were far advanced in pregnancy, or even too ill to move. 'I have seen a mother take the bed-cloaths from her dying daughter, spread them on the floor and prostitute herself in her presence', in order that the visitors should not leave without paying. Every sort of perversion and depravity flourished in this desperate atmosphere, where no excess surprised, since all had happened too often before. 'Three different bawdy houses in an evening was nothing,' notes Stedman of this period. He was fit enough to stand it without damage to his constitution. One night he and his companions 'drank such a quantity of strong spirits, mostly Geneva, that we lay in the street till day-break'. On another occasion, he was so drunk on guard that, while making the rounds, he fell into a senseless rage and almost killed a soldier 'by running my sword through his belt, cloaths and home to his breastbone'. ,

Such moments sobered him. His friends would seem horrible and only his huge dog, Milord, worthy of respect: 'His sagacity, fidelity and strength were without example. He often fought for me, did messages for me and has carried me over the ice.' Milord alone remained uncorrupted by the haunts he nightly visited. Under these conditions Stedman's debts mounted up inexorably. An attempt to recoup himself by betting at billiards failed dismally. He was reduced to bread and cheese. His shirts were in rags. Mrs Stedman refused to send the smallest relief, though continually subsidizing her second son.

There was, however, a recognized antidote to this situation. One applied for a long leave and spent it lodging with a peasant in some remote, cheap village. Week by week, one's pay accumulated. Thus, one was enabled gradually to discharge one's debts sufficiently to obtain a new lease of credit. One might even save a little. Certainly, one's health benefited greatly from the country air, the boring life and plain food.

His spirits reviving, for he was never long depressed, Stedman set out on foot for Boxmeer, to which he had been recommended, Milord trotting at his heels. He had about a shilling in his pocket to last both of them until next payday. Everything would turn out all right in the end, he was sure of it. He would live by his wits when the shilling was spent. Had he not once most successfully posed as a doctor, binding up countrymen's sores, anointing their boils and concocting mixtures, in return for eggs, bacon and beer? Why, he had even had the effrontery to order a meal at an inn, eat it, and vanish before the bill could be presented. A young man of imagination need not starve. Many courses were open to him. Besides, he was personable and gay. In his experience, girls could sometimes be got to feed him free of charge.

His optimism was justified. On reaching Boxmeer, he sat down outside the inn 'below a large elm tree . . . in deep melancholy' on account of his hunger. Sounds of a party came from inside. Soon 'a numerous company of gentlemen and ladies . . . exceedingly chearful and gay', appeared to investigate the sad figure under the tree. He must join them for drinks, for dinner, the whole celebration. His depression lifted at once and he entered so heartily into the spirit of the occasion that everyone took a great fancy to him, enquiring the cause of his troubles, how they could help and giving the name of a farmer who had lodgers.

Here, he might have settled down until affairs righted themselves, had not his host been a catholic. Payday came round and such was the economy of life in Boxmeer, that there was even enough over for a couple of new shirts. But, one evening, a friar came to supper. The conversation turned on religious principles. Stedman insulted the friar, or the pope, or else both. 'In an instant I was attack'd by the whole family, with flails and pitch forks and threatened to be put to death if I did not leave the house that moment.' Though it was midnight and pouring with rain, he dared not resist, for fear of murder. Six people had recently come to a bad end in the vicinity and each time the criminal had bought himself off. Throwing his sword after him, but keeping the shirts, they double-bolted the door, on the advice of the priest.

These were difficult circumstances. Again he was destitute until his pay came through. Next morning Milord 'gave me a look that pierced me to the soul . . . he could no longer fast and I actually became hungry'. However, luck was still more or less on his side. A certain Mr Vonck, a local magistrate whose relatives he had once met, took a strong liking for him, as did his wife. Since it was not safe to invite strangers into the house without some enquiry, they politely asked him to sleep in the barn while they wrote to their relations. This he did; it was free of charge.

Soon, they were treating him as a son and he, for his part, was immensely grateful for their kindness. Their house and farm seemed like a corner of paradise after his late experiences. He busied himself in the garden, the stables, and among the ducks, horses and hounds. He drew portraits and landscapes; built two model warships; played the flute and violin.

In due course, his fortunes having sufficiently mended by the passage of time and cheap living, he was able to leave this rural retreat. Saying an affectionate goodbye to Mr and Mrs Vonck, he rejoined his regiment, full of resolutions for the future and desperately anxious to find some way of escaping from permanent indigence. His father could not live much longer and his captain's commission would then be up for sale. Stedman had no cash, but one of his mother's cousins, called Reygersman, was treasurer to the Prince of Orange at The Hague. Perhaps he might be able to obtain the reversion of Robert Stedman's captaincy with the help of this person.

Full of hope, he set out for The Hague, putting up with two old maids, Reygersman's sisters, rather well-to-do and 'exceedingly religious and bad humoured'. They also drank, particularly during the night, which was the time when they felt most inclined for theological discussion. Their young relative was quite ready to consider higher themes on these terms. They put him through a stiff course of bible study, the sessions never ending before midnight. Meanwhile, Mr Reygersman wrote to General Stuart, commander of the regiment, asking his endorsement of Stedman's application.

'I lived in the highest spirits,' he writes of this interlude. It was true that he had quarrelled with most of the officers and had a fearful reputation for violence and unreliability. But many ensigns were as bad, or worse. It did not affect their chances, provided they had enough cash to buy promotion. Surely Mr Reygersman's influence and the fact that General Stuart liked him, in spite of all his escapades, would make up for lack of money. Stedman had no doubt that this was so.

He was, therefore, quite unprepared for the general's reply 'which was that he not only begg'd to be excused from giving his approbation, but would actually oppose the endeavour and solicitation with every nerve, etc'. He dared not be responsible for an appointment which, since it had not been bought, must be presumed to rest on extraordinary merit and aptitude for military affairs.

The sudden prospect of a lifetime in his present position overwhelmed Stedman. 'I was desperate and ready to commit any extravagance,' the more disgraceful the better. He went to Amsterdam where the brothels were reputed more exciting and various than those of other towns he knew. Thence, he 'escorted the wh-res like a wildman to Rotterdam to which place they are sent, with whole waggon fulls, to remain during the week of the (annual) fair'. He stayed there, fighting, dancing and drinking with whores, Milord at his heels, until the fair ended.

His money spent, he then returned to the Misses Reygersman at The Hague. The nightly discussions of knotty biblical problems now became wilder than ever. Finally, the old ladies became so hysterical, what with gin and the contradiction of their opinions, that fearing they might fall down dead in a fit, he called a doctor.

They were unable to forgive him this unnecessary exposure of their private habits. How could they now hold up their heads as respected members of the best society, sisters of the Prince of Orange's treasurer? They ordered the footman to pitch him out of the front door, forthwith.

V

ARRESTED FOR MURDER

Thereafter, he continued his career of aimless dissipation, broken by occasional fits of sobriety, when he would make good resolutions, such as learning navigation in order to ship on a Dutch East Indiaman and make a fortune in Ceylon, where another of Mrs Stedman's relations was a governor. But the lessons were interrupted by his falling in love with a wonderful girl, which caused him to feel strongly that it was impossible to leave Holland for any reason, however superficially advantageous. By the time this impression had worn off, his interest in navigation had entirely evaporated.

There was nothing in his circumstances to induce a calm view of things. Sometimes the men were quartered in barns which went on fire, through careless smoking in the hay, and everyone was burnt to death, except those near the door. The private soldiers might escape deserved punishments, or be executed for trivial offences. 'I have known a poor fellow shott for menacing a scoundrel sergeant' who, mad drunk, was beating him for no reason. Another 'was only pardon'd on the spott after he had already kneel'd down with a handkerchief tied before his eyes'. This unfortunate had 'opposed a Corporal when in his cups'. In subsequent adventures, Stedman never saw worse incidents than these.

Arriving at his lodgings one day, he was suddenly accosted by a miserable 'boy of twelve years old, new come from Scotland', a fugitive from the violence of his uncle, to whose guardianship he had been entrusted by parents anxious to launch him on a suitable career. 'He had a cut in the forehead by a hatchet'; his feet were so swollen with cold and chilblains that he could hardly stand; 'he had not ate or drank for five days and nights, only two apples and a raw egg excepted'. This wretched object implored Stedman to save him. 'If you return me to my uncle,' he cried, 'I shall put an end to my life.'

Stedman took him in, nursed him and, when he had sufficiently recovered, smuggled him out of the town with a recommendation to a captain of his acquaintance. For the uncle was roaming the streets, breathing murder against his ungrateful nephew. The captain proved as sympathetic as Stedman had hoped. It was arranged that the child should be made a sergeant so that he would have enough money to live independently. It seemed to be the only way of dealing with the situation. No formal accusation was ever brought against the uncle.

How could anyone imprisoned in such an atmosphere pursue good resolutions for a life of sobriety and devotion to literature, art and music? Certainly not Stedman. These were dreams he had as a reaction from a particularly hectic night out; or when his funds were in such a state as to oblige him to stay in, sustaining himself on bread and cheese, and not much of it at that. But pay-day came at last and, throwing pencil, paper, books and violin into a corner, he would sally down the stairs in the highest spirits, dressed in his least ragged shirt.

Such evenings were liable to end up in fights, though they might begin most respectably by his taking part in a small concert at a coffee-house. After music and coffee, however, gin came on and the renowned Dutch placidity and silence gave way to the reckless brutality which was equally ingrained in the national character. In this state of mind, one was easily insulted and obliged to defend one's honour. One's native country, one's whole moral code had been outraged. During the scrimmage, one might be killed, or half killed. If the latter, one had afterwards to demand satisfaction, or take revenge, unless one wished to lose the respect of all one's acquaintance.

Stedman unfortunately reached this impasse in connection with the proprietor of a coffee-house. The man refused to apologize and, in addition, used some very objectionable expressions. Stedman jumped on him, hammered him, battered him. His wife called out the guard. Somewhat cooled by his exertions, Stedman prepared to go quietly, but, taking sudden exception to the officer in charge, 'I flew upon him like a tiger'. As the officer was one of the most unpopular in the regiment, the soldiers were glad to see him lying on the ground covered with blood and made no attempt to interfere. An enthusiastic crowd, gathered by the noise, shouted, 'Bravo! Bravo! Mynheer, make an end of the barbarian at once.'

After sobering up in the guardhouse, Stedman was next day taken to prison. A complaint had been laid before the town magistrate and no one offered the cash for a bribe. Stedman was given to understand that the coffee-house owner was likely to die from his injuries. If so, the charge would be murder. Thus were his mother's most gloomy prognostications fulfilled. She had foretold precisely this end innumerable times during the last twenty years or so.

The gaoler proved a man of humour and ingenuity. Arriving in the cell 'with clean straw and a broom to clear the place from bats, dead rats and cobwebs', he remarked: 'You are heartily welcome, sir . . . The last gentleman we had in this apartment, sir, had kild a man, sir, as I suppose you have done.' Yet, he escaped the consequences because, 'he was a generous gentleman to me', the gaoler explained. It had been possible to arrange matters so that 'when they came to fetch him to execution, they found him dead by poison.'

The memory of this occasion remained very vividly in his mind, the gaoler said. 'Methinks I see him still in that very bed where you shall sleep tonight; with his eyes fixed and his jaw dropt.' To follow so excellent an example would, of course, be rather expensive. Possibly Stedman was not sufficiently in funds. But there were other, cheaper, comforts of which he could avail himself: 'I sell brandy, Geneva and small beer.'

He might have run on a good deal longer in similar vein, but two officers now appeared. The coffee-house proprietor was dying, they said, wiping tears from their cheeks. Stedman must prepare himself for the worst. They shook him affectionately by the hand and left with expressions of sorrow, shooting the bolt behind them. 'A flood of tears came to my relief,' writes Stedman. 'I threw myself down resolving to wait with resignation the event of future fate, but to partake of any subsistence or sleep was impossible on account of the clanking of neighbouring chains and my own melancholy reflections.'

In the morning, however, he was cheered by the visit of a friend from the Hanoverian regiment who, having bribed his way in, arrived with 'two bottles of claret and some biscuits'. Alarmed by the miserable state of mind into which Stedman had fallen, he made arrangements to stay in the cell with him for a few days, in case he should hang himself. This 'was exceedingly kind', as Stedman remarks, 'and I was sorry to hear he was since drown'd on a sea voyage with many others'.

Perhaps the young Hanoverian saved his life. For, as it turned out, he was never in any danger from the law. The whole elaborate affair was a cruel trick, played to teach him better behaviour. The coffee-house owner was not really badly injured at all. He could expect to be released almost immediately. Such news called for celebration. Drink was sent for and the gaoler invited. It was a good party, lasting till reveille 'when we had finished all the bottles, besides near a quarter of gin'.

The treatment utterly failed to reform Stedman. Rejoining his regiment, he plunged into the accustomed round of amusements. There were no others to be had. His debts mounted at a frightful pace.

It was now 1770 and news came from Breda that old Captain Stedman was growing increasingly weak. His cheerfulness did not fail – he continued to sing his favourite songs – but he seemed to be fading away. Mrs Stedman must have been in a terrible state of rage and agitation, for she was devoted to her husband. One day in June, she found him in his chair, not enjoying his usual nap, as she had thought, but dead. Such was the end of this daft, good man who had struggled all his life to make the best of a situation which it was beyond his powers to master.

'I cried most bitterly,' Stedman recounts, 'having lost a friend who doated upon me, a friend who never, during my whole lifetime, did so much as once disoblige me, who was my whole ambition and I his only delight.' On account of his poverty, a piece of crape round his arm and another on his sword hilt, were all he could manage in the way of suitable mourning. He had, for remembrance, the old man's books, a steel penknife, a silver St Andrew's cross and the portraits he had drawn of him. He would have liked also the gigantic human jawbone picked up on the field of Fontenoy so many years ago, but Mrs Stedman threw it down the lavatory in disgust before he could prevent her. He was lucky to get hold of the books, for she had been on the point of giving them to his brother, whom she considered more deserving of the property.

Stedman was, however, obliged to part with his inheritance almost immediately. His creditors were so vociferous. He managed to obtain ten pounds at an auction held in the regiment, as they were all military works. The only deduction was for a bottle of gin, without which it was generally felt to be impossible to do any sort of business. Next, he applied for nine months' leave to visit relations in Scotland. In fact, he planned to spend it as a seaman, shipping to America, the Mediterranean or even, if all else failed, to the Baltic. His finances ought to have righted themselves by the gradual accumulation of his pay by the time he returned.

He put the plan into operation at once, presenting a self-portrait to an Anabaptist girl with whom he happened to be in love and taking her portrait and a lock of her hair to cheer him in moments of homesickness on the high seas. His luggage was small, consisting simply of a change of clothes, a bottle of gin, a bible, tobacco, a knife and a rather smart green silk purse with the remains of the ten pounds in it.

The first stage of the journey took him as far as London, where he hoped to pick up a ship for America. He did not want to sign on with a Dutch merchantman, in case he should happen to meet anyone who would recognize him in the disgraceful position of common sailor. Everything went well to begin with. He nearly set off for Carolina, but something occurred to prevent the voyage at the last moment. This was unfortunate, for he then became acquainted with a delightful sailmaker's daughter and missed opportunities he might have seized, had his attention not been distracted. As a result, he was obliged to take such odd jobs as playing the fiddle in public houses and heaving ballast on the Thames, in order to keep body and soul together sufficiently to amuse the sailmaker's daughter.

Thus, his nine months' leave passed quite agreeably and rather less dangerously than if he had voyaged to Carolina. He got into a great number of fights with London toughs, particularly in Kensington Gardens, and was once or twice arrested, though he managed to break away before they got him into prison and turned the key. But he escaped drowning and all the fatal diseases to which the seamen of those days inevitably were subject from the conditions of their employment. He was just able to scrape up enough money for a ticket to Rotterdam and to rejoin his regiment, as if from a nostalgic visit to friends and relations in Scotland.

He found his Anabaptist love faithfully waiting at Deventer and at once took up the old round with enthusiasm. He had now nine months' pay to spend and, after staving off the worst of his creditors, still had something left. The perennial dissatisfaction with military life was less difficult to support at times like these. Yet, he still longed to escape. On the 29th October, 1772, the chance suddenly came. As he prepared to mount guard, someone remarked that there had been a rebellion by the Negro slaves of Surinam and that volunteers were being sought for an expedition to suppress them.

He had been too dilatory to join the force sent to Berbice in 1763. Now, he wasted not a moment. Running to the commandant, he obtained instant permission to leave. Another officer was sent to take his place on guard while he said goodbye to the Anabaptist and jumped on to the next *trek schuit* for The Hague.

VI

THE VOYAGE TO SURINAM

Arriving at The Hague, he took lodgings at a public house, for the Misses Reygersman had never yet been able to forgive the exposure of their secret drinking habits. He sent in his application at once, passing the next fortnight 'between hope and fear'. Was the great adventure to materialize? Or was he fated to rot in the garrison towns of Holland? In an effort to take his mind off the question, he spent all his money 'in dressing, going to coffeehouses, gaming wh-ring and d-mning'.

At last the news came through. He had been appointed a captain 'under Colonel Louis Henry Fourgeoud, a Swiss gentleman from the Alpine Mountains',* who was to be commander-in-chief. This Colonel Fourgeoud had been with the expedition to Berbice in 1763. He knew the country, the climate, the tactics, the Negroes and their masters from hard experience. Though now rather old for active service in tropical forests and swamps – he was over 60 – his physical toughness, the resoluteness of his character and his unrivalled knowledge of the conditions to be encountered made him the obvious choice. He was also extremely eccentric, as his officers were to discover, sometimes to their cost.

Now in the highest spirits, Stedman set off on a round of farewells to his mother and friends, galloping from town to town on a hired horse by day and drinking huge quantities of gin by night. Mrs Stedman, still living in Breda, rose to the occasion in a practical manner. It might well be that she would never see her son again. He must be sent off with an outfit as worthy of a captain as straitened means permitted. She produced a silver spoon and fork in a special box, six bottles of liqueur, a dozen serviettes, a fine red handerkchief, two pieces of Spanish brown sugar and a small, but powerful, bottle of medicine. She bought also a hammock with cushions and four blue shirts. These things were

* Stedman's *Narrative of a Five Years' Expedition Against The Revolted Negroes of Surinam*, 1796. All future quotations are from this source, unless otherwise stated.

properly packed in a chest and sent in advance to the port.

One feels that in the pride and agitation which were so remarkably interwoven in her character, Mrs Stedman must have lavished much advice and many exhortations, not all very agreeable, on her son. She must have had great hopes of his coming back a hero, if he followed her instructions as to moral conduct; and deep fears that he would succumb to wounds, enemies or some foreign disease against which the bottle of medicine would prove ineffective. It may be that she abused him up and down and said he had been the death of his lamented father, while trembling with horror and loneliness at the thought of his departure. For this is the sort of woman Stedman describes to us in the person of his mother whom he loved and hated so well.

It was now December 1772, a cold and stormy month to put to sea. Everyone was ordered to assemble on the island of Wieringen in the Texel road, where three new frigates were moored, together with two ships of the line. By the 7th December, Colonel Fourgeoud had arrived to take charge. The 'five hundred fine young men' who had volunteered, were formed into a company of marines and ferried across to the frigates, being saluted by seven guns as they stepped on board.

The quarters were rather cramped: 'I creep on all fours between decks, to help range the chests and sling the soldiers' hammocks. Get my self cover'd with lice,' Stedman notes. As they lay windbound in the Texel road for the best part of three weeks, the men must have been hard put to it to amuse themselves, even with the help of trips ashore to the nearest tavern.

On Christmas Day, 1772, the wind shifted. The fleet weighed anchor 'with a fresh breeze from E.N.E. in company with above one hundred vessels bound for different parts of the globe, and the most beautiful clear weather'. He was now twenty-eight and the important part of his life had at last begun.

Soon, they were passing 'the North Foreland, the Isle of Wight and Portland Point'. One of the warships was found to be leaking badly and had to bear away to Plymouth for repair. The rest sailed on towards Biscay. The course lay due southwards to the tropics, where one caught the trade wind in the sails and was blown across the Atlantic, expeditiously. Tales of prolonged becalmings near the equator were usually due rather to faulty navigation than inescapable fate. If one kept one's bearings correctly, the wind did not fail, except in extraordinary circumstances, and the passage could be accomplished in five weeks, or so, from port to port.

Stedman was filled with excitement. He felt very sure that a new and better chapter in his life had opened. The idea that many would die during the adventure, perhaps himself also, he did not seriously consider. He was strong and in perfect health, had never had a bad illness, except on two occasions when suffering a kind of nervous collapse. But these were purely temporary. No amount of drink and dissipation had undermined the essential soundness of his constitution. Others might succumb, some of his seniors, for instance, even the old Colonel Fourgeoud. This would cause vacancies in the higher ranks which would be filled by the most active and efficient survivors available. He was resolved, therefore, to embrace with the utmost fervour the opportunity the Negroes of Surinam had offered him of permanently improving his prospects. Already these accommodating blacks had enabled him to become a captain. Before they were done, he might be a colonel, or at any rate a major.

He had kept a journal for years. At last, he would have something interesting to put in it. The time he had wasted, stunned with boredom in brothels and bars, vanished into its proper insignificance. He prowled the ship watching for unusual sights, or incidents with which to enliven his pages. 'The mate of the vessel directed my particular attention to a kind of sea-swallow, commonly distinguished by the name of the stormbird, from its supposed property of foretelling an impending tempest,' he notes and goes on to describe its colour, size and habits. He watched it fascinated 'for a considerable time, skimming with incredible velocity around the horizon'.

Sure enough, as the sailor had said, a terrific gale sprang up next day in the Bay of Biscay. Two of the ships were blown out of sight amongst the enormous waves. The expedition to Surinam lay under battened hatches. The smell was frightful in the narrow space, since it was impossible to have any ventilation and everyone was sick.

Two days later, as they neared the coast of Africa, 'we spied a stout ship to windward in the offing, bearing straight down upon

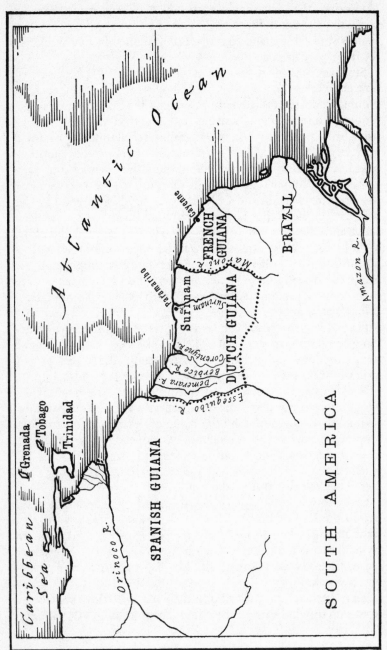

Dutch Guiana

us'. Some people were of the opinion that it was a pirate from Algiers. Only two small ships were now left in company out of the five that had sailed from the Texel. They prepared for battle. However, it proved a false alarm. As the supposed pirate came more clearly into view, they recognized the *Boreas* from which they had been parted in the Bay of Biscay.

As they neared the equator, the weather became more settled. Colonel Fourgeoud drew up a regular programme to keep the men occupied. There was drill and firing practice every day. Unfortunately, the colonel had further ideas for improving physical fitness which were not so well appreciated by his juniors. On his orders, only 'salt beef, pork and peas' were served to officers and men alike, as though all were 'common sailors'. This was 'to enure us (he said) to such food as we were likely to be alone supplied with in the woods of Surinam'. Moreover, 'instead of plate, our meals were frequently served up in small wooden tubs of not the most cleanly appearance and only once a day'.

There was a good deal of insubordinate language among the officers as they faced this unappetizing provender seven times a week and meditated on 'the European refreshments – such as live sheep, hogs, fowls, ducks, bacon hams, bullocks' tongues, preserved vegetables, pickles, spices, etc., all of which were provided by the town of Amsterdam in profusion'. It was rumoured that the colonel intended to present these delicacies to his friends and to important people in Paramaribo, the capital of Surinam, thus endearing himself to all and sundry immediately on arrival. No doubt there were sound strategic conceptions behind this plan, but, in the circumstances, no one was prepared to admire him for that. 'Good intentions do not always meet with their rewards,' Stedman remarks, 'since the worms, without anyone's permission, laid hold of the greatest part of the dead stock for themselves; who were, for punishment, together with their plunder, thrown overboard into the ocean.'

One could only laugh sarcastically as the dolphins gathered round this unexpected banquet. They were a sight worth seeing 'being enamelled with spots between azure blue and a reflecting light sea-green, on a very dark ground, which appears as be-spangled all over with jewels ... The fins and tail are of a golden dye,' Stedman noted industriously, making the best of a bad business.

Sometimes shoals of tropical jellyfish floated past the ship and were easily caught and examined by the curious. Or flying fish would drop down on the deck to die, having intended to plunge back into the sea, but missing the way. Other happenings were more sombre: 'the scurvy and other loathesome disorders began to make their appearance'. People became low-spirited, regretting the romantic impulse which had made them volunteer for an adventure on the further side of the world. Perhaps it would have been better to endure the dismal garrison round in Holland.

What could be more brutal than this shipboard life? A strange lassitude pervaded the decks. The boatswain's mate of the *Boreas* fell off the foreyardarm into the sea. No one threw him a rope as he struggled near the ship's side. No orders were given to launch a boat, shorten sail or heave to, 'in consequence of which, after swimming a considerable time within view, the unfortunate young man went to the bottom'. It was true, there was 'some murmuring' from those who felt a 'peculiar compassion' while watching this slow murder. But it is not recorded that any real protest was made.

In order to escape melancholy reflections, quarrels in the communal cabin caused by heat, close proximity and indifferent health, Stedman opened his box of books. He does not tell us exactly what he read, yet some of it, at least, must surely have been about Guiana, a country where he hoped to realize the dreams and aspirations of too many wasted years.

For this part of South America, stretching from the Orinoco to the Amazon, had been a place of dream and legend since the days of the Spanish conquistadors in the sixteenth century. Somewhere among these impenetrable forests, mountain ranges and cascading rivers lay the mysterious Lake Parima; and on those shores was built the magic city of Manoa, inhabited by golden people, ruled by El Dorado, the Golden King. Here were gathered riches far exceeding anything discovered by Cortes in Mexico, or Pizarro in Peru. It was better than paradise: one might hope to find and to enjoy it in this world, without waiting for the next.

It was said, and confidently believed, that the remnants of the

Incas, fleeing before the Spaniards in Peru, had taken refuge in the fastness of Guiana. Manoa was their capital. There were many other cities round the Lake Parima and elsewhere, all rich and populous, though not actually constructed out of gold as was Manoa. Gold and silver mines abounded, if one could but find them. Temples, tombs and warehouses of treasure lay a little further up the rivers than it was ever possible to go, another week's march hacking through the undergrowth, scrambling up the cliffs, negotiating with savage tribes inhabiting the perimeter of the fabulous kingdom. These latter did not wear clothes, but some had gold bracelets and certain gold plates, or discs, which they might be induced to part with for a hatchet, or a handful of nails.

The Spaniards on the Orinoco thought that if they followed that river to its source, they would surely discover Lake Parima. Indians living on the banks encouraged them in this belief; for it meant that the strangers would move on. Yet, nothing certain could be gleaned, though several persons of doubtful character asserted that they had been to the golden city, had lived there as the king's guest and observed his sumptuous habits. They had left laden with presents: gold plates, beads, fish, birds, clothes, vessels and ornaments of all kinds. Unfortunately, savage Indians had attacked them as they floated down the river and stolen everything. Nor would they ever retrace their steps though urged to do so. They could not remember; it was too difficult; vague but insuperable obstacles presented themselves.

Reading these accounts with tremendous excitement, Sir Walter Raleigh determined on a voyage of exploration. He would reach Manoa – the very name was like a bell, pealing through a dream. He would force the gates of paradise and so attain the greatest glory possible for mortal man. In 1595, he arrived on the Orinoco in a small boat, 'having with me an Indian that spoke many languages, and that of Guiana naturally. I sought out all the aged men and such as were greatest travellers', he wrote in his account of the voyage.*

The Indians, when consulted, said that if he continued upstream, he would come to a great plain on which the people lived

* *The Discovery of the Large, Rich and Beautiful Empire of Guiana.*

57

as thick as grass. Everything they used was made of gold. They spoke, too, of a white sparkling mountain composed entirely of diamonds; they referred, in passing, to silver, sapphires, crystal and most other kinds of jewel. Some, however, counselled Raleigh to go home. The time of year was wrong, they said, the rains were about to begin. The Emperor of Manoa had given orders that intruders were to be killed at sight. Let him return next year, or the year after, and things would be different. They promised to arrange military expeditions, embassies, everything. But it would take time and couldn't be done this season.

These conferences took place in a gay atmosphere. The Indians loved parties and seized every chance of holding one. They were 'marvellous great drunkards', Raleigh noted, and their spirits were so strong that a very small quantity sufficed for those more accustomed to the products of Europe. In Manoa, they were reported to smear themselves with gum and then with gold dust 'and in this sort they sit drinking by twenties and hundreds . . . sometimes six or seven days together'.

Raleigh was obliged to go home empty-handed, but the spell of Guiana had fallen on him and changed his life. This was to happen to Stedman also. Though he did not hope to meet with El Dorado, the magic lake, or the treasures of the earth, yet he was ever after haunted by his memories of the country, the people whom he knew there and the adventures which he had. The five years' expedition to Surinam was to concentrate his energies and give his whole existence a strange, exotic tinge it never otherwise could have acquired. He had a presentiment that this would be so as he lay on the deck, reading the days away.

Failure hardly lessened people's belief in El Dorado. It must be somewhere, for all the Indians swore to it. If they could only have given more precise directions than a finger pointed towards the interior. Evidently, the Orinoco did not provide the best approach. Perhaps the Essequebo would prove easier. Why, yes, the natives eagerly said, it rose 'within one day's journey of golden Manoa . . . But both our English and the Dutch, who have diligently endeavoured to make entrance into the continent by this river, have found it in two or three days not passable, by reason of many great waterfalls, three times as high and more heady than is the fall of London-bridge.'*

As time went on, the Guiana coast began to be settled by European planters, for, whatever the truth about El Dorado, the soil was extraordinarily rich, especially in the swampy areas near the sea. Sugar, tobacco and coffee, for which there was a rising market, could be grown with success along the banks of the mysterious great rivers that might, or might not, have their source in Lake Parima. The only means of communication between the plantations was by boat. French, Dutch, English and Spaniards resigned themselves to making their money in a more humdrum way than by the sack and spoliation of Manoa.

Yet, the dream still lingered. The evidence for its existence and for its non-existence seemed equally cogent. To become really friendly with the Indians of the forests seemed to offer the best hope of solving the riddle once and for all. But they were not an easy people with whom to strike up an acquaintance. Though superficially gay and fond of drink, they lived a secret life, ruled by signs and portents very different from those observed by western civilization.

'Their dreams are to these people instead of prophesies, revelation and rules in all their undertakings; whether in war, peace, commerce, or hunting. They look upon them as oracles; and this opinion puts them under a necessity of being entirely directed by them.'† If their nightmare, on being explained, meant that they ought to kill you, they did so immediately. Their priests were much respected for the gift of interpretation they had and their ability to control the weather and luck in the hunting field. They could produce fruitfulness, or barrenness, illness or health, if suitably approached and paid. 'Thus they gain the reputation of men of great sanctity and extraordinary qualifications, tho' generally of a leud conversation.'†

Those who had travelled among the Indians found them almost

---

* William Castle, *A Short Discovery of the Coast and Continent of America*, in *The Harleian Collection of Voyages and Travels*, 1745. The piers of old London bridge were so constructed as to have the effect of a weir when the tide was out. Shooting the bridge, as it was called, could be done only by small boats at, or near, the time of slack water.

† John Barbot, *A Description of the Province of Guiana*, in Churchill's *Voyages*, 1746.

invariably mild and charming, despite their enigmatic ways. They were hospitable and handsome, particularly the women, whose 'pretty bashfulness (especially while virgins) in the presence of a stranger, adds such a charming grace to their perfections (too nakedly expos'd to every wanton eye) that whoever lives amongst them had need to be the owner of no less than Joseph's continency not, at least, to covet their embraces'.*

The French settlers on the river Cayenne, however, had had experiences that shed another light on these Arcadians. 'They look upon them as fierce, cruel and perfidious to their guests; and it is true,' admits Barbot in his account of Guiana, 'they have not long since extirpated a small nation of Indians and eaten some of them: but this inhumanity is rather the effect of a barbarous custom, than the natural disposition of the people.'

It was felt by certain French Jesuits that to sow the word of God among these heathens would be particularly meritorious. What better way to gain the confidence of such shy denizens of the forests than to open their eyes to the truth about the hereafter and give them the chance of attaining to paradise? One could enquire also, very conveniently, about Lake Parima, for it was not possible that they really were ignorant of its location. One might convert the whole population of Manoa and its dependent cities, explaining to them the great advantages to be obtained by putting themselves under the direction of the church and contributing substantially to religious funds.

Inspired by this vision, two Jesuits set out into the forest from Cayenne. The first tribe they met with seemed to 'take delight in hearing their discourse of the creation of the universe'.† Soon they were repeating in a chorus, 'God made the heavens, God made the earth, etc'.† Hymns took their fancy strongly and they sang them three times a day with gusto. They were not at all put out to hear that it was a terrible sin to have more than one wife, for they did not regard this part of the new dispensation seriously.

Indeed, the good fathers began to wonder exactly what impression they were making. On the one hand, their brighter pupils 'learnt to answer to the litanies ... and made all the children say

* George Warren, *A Description of Surinam*, in *The Harleian Collection of Voyages*, 1745.
† Barbot.

Captain John Stedman in 1772. A wounded rebel slave lies on the ground

Monkeys of Guiana

The slave at Fort Amsterdam

A Surinam planter

A private of Colonel Fourgeoud's force

A black ranger

Joanna

Negroes imported for sale. The masts of the slaving ship from which they have just landed are in the background. A sailor herds them towards the auction rooms, assisted by a dog.

their prayers morning and evening, baptizing some of them and some women'.* On the other, it was impossible to persuade them to leave off their 'juggling tricks and divinations, much less the plurality of wives'.* There were, moreover, three old men who considered the foreign magic dangerous.

Matters came to a head when 'a serpent came in the night into the hut where the missioners lay, and bit a hound; so that he died thirty hours after'.* Nothing could prove more conclusively that the three old men were right: it was no accident but a supernatural happening, brought on by the singing of litanies and hymns. Jesuit influence declined sharply in the village. Nor would anyone give the smallest information as to the whereabouts of marvellous Lake Parima, ringed with sands, the grains of which were 'gold, silver and copper.'* Plainly, it was time to move on, pressing further into the endless, hot, damp forest.

The next tribe, being more remote, were much excited by the arrival of two Europeans 'and in three days became so familiarly acquainted with the missioners that not one of them refused to pray'.* Obviously, these strange white beings were the servants of a powerful god – were perhaps even gods themselves – so that it was only prudent to perform the proper rituals. The news went round and people began to arrive from a distance 'and admir'd their garments, their guns, the pictures in their breviaries, their writing and the songs of the church, which they desired to hear several times a day'.* They seemed most struck by the fact that the French had once been pagans, like themselves.

Yet, in spite of their cordiality, they remained evasive on the subject of Lake Parima, saying only that there was a tribe situated a week's journey to the southwest which might be able to give more precise information. The guides, also, became restive, for some reason not plainly expressed. They did not think they could conduct the foreigners any further up country. There were obscure dangers. It would be better to go home to Cayenne. The fathers had caught 'a tertian ague'* and were much weakened by this time. It may be that their hosts were afraid of having two unmanageable ghosts on their hands.

In the circumstances, it seemed best to comply. The Indians became more insistent on their immediate departure. Evidently,

* Barbot.

bad omens had been noted. They were also very greedy, whether for magical or mundane purposes, and tried to persuade their guests to leave behind them the guns, saucepans, knives, bottles and whole wonderful array of possessions they had. However, the Jesuits managed to put them off with a proportion, endeavouring to extract promises of monogamy from the recipients.

Thus, they embarked in a canoe and paddled downstream sadly, in considerable doubt as to whether Lake Parima of the golden sands actually existed. Perhaps it was only a dream, like Utopia; or to be understood in a symbolical sense, like the Holy Grail, or the philosopher's stone. Who could say? Certainly, nothing could be got out of those natives. It might be true that they could not direct one to Manoa simply because there was no such place. Or it might not.

By the eighteenth century, belief in El Dorado had much declined. But the interior of Guiana remained mysterious and unvisited. Mountains of a strange shape, reminiscent of pyramids, could be observed from afar. Also white hills, gleaming like diamonds, such as Raleigh had heard of almost two hundred years before. There was certainly gold, for the natives had these tantalizing bracelets, collars, ornaments, finding the metal in alluvial deposits along the rivers. If one could only discover the source from which it was washed down. Stedman was merely one of many needy adventurers hoping to recoup their fortunes in various ways among the swamps and fevers of Guiana, or the Wild Coast, as it was alternatively named.

VII

SLAVES

Once the New World had been discovered and the first flush of gold fever had died down, emigrants turned their attention to the profits of agriculture. The land was there for the taking. It was only necessary to clear the natives out of the way. In the Caribbean Islands, along the Guiana coast and in the southern colonies of North America, soil and climate were such that anyone with capital to sink in a large estate might hope for good returns on sugar, tobacco, coffee, and, in Guiana especially, certain subsidiaries such as, indigo, anatto dye and tropical woods. The Spaniards were first to see the possibilities and to encounter a fundamental difficulty.

The local Indians would not take jobs on the plantations. If enslaved and put to work in gangs under an overseer, they pined away and died. Forced labour was so alien to their whole outlook on life, their system of thought, the mysterious hierarchies of the forest, that they could not sustain it. In any case, the Spaniards found, they had not sufficient physical strength for long hours under the sun. Even the stoutest sank quickly. The world was not worth it on these terms. Every principle of existence had been violated.

This did not matter much, to begin with. There were plenty of Caribs. One got hold of another tribe. Or bought prisoners taken in some fratricidal raid. Or simply let it be known that knives, beads, looking-glasses, hats and coats were to be had in exchange for healthy men and women. It was no good. The wretched natives were never able to adjust themselves to the new order, except in a very minor degree. You could set them to hunting and fishing for you, if they were not too strictly treated.

Under these circumstances, the West Indies and the coast of Guiana became depopulated. The question was, with whom to replace them? There were plenty of impecunious European peasants and workmen who might be tempted to emigrate for low wages. But experience had shown that white people were soon prostrated by heat and tropical climate.

Africa provided the answer. The Negroes were strong and energetic. They had the resilience to stand the psychological shock of transplantation to an unknown country, governed by strange and powerful masters. Above all, they were willing to sell each other at a reasonable price. Had this not been so, the slave trade could never have been established on a regular basis.

The Portuguese, the Dutch, the French and the English were the chief slaving nations. Each founded a chartered company to which was granted the monopoly of this lucrative trade. It was hoped that the companies would pay fabulous dividends and every shareholder become immensely rich. In actual fact, these arrangements proved not to be the best. Overheads were too high, for one thing. The companies maintained their own forts on the West African coast – the Dutch had eleven – with resident staff, soldiers, inspectors and so on. There were also agents, or factors as they were called, stationed at various points on the main rivers in contact with tribes and kingdoms further inland. On top of these expenses, the ships had to be fitted out. There was no certainty that a full cargo could be collected. It depended on local circumstances. Mortality amongst the slaves was sometimes very heavy during the passage across the Atlantic. Half might be lost.

The most serious difficulty, however, was the presence of the illegal traders, or interlopers. It was impossible to police the whole vast western coastline of Africa. Arriving at some unfrequented beach, these individuals would bargain with the local king directly and, passing up and down from place to place, gradually fill their holds. Sometimes they bought cheap, having come just at the moment when a king had concluded a successful war against his neighbours and had more prisoners than he knew what to do with. But, if times were peaceable – which was luckily not often – and slaves consequently dear, the interlopers could still afford to undercut the official price in the West Indies. For they contributed nothing of their profits towards the elaborate organization maintained by the chartered companies.

From 1740 to 1770, the price of sugar rose steadily and the plantations expanded as fast as they could obtain the necessary slaves to work the extra acreage. Interlopers increased to such a degree that it seemed most sensible, in England at any rate, to disband the Royal African Company in 1750 and open the trade to everyone. Under the new arrangements, the English forged ahead. Ships from London, Bristol and, in particular, Liverpool carried by far the largest number of slaves from Africa to America. It has been estimated that 50,000 were transported every year.

Throughout the eighteenth century, there were people who condemned the traffic in human beings, the Quakers, for instance, and the Baptists. The philosophers also thought it wrong for intellectual and humanitarian reasons. But these were faint voices beside the vociferous merchant and planter interests. Were the riches of Liverpool to be undermined for a reason like this? Were the West Indian proprietors, many of them absentees living comfortably in their home country with a seat in parliament, going to allow themselves to be ruined by sentiment? For it seemed obvious that plantations could be worked only by slaves. You had to have blacks, on account of the heat. If they were to be emancipated and become wage earners, with the right to refuse a job if they didn't fancy it, how would one manage at all? One would never get enough work out of them. The expense would be terrific. Cultivation would suffer. In short, it was impossible.

Mere decency and right feeling could never prevail against such powerful arguments. It required the fervour of a missionary, the excitement of a crusade, the joyful certainty that one was suffering obloquy in a good cause. The religious revival of the last decades of the eighteenth century provided the necessary impulse. The movement for the abolition of the slave trade was conducted by a close society of earnest evangelicals. They were much influenced by the principles and preachings of John Wesley, that strange, indefatigable man, whose whole approach to life was the negation of the reason, calmness, classical balance and cool intellectuality to which the philosophers aspired. It was not until 1807 that the slave trade became illegal for English merehants. Slave owning continued however, being abolished in Demerara, Berbice and Essequebo in 1834. It lingered on in Surinam until 1863.

Those actively engaged in the business of collecting, buying and selling slaves rarely suffered from doubts of any sort. The people they loaded into their holds on the coasts of Africa were already slaves in their own country: they had been born into that condition; or fallen to it through debt, the fortunes of war, or the results of crime. Their black masters offered them for sale freely, along with other natural products, such as ivory, gold dust and provisions for the voyage to America. If supplies were rather short, they would round people up in the fields and villages, enslaving them on the spot.

To Nicholas Owen, wandering Irishman, retired sailor, and, at the last, resident slave dealer on the Gold Coast from 1754 to 1759, the routine of collecting live cargo for visiting captains was so unremarkable that he says hardly anything about it in his *Journal*, observing merely: 'Our chiefest busness is in the pur-chaceing of slaves which is very troublesome. In the first place you are obliged to treat them all to liquer before you purchase anything or not; at the same time you are liable to their noise and bad language without any satisfaction.'* A quarrel could only end disastrously for one white man alone in his hut on the bank of a river full of crocodiles.

He could not have survived had the local king not found his presence convenient and profitable. 'These people that goes by the names of kings and princes are only so in title,' he notes severely. 'Thier substance consists of nothing more then a lace hat, a gown and a silver-headed cane and a mat to sit down upon.' Unsophisticated they might appear, but when it came to business, no one could be tougher: 'You are obliged to take all advantages and lave all bounds of justice when tradeing with these creatures, as they do by you,' or else submit to being swindled. 'Some people may think a scruple of congience in the above trade,' he admits, 'but it's very seldom minded by our European merchts.'

This extraordinary Irish relic was, in general, perfectly contented with his life. 'It's a dail of comfort to me that I can sit down in my own cabin, after all my sufferings and hardships and injoy the fruits of a quiet retirement,' he writes, his native brogue still as thick on his tongue as the day he left the bog.

But a factor's job was a lonely one, even if he was stationed in one of the forts with a few of his countrymen and a pretty mulatto girl for wife. One was so cut off, so cast away in a measureless wilderness, at the mercy of savages whose mental processes it was impossible to understand and whose actions, consequently, one

* Nicholas Owen, *The Journal of a Slave Dealer*, ed. Eveline Martin, 1930.

could never predict. Owen believed them to be in league with the devil. He had watched elaborate ceremonies conducted by witch doctors and seen people wither away and die after spells had been cast on them. 'There's a great many whites that thinks all these things are false,' he remarks, 'but what a man sees and imploys his reason upon must have some grounds of truth.' They could also foretell the future and discover thieves. He had had personal experience of it. Yet, he considered himself a happy man, for he was a dreamer and, like all such characters, valued his independence extremely.

Persons of a more sociable disposition were inclined to suffer from sinking feelings and as soon as they saw any ship in the offing would fling themselves into a canoe and paddle at top speed. 'The Dutch factor Mr Rawlisson came aboard us to enquire news from Europe,' wrote Captain Thomas Phillips* who had just anchored 'in eight fathom water about two miles from the Dutch fort'. What were two miles through surf and swell? What did it matter that it was against the regulations for him to board an English ship? He bounded on to the deck and, we 'having told him all we could remember' of current events, 'he stay'd to dine with us; and after dinner we found him to be a boon companion, taking his glass off smartly and singing and dancing by himself several jiggs', such were his sensations of release and happiness. The captain was unable to join him in his figures 'being indispos'd and in no dancing humour', as he explains. But 'I was glad to see he could be so cheerful that had lived so many years in such a dismal country.'

Despite an appearance of joyful abandon, however, Mr Rawlisson was keeping a sharp lookout. 'His mirth was suddenly dampt, upon sight of a great twelve-hand canoo with a flag in it.' Instantly, he was overcome by 'terror and confusion . . . and leap'd into a small canoo that was selling fish by the ship's side to our seamen . . . and squatting himself down in her flat upon his belly, made the canoo men row away . . . with all the force they could.'

The captain was greatly astonished, for Rawlisson had not had leisure to explain that he thought a Dutch inspector was approaching. These officers travelled from fort to fort unannounced.

* Thomas Phillips. *A Journal of a Voyage to Africa and Barbados,* in Churchill's *Voyages.*

If they discovered a factor on board a foreign ship, it was to be presumed that he was trading on his own account with interlopers, to the prejudice of the Dutch West India Company, his employers. The penalties for this were severe.

Later in the evening, Mr Rawlisson found out that the canoe carried officials from the English fort, not far off. He therefore 'resolved to have t'other jigg with us; and accordingly we soon had him aboard, where he continued till late at night and was carried ashore well balasted with wine and punch'. It had been a rare and wonderful party for one whose daily work consisted in trying to collect, at a low price, a sufficient store of slaves, gold and ivory to freight the next Dutch ship. A dinner of proper English food was an event to remember.

'O, how I long for the produce of Europe, sich as milk, sallit and a hundred other things that's good for a sick man which I can't get here,' cried Owen, lying in his cabin in the grip of 'a voilant favour the 5 or 6 days' past. But there were only black voices and black cooking near at hand, and in the distance, faintly, the tremendous boom of Atlantic rollers on the beach.

After 1750, the English slaving ships all belonged to independent merchants. The forts built by the old Royal African Company were maintained, in a vague way, by the government. They had no longer any particular function except that of protecting English interests in the vicinity of their battlements. More they could hardly do. Besides, captains engaging in the African trade were resourceful characters, accustomed to looking after themselves, their ships and their money in whatever circumstances arose. Each ship was on its own to make a fortune or go bankrupt, cruising up and down the torrid coast, looking for beaches where the inhabitants were moderately sophisticated: one wanted to get slaves cheap, but it must be a place where they were prepared for callers and had collected sufficient stock to make a halt worth while.

The climate on the Guinea coast was inimical to the European constitution. Heat, rain and mists, sometimes of a strange reddish tinge, bred fevers from which it was difficult to recover. The African villages were full of flies and maggots and smelt horrible, even to persons accustomed to the crowded conditions of eighteenth-century shipboard life. Everything was full of maggots everywhere. They grew like mushrooms. Sometimes, instead of a burning sun, there were 'dark gloomy days inspiring horror and dread'.* Terrific thunderstorms were not unusual: 'The lightning is sometimes so frightful that it really looks as though the world were going to be consumed by fire.'* One might have to drop every anchor one possessed in order to ride out a tornado, praying that the cables would hold and prevent one being splintered in the surf on the beach.

Nor could the seamen be induced to take care of themselves. They would lie down in the open in wet clothes at night. It was impossible to prevent them overstraining themselves with black women. On some days in June and July, a piercing wind would spring up: 'Tuesday 11th June,' noted Captain John Newton in his journal as he lay off the Niger river in 1751. 'Close dark weather and incredibly cold, considering we have the sun almost in the zenith. I think I have felt it (sensibly) much warmer in England at Michaelmass.'†

Of course, no sailor had warm clothes to put on. Any he had had on leaving home had long since worn out, been gambled away or exchanged for what some smiling Negro assured him was real gold, real ivory, real pearls, etc. What wonder that they were carried off apace by 'fevers, fluxes, cholicks, consumptions, asthmas, smallpox, coughs and sometimes worms and dropsies'.‡

Much hard work had also to be done by everyone able to stand, especially on independent merchantmen. The slaves' quarters had to be prepared for their reception. Water and provisions loaded. The ship's boats unslung and sent up the rivers for voyages lasting perhaps ten days, trading with villages and tiresome kings up-country. The goods to be exchanged for slaves, gold, ivory and beeswax had to be unpacked and laid ready.

These consisted of old sheets, red hats, bugles, gloves, glass beads, rolls of coloured cloth, turkey carpets, hammers, bells, drink, powder, shot, muskets, fishing tackle, knives, pewter plates, copper kettles and saucepans, iron bars, sheepskins, pins,

* John Barbot, *A Description of the Coasts of North and South Guinea*, in Churchill's *Voyages*.
† John Newton, *The Journal of a Slave Trader*, 1750–54, ed. Bernard Martin and Mark Spurrell, 1962. Newton was later converted, becoming a fervent abolitionist and a parson in Buckinghamshire.
‡ Barbot.

looking glasses, bottles and any other knicknacks the vendors hoped might catch a black fancy. For one could never be sure what they would like. There might be a rage for blue beads. Or cloths of a pattern previously thought attractive might have been found unlucky in wear and, consequently, were refused with horror on subsequent occasions. It was a terrible life dealing with such uncertainties.

In addition to their curious predilections, the Africans were very sharp at business. Gone were the days when, having got an unsuspecting crowd on board by inviting gestures and acquiescence in certain wordy rituals involving long, incomprehensible addresses and offerings cast into the sea, one could suddenly weigh anchor, kidnapping the lot for nothing. This had, in any case, always been a short-sighted practice, if one hoped to return on later trips.

There were still places, however, particularly southwards, towards Angola, where the inhabitants were not such keen bargainers as they had become on the Gold Coast. 'Some years ago,' relates Captain John Barbot, 'a Dutch ship happening to anchor' off a lonely beach on which a village stood, 'a sloop soon came aboard with twenty-eight Blacks, one of whom had a drum and a hollow stick like a flute; and another whose face, arms and breast were white, held in one hand a green branch and a bell and in the other a little bird about as big as a sparrow, which he now and then let fly off upon the deck, and while discoursing with them he often rung the bell, as it were to express surprise at what the Dutch gave them to understand by signs and gestures.'

Such people were really too poor and ignorant to be worth bothering about, unless one was obliged to stop to take in water and whatever food there was to be bought. Yet, they had their dreams and aspirations. They had glimpsed the great world and wished to share its wonders: 'They take a great vanity in wearing the old hats, periwigs, coats, etc., of our sailors, who sell them for wax, honey, parrots, monkeys and all sorts of refreshments.'*
They would also call themselves by the grandest foreign names they could hear of: Duke of York or Duke of Monmouth in those parts where English ships called, and corresponding titles in Dutch, Portuguese, French and Danish. 'They are all excessively fond of

* Barbot.

brandy and other strong liquors,' Barbot continues informatively, 'which they will drink out before they part, and sometimes before they go out of the ship'. In their cups they were quarrelsome, the new 'coats, hats and perukes' flying overboard in the mêlée. It was sometimes possible to deceive them with coloured water and a little soap added to it for froth.

In most places, however, they were highly educated in the niceties of barter by the 1750's. Negotiations took time, for they insisted on unrolling bales of cloth to see whether a piece had been cut out of the middle; uncorking the brandy to give it a knowing sniff; opening kegs of gunpowder to make sure they were full and had no false bottom. On their side, they would arrive with gold dust that was mostly brass. The captains were prepared for this: 'We pour some *aqua fortis* upon it, which immediately turns all the brass that is amongst it green, to the great admiration and confusion of the cheats.'* Or they might produce ornaments consisting of gold foil over a clay core and insist on having the whole weighed as gold. Here, one had to try and redress the balance as best one could by wedging the scales and using false weights.

Finally, having bought, perhaps, gunpowder, drink and tobacco, for which they had acquired a marked taste in some parts, the Negroes would be in a most happy frame of mind. The canoe was heavily loaded, the distance to the shore might be a couple of miles. They would paddle better after a dram, or two. Thus, they would begin 'drinking and smoking tobacco till they were drunk, all the while sitting a top of the barrels of gunpowder and letting the sparks from their pipes fall upon them . . . by which means they are frequently blown up,' notes Captain Phillips, who had given strict orders that purchasers of these particular goods were 'to put off and lie about two hundred yards from the ship' at least, before starting their party.

'Take heed of such as come with rush baskets,' warns Captain Barbot. Sometimes, they all have them and the minute your back's turned, they fill them with any little trifle that catches their eye, neatly unscrewing bolts and bars, picking your pocket, snatching up objects left lying on the deck, such as hammers, saws, cooking pots, trousers. Never let them wander about the ship unaccompanied, baskets at the ready. Locks, knots, packages,

* Phillips.

barrels may look the same as before they passed, but later it will be found that every container is empty.

Sometimes the local king paid a state visit during negotiations to fix the price of slaves. 'We saluted the Black king of Great Bandy with seven guns,' writes Captain Barbot. The potentate came over the side accompanied by his entourage: Captain Forty, his general; Captain Pepprell, his brother, 'a sharp blade and a mighty talking Black'; Captain Boileau, Alderman Bougsby, Lord Willoughby, the Duke of Monmouth, 'drunken Henry and some others'.

There was much to be settled besides the price of slaves, which were dear this year, the king explained, because so many ships had called that supplies were short and the inland markets were putting up their prices in the most barefaced way. However, he had such 'a great esteem and regard for the whites, who had much inriched him by trade' that he was ready to cut his profits almost to nothing. After a good deal of talk on these lines, the matter was settled and it was possible to pass on to the question of tips, fees, port dues, presents, all of which were payable mostly in brandy. During the discussions, the royal party were regaled with bowls of punch 'at such a rate that they all, being about fourteen with the king, had such loud clamorous tattling and discourse among themselves, as were hardly to be endured'. But, at last, agreement was reached. 'The king order'd the publick cryer to proclaim the permission of trade with us, with the noise of his trumpets, being elephants' teeth.'*

Next day, they came again to confer on the price of wood, water, yams, hogs, calves, porterage and how much credit for goods they could obtain in advance of delivery of slaves. This time, business concluded with a dinner party. The royal table manners were uninhibited, 'both king and subjects making a confused noise, all of them talking together and emptying the dishes as soon as set down, everyone filling his pockets with meat as well as his belly; especially of hams and neat's tongues,' Captain Barbot observed, 'falling on all together without regard to rank or manners, as they could lay their hands on it.' They seemed to munch the gristly bits with particular relish.

'After having drunk and eat till they were ready to burst, they
* Tusks.

72

returned ashore, being again saluted with seven guns.' The entertainment had been marvellous. There was nothing like white men's food. Soon, his majesty's canoe was back again. He wanted to see some samples of the captain's goods, he said. So did the Duke of Monmouth and Alderman Bougsby. 'But it was only a pretence,' his host found, 'for instead of that, he fell a drinking and eating all the while, and returned to town with his company, being saluted with three guns' only, this time.

Such were the rigours of the slave trade. In some ways, it was better to brave the entertainments offered on shore. Arriving at Whydah, for instance, one was expected to pay one's respects at the palace, 'which was the meanest I ever saw,' remarks Captain Phillips, 'being low mud walls, the roof thatched, the floor the bare ground with some pools of water and dirt on it.' A good deal of ceremony was, however, observed by the courtiers: 'When we entered the palace-yard they all fell on their knees near the door of the room where the king was, clapping their hands, knocking the ground with their foreheads and kissing it.'

They found the king seated on a dais 'about six foot square, surrounded with old dirty curtains . . . He had two or three little black children with him and was smoking tobacco in a long wooden pipe, the bole of which, I dare say, would hold an ounce and rested upon his throne, with a bottle of brandy and a little dirty silver cup by his side.' He greeted Captain Phillips very politely, saying that he loved all Englishmen like brothers. He was particularly fond, he added, of the Royal African Company. To this Phillips replied that the company was so impressed by the wisdom and justice of his rule that 'notwithstanding there were many other places, more plenty of negro slaves that begged their custom, yet they had rejected all the advantageous offers made them out of good will to him.'

It was now time for brandy. They drank to the King of England, the Royal African Company and each other. Next, 'there came a repast on a little square table, with an old sheet for cloth', laid out with plates and spoons, for the king knew how to entertain in a metropolitan manner. The meal consisted of stewed chicken in 'a large pewter bason of the same hue with his majesty's complexion' and a bowl of something resembling potatoes.

The king had very definite ideas on polite behaviour, for he

73

had studied these things carefully. 'He would bow to us' during the dinner, 'kiss his hand and burst out often in loud screaming laughter'. But whether this last was because he thought he ought to, or because the sight of people eating with spoons was excruciatingly funny, it was hard to determine. When his guests had finished, he graciously divided what was left between the children and 'his nobles who scrambled for it on their bellies . . . making spoons of their hands, which they would dip in the broth and then lick'd them'.

Conversation continued with the king asking after his friend 'Capt Shurley and we acquainted him that he had died on the Gold Coast at Acra'. Instantly, the king left off laughing and began 'a loud howling and crying, wringing his hands and often wiping his eyes, tho' no tears came out', and declaring, as well as he could, that the people of the Gold Coast must have poisoned the brandy. When he had recovered sufficiently, he asked after certain presents Captain Shurley had promised to send him by the next ship. On being informed that Phillips had none, had never heard of them or been approached by anyone on the subject, the king was angry. He was convinced that Phillips had stolen them and could only be soothed by promises of 'blunderbusses, silks, etc'. He then consented to discuss business seriously.

Not all royal personages were as exigent. There was something engaging and simple-hearted about the Queen of Winiba, for instance, whose capital was a village of 'not above 20 houses', Phillips reports, surrounded by 'pleasant fields inclos'd with good hedges and full of Indian corn'. Her majesty was fifty, stout and 'as black as jet . . . We went with Mr Buckerige (the resident factor) to pay our respects to her under a great tree where she sat. She received us very kindly and made her attendants dance after their manner before us.' During the performance, she bestowed many smacking kisses on Mr Buckerige 'whom she seemed much to esteem'. Truly, remarks Phillips, she was quite right, for he was a most good-natured man.

In return, the visitors 'presented her with an anchor of brandy each and some hands of tobacco, which she received with abundance of thanks and satisfaction', and was 'so extremely civil before we parted to offer each of us a bed-fellow of her young maids of honour'. She was even prepared to do without their services until the captain sailed away, having concluded as much business as was possible in her domains.

The King of Benin was equally affable, but in a far grander way. There was besides a sinister aspect of the arrangements in his kingdom which seems to have been absent from the life of the delightful queen under the tree, and also of the King of Bandy. In the first place, he was powerful, rich and organized: 'The metropolis of Benin is prodigious large, taking up above six leagues of ground',* surrounded by walls and containing 'thirty very great streets, most of them prodigious both in length and breadth, being twenty fathom wide and almost two English miles long . . . and besides these a great number of cross-streets and lanes'. In the markets one could buy 'cattle, elephants' teeth, cotton wool or yarn and many sorts of European goods: and all those streets . . . are by the women kept very neat and clean'. The royal palace was spacious, elaborately carved and ornamented with bronze figures.

'The king of Benin is absolute; his will being a law and a bridle to his subjects which none of them dare to oppose', for death was the penalty. Not only were the laws severe and promptly enforced, but the religious system included human sacrifice. Anyone of substance had thirty or forty slaves, at least, killed at his funeral, in order that he should be properly attended in the next world. In the case of a king, hundreds were buried alive with him in the tomb.

There was also a certain festival when the king rode through the town with his ministers and officials, everyone 'richly equipp'd and habited'. The procession was headed by 'tame leopards or tygers in chains, attended by dwarfs and mutes'. In the middle were 'a great number of musicians, playing on all sorts of their instruments, sounding at the same time something rude and pleasant'. The ceremony ended with the sacrifice of a dozen, or so, slaves.

This formidable king was well able to appreciate the benefits to be obtained from trade with European nations. Business had to be conducted through royal brokers who were 'very honest and just in their dealings', reliable when given credit and extremely 'genteel, courteous and easy to be dealt with', Barbot found. They

* Barbot.

75

were generous with presents of food and drink, even providing too much, in some cases. The only drawback was the length of their deliberations. 'Sometimes it is the work of eight or ten days to bring them to strike a bargain for a parcel of elephants' teeth.' Yet such were their politeness and geniality that it was 'almost impossible to be angry at them', even though the season might be passing and one's crew dying of malignant fevers, which spread also amongst the slaves one had already bought.

If necessary, one could apply to the king himself who was always willing to grant an audience. 'He sits in a room appointed for that purpose, before a fine tapestry, having on his left hand seven very clean bright elephants' teeth on pedestals of ivory.' No one except his ministers was allowed to approach closer than twenty-five yards, for fear of assassination 'or poisoning of the king's idols', which amounted to the same thing, since the king was a god. One had, therefore, to address the ministers, who conveyed the message to the throne and brought back the answer. 'Next, the European's presents, consisting of some silk garment, or night-gown', were handed over, but it was not possible to say whether or not they met with his approval, as he only examined them afterwards, in private.

All these preliminaries being over, one had to get down to the arduous business of actually buying and shipping the slaves. In Benin, it was easy, for the king had seen to it that every convenient arrangement was made. Slow they might be, but one was not cheated and there were plenty of slaves to choose from.

At Whydah, the stock was equally large – Captain Phillips bought 1,300 – but one had to look after oneself rather more carefully. On the surface, nothing could surpass the royal cordiality. 'We were every morning during our stay here invited to breakfast with the king, where we always found the same dish of stew'd fowls and potatoes.' He would also send along a hog, goat, sheep or pot of palm wine for their dinner. 'We usually return'd his civility with three or four bottles of brandy.'

Meanwhile, a man with a bell 'which made a small, dead sound' went about calling on the people to bring what slaves they had for sale to the central depot, or trunk, as it was named. Here, every day, the captain and his officers posted themselves. They were mostly trembling with fever by this time and Captain Phillips had 'such convulsions and aches in my head that I could hardly stand or go to the trunk without assistance and there often fainted with the horrid stink of the negroes, it being an old house where all the slaves are kept together and evacuate nature where they lie'. What a way to have to make one's living. It 'quite ruin'd my health, but there was no help'.

'The king's slaves, if he had any, were the first offer'd to sale.' These were 'generally the worst slaves in the trunk and we paid more for them than any others'. One was obliged to submit to this imposition, as it was a recognized royal perquisite. Next, the most important people produced their goods, each in order of rank.

The ship's doctors examined every individual with the greatest care 'to see that they were sound in wind and limb, making them jump, stretch out their arms swiftly, looking in their mouths to judge of their age'. For the blacks were very cunning and could shave a man so closely that it was impossible to tell whether, or not, his hair was grey. They would rub an old fellow with palm oil till his skin was sleek and shiny and give him a drink to brisk up his wits and gymnastics. If the examination was hurried, one might not discover until several days after, when it would be too late, that one had mistakenly purchased an old man with white wool, fallen chaps and insufficient strength to survive the voyage, let alone fetch a decent price at the end of it.

Anyone stunted, or with venereal or other diseases, had to be refused. Boys and girls must be large enough to be of some use to a planter immediately on arrival. Those too much starved and beaten by previous owners could not be accepted. Sometimes there were complications. In a fit of rage, or avarice, the king would send one of his wives to the trunk. But, next day or the day after, 'he would relent and desire us to exchange for another, which we freely did often and he took very kindly'.

The drinking, swearing, wrangling and general sales talk were terrific. Captain Phillips's convulsions became worse and worse. 'We were oblig'd always to carry three or four bottles of brandy to drink at our bargains; and they would often beg brandy of us under pretence they had married a new wife and must make merry, which we always gave them to keep them in a good temper.'

In other ways, they showed a touching faith in the white man's good nature and magical powers. One night, Captain Phillips was summoned mysteriously by the king who explained that he must not only have a keg of brandy for his new wife, but also a mixture to ensure potency, for he was much afraid of disgracing himself. Promising to send the doctor, Phillips 'took leave and wished him a merry Christmas'. The spell worked. At breakfast, the king was in excellent spirits, 'making large harangues upon the charms of his mistress and other impertinences relating to his last night's adventure'. Precarious health, combined with eternal stewed chicken and so-called potatoes first thing in the morning made it difficult to show a very keen interest.

Besides, Phillips himself seldom had a decent night, on account of two sacred dwarfs who 'would often come begging cowries of us', he relates, 'which we durst not refuse them, tho' they deserved hanging more from us, for we were . . . constantly disturbed by them with a most unnatural sort of houling they kept all night under the trees by our lodgings'. They explained that it was impossible to leave off, as they were communing with a god who spoke to them through a great wooden image.

Phillips was curious to hear the supernatural discourse and went to the ceremony accompanied by 'four of my men, well arm'd with pistols and cutlasses'. He listened for hours and the image made no reply whatever to any of the petitions and prayers addressed to it, 'at which the blacks seem'd to be much surpriz'd, saying, They never knew it so long without speaking before'. Finally, the captain became irritated 'and fir'd at the ill-favoured image, and the bullet went in under its left eye'. The dwarfs and other devotees immediately fled in terror. Phillips seems to have been half convinced of the idol's divinity, for he waited a good thirty minutes in hopes of some communication, before going back to bed.

The dwarfs were astonished to see him still alive in the morning after having perpetrated such a frightful sacrilege. The king placidly explained, over breakfast, that, of course, the god would not speak while an unbelieving white man was present. He knew perfectly well that the idol was made of wood, he said. It was not, itself, divine. The god came down into it at certain moments.

It was a terrible country, full of devils, 'monstrous bats . . . most hideously deform'd and as big as one of our blackbirds' and music 'consisting of a loud grating bellowing noise like a company of bulls'. As for the dancing, nothing could be more ungraceful, he thought. On their side, too, the people of Whydah found things to criticize. There was the question of disrespect to the gods, which was serious, but in other matters, they were inclined to take a lighter view: the king's wives, for instance, found the mere sight of them irresistibly funny. 'As they pass'd they would salute us by bowing their heads and kissing their hands, laughing often very loud and staring on us as if we were so many monsters.'

At least, however, Captain Phillips was able to make all his purchases at one place. One might have to send boats scouting up and down the coast in an effort to fill the slave decks. Barbot was obliged to send his sloop a day's voyage from Bandy, where the main ship lay, to Calabar. There King Robert ruled, assisted by the Duke of York and Captain Jan Alkmaers. 'Every evening they club together at one another's houses, by turns; providing two or three jugs of palm wine, each of them containing twelve to fifteen gallons.' They sat in a circle on stools, drinking each other's health, 'singing and roaring all the while till the liquor is out'.

It was best to do business early on in the day. For they had plenty of slaves and were quite energetic and efficient when sober. They had scoured the markets inland and captured whole villages by sudden armed descents. Though it poured with rain in the most abominable manner the whole time Barbot's agents were there, they managed to keep the sloop sailing backwards and forwards every day, laden with slaves. The Negroes attributed their success in trade to an assiduous devotion to the gods. They never did anything without consulting them. 'Every house is full of idols, as well as the streets of the town.' Hens were perpetually being sacrificed before them. King Robert's subjects had also a particular fondness for old hats and were always ready to give three, or even four, monkeys for one.

Expeditions to villages along the shore were tedious enough, but sometimes it was necessary to penetrate the enormous forest: 'From the factors here we learned that the Ebo and Golo Kings had been at war,' wrote Joseph Hawkins, a young American in 1793.* Ebo had won and captured the whole of the opposing

* *The Voyage of Joseph Hawkins*, 1793–5, in *Documents Illustrative of the Slave Trade to America*, ed. Elizabeth Donan, 1935.

army. Anyone with the necessary health and perseverance could secure the finest and most profitable cargo: warriors in the prime of life, free of disease and dirt cheap. One had only to go to a certain river, the factors said, 'and from thence by land about three hundred miles'. This prodigious journey Hawkins performed, carrying with him samples of goods for the purchase of 100 slaves. The balance would be brought later, if business proved up to expectation.

At last, they reached the Ebo king, who received them politely, being glad of the opportunity to get rid of his prisoners on favourable terms. He personally conducted his guest across 'the town where we found them confined in a large area within a thick stockade . . . and the entrance as well as the whole circuit was guarded by men with spears', Hawkins relates. 'The captives were destitute for the most part even of their necessary covering and bound indiscriminately together by the hands and legs, the cords being again fastened to the ground by stakes.'

Rations were at starvation level and many had infected wounds received during the battle. Those not sold would probably die fairly quickly. 'I was fully convinced the removal of these poor wretches even into the slavery of the West-Indies, would be an act of humanity, rather than one exposed to censure,' remarks Hawkins uneasily, memories of plantation life before him as he writes. At this time, too, the humanitarian movement for the abolition of slavery was at its height in England. He had taken up slaving purely because it seemed the best thing to do in the financial circumstances in which he found himself in 1793.

He spent a week choosing the fittest and haranguing them on the delights of their future prospects; for, if they could be induced to go with him willingly, it would be much easier to manage them during the long trek back to the ship. He assured them, therefore, that, although they would have to work, certainly, yet there would always be plenty to eat. They would not be chained. They would join a community of their own nation. The benefits of the Christian religion would be open to them, together with the chance of paradise hereafter. Some were dazzled by these promises; others only partially so.

However, they started off fairly buoyantly, each slave with a load of provisions on his head. 'They were tied to poles in rows, four feet apart; a loose wicker bandage round the neck of each connected him to the pole and the arms being pinioned by a bandage affixed behind above the elbows.' But when they arrived at the ship's boats and found themselves being put in irons, they realized that everything Hawkins had said was a lie: they had been bought as a sacrifice to the great white gods of the ocean. Their fate was to be killed and eaten. Some had suspected as much from the very beginning.

They now despaired. 'We furnished the slaves with provisions,' writes Hawkins, 'but whether through grief or sullenness, very few of them would partake of any refreshment besides water.' Even a tot of brandy failed to revive their spirits. They seemed so lethargic that a few in the largest boat were left out of irons, as it happened to be more convenient. In this manner, they began to drop down the river towards the ship. At a certain point, the stream narrowed. Seeing a chance, two of the loose slaves jumped overboard. One reached the bank and the other was seized and dragged back 'though not without some difficulty'.

Meanwhile, the others who were loose, tried to throw the sailors into the water and 'set up a scream, which was echoed by the rest'. They snatched up the oars and laid about them to such effect that one of Hawkins' fingers was cut off. Five of the ones in irons got free and the rest caught hold of the sailors' legs as they fought to regain control of the situation. One person was dead and fourteen severely wounded before the mutiny could be quelled.

Sudden explosions like this were one of the recognized dangers of the slave trade, especially while the ship was still anchored off the African coast, having bought perhaps half, or three quarters, of a full cargo. What with sickness and manning the boats, there might only be a dozen fit men to guard several hundred slaves. Often the blacks deceived their masters by a period of docility and good behaviour. They would appear to have been persuaded that they were not destined to sacrifice for ocean gods, but were being transported to a new and delightful existence, passing, in due course, to the joys of heaven. They would seem to be in excellent spirits, singing the songs of their country and dancing as best they could in chains.

But, in reality, they were chanting spells to poison the white man's food and drink; to cause him to wither away and die; to summon all the spirits of the forest to their aid; to rouse their greatest gods to battle with Christ and the Trinity, on whose altars they would otherwise be killed. They also took practical measures. Soft manners sometimes earned them knives with which to cut up their food. In the appalling darkness and squalor of their quarters, they concealed pieces of iron, chisels, shot, anything they could pick up during their airings on deck.

Captain Barbot relates the history of one such desperate insurrection: 'Seeing all the ship's company at best but weak and many quite sick', they suddenly broke out 'about one in the afternoon, after dinner', at a moment when they had knives in their hands. They had weakened their shackles and now snatched them off to use as weapons. 'Thus arm'd they fell in crouds and parcels on our men upon the deck unawares'. In an instant, they had cut the cook's throat, hamstrung the boatswain, wounded three sailors and thrown another overboard. Above them, on the quarter deck, the captain and officers 'stood in arms firing on the revolted slaves of whom we killed some and wounded many'.

Dinner knives and iron bars were no match for steady fire from a superior position. When the slaves realized that their gods could not prevail, they lost heart and 'many of the most mutinous leaped overboard and drowned themselves in the ocean with much resolution, showing no manner of concern for life'. Were they not dead men anyway? The rest resigned themselves to fate and punishment. 'We caused about thirty of the ringleaders to be very severely whipt by all our men that were capable of doing that office.'

Some ships carried thumbscrews, spiked iron collars, which could be tightened round the neck, and other instruments of torture for use in emergencies. 'Monday 11 December 1752,' notes Captain Newton, at anchor off the Gold Coast. 'By favour of Divine Providence made a timely discovery today that the slaves were forming a plot . . . Surprized 2 of them attempting to get off their irons and, upon further search of their rooms, upon the information of 3 of the boys, found some knives, stones, shot etc and a cold chissel . . . Put the boys in irons and slightly in the thumbscrews to urge them to a full confession . . . In the morning, examined the men slaves and . . . put 4 of them in collars.'

Though the most dangerous time was while Africa was still in sight and the influence of the gods consequently strong, as well as the hope of reaching the shore, it was never really safe to relax precautions unless one had sufficient men to stand permanently on guard at strategic points, with loaded muskets. Disease and an eye for economy usually prevented this. 'Sunday 25 May 1751,' wrote Captain Newton, *en route* for Antigua. 'In the evening . . . discovered a conspiracy among the men slaves to rise upon us. . . A young man who has been the whole voyage out of irons, first on account of a large ulcer and since for his seeming good behaviour, gave them a large marline spike down the gratings.' Within an hour, twenty had broken their chains and removed most of the nails from the bulkhead separating them from the rest of the ship.

The successful management of slaves during the voyage was very important, for profits could be sharply reduced by captains who were careless, drunk or being 'of a morose and peevish temper are perpetually beating and curbing them even without the least offence, and will not suffer any upon deck but when unavoidable necessity to ease themselves does require; under pretence it hinders the work of the ship and sailors and that they are troublesome by their nasty nauseous stench, or their noise; which makes those poor wretches desperate, and besides their falling into distempers through melancholy, often is the occasion of their destroying themselves'.*

All sensible persons agreed that they should be treated with as much kindness and given as much liberty as was consonant with safety. The agents in America were particularly insistent on this. One could not hope to do business if the slaves offered for sale were all half dead and wandering in their wits. 'Be sure to give them good covering and victuals and secure the promise of the master by whom you send them to treat them with humanity and keep up their spirits,' wrote Henry Laurens of South Carolina to Lloyd and Barton, importers, of Jamaica in 1764.

The Portuguese kept them in special enclosures on shore until they were ready to sail. There they were fattened and got into a really good state of health before facing the rigours of the voyage. They were also baptized, as only Christians were allowed into

* Barbot.

Brazil. Captain Barbot commended the Portuguese practice of providing 'coarse thick mats to serve as bedding under slaves aboard . . . which besides that it is softer . . . must also be much healthier for them, because the planks, or deals, contract some dampness more or less, either from the deck being so often wash'd to keep it clean and sweet, or from the rain that gets in now and then thro' the scuttles . . . and even from the very sweat of the slaves; which being so crouded in a low place, is perpetual and occasions many distempers.'

'With our ships,' wrote ex-captain Newton after his conversion and retirement to a parsonage in 1764, 'the great object is to be full . . . Their lodging rooms below the deck . . . are sometimes more than five feet high and sometimes less; and this height is divided towards the middle for the slaves to lie in two rows, one above the other, on each side of the ship, close to each other, like books upon a shelf.' In Dutch ships, however, it was remarkable that no one ever had less than two foot six headroom and extra scuttles and portholes were provided so that the air could circulate, at least in calm weather.

'Let it be observed,' continues the reformed Newton, 'that the poor creatures thus cramped for want of room are likewise in irons for the most part both hands and feet, and two together, which makes it difficult for them to turn or move, to attempt either to rise or lie down without hurting themselves or each other . . . They lie athwart or cross the ship (which) adds to the uncomfortableness of their lodging, especially to those who lie on the leeward, or leaning, side of the vessel.' Such were the conditions under his command in his unregenerate days, together with thumbscrews and spiked collars.

Yet, courage and ingenuity enabled one to work miracles. A certain captain known to Phillips used to cast spells on the slaves. In an elaborate ceremony, he boiled up 'English beer with a little aloes in it to imbitter it'. This he made them drink, saying that if they ever afterwards tried to escape, or mutiny, they would instantly fall down dead. He 'then would let them out of irons' with perfect confidence. Beatings and torturings were never necessary on his ship.

It required a good deal of personality to carry off such an act. Other captains preferred more orthodox methods, while endeavouring to treat them like human beings, as far as possible. 'We must not be too severe and haughty with them,' remarks Captain Barbot, 'but on the contrary, caress and humour them in every reasonable thing.' The first essential was to impose proper discipline on the crew. They must not be allowed to be perpetually drunk and time spent enjoying themselves with the women slaves, who were segregated from the men, should be curtailed. Officers should have only a reasonable number of black wives for the voyage and not too many men for sale on their own account. For, besides distraction from duty, these favourites caused jealousy, being given, sometimes, better rations than the seamen to keep them sleek and raise their price at the journey's end. They might also be taught carpentry, or coopering, which made them much more valuable.

If, by these measures, the crew were kept alert and prompt to obey orders, guarding the decks with cannon and muskets whenever the captives were let out of their cabin, searching daily for stolen knives or other weapons, it was possible to allow the women and children the freedom of their part of the deck. 'Nay,' writes Barbot, 'even many of the males had the same liberty, by turns, successively; few or none being fetter'd or kept in shackles and that only on account of some disturbances, or injuries offer'd to their fellow-captives.'

Another useful move was to select one particular tribe among the slaves and appoint them overseers over the rest. This was found to work well. They could be given whips as badges of office, told to organize the cleaning of their quarters and watch out for plots, 'which trust they will discharge with great diligence', says Captain Phillips who made a habit of it.

In a properly regulated ship, the health of the slaves was a major concern. 'Thrice a week we perfume betwixt decks with a quantity of good vinegar in pails and red-hot iron bullets in them.'* One ought, also, to set aside a special cabin for the sick so that the doctors could 'with more conveniency and time administer proper remedies; which they cannot do leisurely between decks, because of the great heat that is there continually, which is sometimes so excessive that the surgeons would faint away and the candles would not burn'.* A sick bay restricted the spread of

* Barbot.

infection and ensured the medicine and extra nourishment prescribed were not seized by healthy prisoners.

Two meals a day were provided together with wooden spoons for preference, so that they could be eaten in a safe and civilized manner. The most suitable food, cheap and fattening, was 'large beans boil'd with Moscovy lard, which we have from Holland, well pack'd up in casks'. And, in the evening, 'pease, or Indian wheat . . . boil'd with either lard or suet or grease by turns'.* This revolting provender was evidently much appreciated. 'Three days a week they have horse-beans boiled for their dinner and supper,' notes Captain Phillips. 'These beans the negroes extremely love and desire, beating their breast eating them and crying, Pram! Pram! which is, Very good!'

Each day that passed without sacrifice to the white gods of the ocean, followed by a cannibalistic feast, calmed black fears. The lovely beans floating in grease came up regularly. On a good ship, no particular violence was offered them, if they obeyed the rules. 'We often at sea in the evenings would let the slaves come up into the sun to air themselves, and made them jump and dance for an hour or two to our bag-pipes, harp and fiddle.'† Only under incompetent captains, with no head for business and a sadistic turn of mind, were the full horrors of the slave trade apparent.

Unfortunately, there were too many of these. Often, they were masters of very small ships and their low and brutal character was turned against everyone in their power. Not only would they flog and murder the slaves, but also the crew, cheating the survivors of their proper wages into the bargain. On such ships, sanitary precautions went unheeded. Sometimes the slaves were so crowded that they could not even lie flat on their backs. Food and water were inclined to run short during the voyage from bad management. Slaves might be thrown overboard to drown in order to avoid further reduction of everyone's rations. The evening dance was conducted under the lash to keep the circulation brisk. The songs were laments and a wooing of death. For only as spirits could the singers regain their own country and freedom. Some committed suicide, or fell into a decline, refusing to eat, even though their teeth were broken as food was forced down

* Barbot.
† Phillips.

their throats. Others burst their bonds in the fury of desperation, ready to die in the attempt to murder their tormentors. There was seldom any profit to be made from ventures conducted by captains of this temper.

The course set for America was called the middle passage and was the same as that followed by Stedman's ship. His experiences of heat, disease and over-crowding were bad enough. But, at least, the soldiers' cabin was a full five feet high and not divided by a shelf at two and a half feet. The occupants, though near enough together, were not so closely packed as books in a case. Their chances of survival, on reaching Surinam were scarcely better than those of an African: their labours were hard, the food inadequate and they had no resistance to tropical illnesses. Few returned home.

VIII

ARRIVAL AT PARAMARIBO

It seemed to the soldiers that their journey would never end. They would, perhaps, sail for ever over this hot sea, suffocating in the cabin by night, confronted by the most horrible food each day, suffering from diseases for which no one knew the cure. For, though Captain Cook insisted on everyone eating pickled cabbage during his expedition to the South Seas, this was considered very mad by most people, who were not prepared to believe that scurvy had anything to do with wrong feeding. If his ships were free of it, pickled cabbage could not be the cause. The accepted theory was that there were certain miasmas rising from the sea inimical to human beings, whose proper element was land. The only cure for scurvy was to make for the nearest shore and put the invalids upon it, where those in whom the disease had not progressed too far recovered. It was noted that they had a great desire for fruit and vegetables, but this was thought unnatural and a mere phase of their illness.

'Becoming extremely low-spirited towards the close of our voyage, I now had recourse to daily sea-bathing, and to a chearing glass of claret,' writes Stedman, not attributing his malaise to anything worse than lack of variety in his daily life. 'These means proved efficacious,' he continues, 'and I found myself in a few days perfectly recovered from my complaint.'

On 31 January, 1773, they sighted 'several large black rocks to windward called the Constables'. These lay off the shores of Cayenne, French Guiana, immediately east of Surinam. The first view of land caused great excitement after weeks of empty horizons. 'Large forests of trees extend along the coast even to the beach which appeared to consist of mud, with but few intervals of sand,' wrote an English traveller to these parts. 'This prospect . . . was not the most flattering, but it being the end of my journey, and the first land I had seen for several weeks, I beheld it with glad eyes and really thought it a most delightful place. I looked on the forests of trees as so many pervious groves and pleasant plantations, and compared the situation . . . to some of our watering places in England – I hugged myself with the idea of traversing those rural retreats of wood and hearing the dashing of waves against the lofty mangroves in my supposed walks of retirement.'*

Such, more or less, were the feelings of Stedman and his companions also. With intense interest, 'we observed the narwhal, or sea-unicorn, and one or two large turtles, floating past the ship's side', as they lay at anchor. For this was a treacherous coast, swept by tremendous currents and only to be traversed in full visibility, at times when the tides were favourable. The country was confusing in its monotony. It was difficult to know exactly where one had got to. The mouths of the rivers all looked the same. This was particularly the case with the River Maroni, which formed the boundary between Surinam and Cayenne and 'has occasioned the loss of many ships, by seamen fatally mistaking it for the river Surinam'. 'Those who have the misfortune to enter rarely come out again, on account of the great number of sandbanks, and various rocks, there to be met with.'†

Fatalities were so frequent, that a small fort had been built about twelve miles short of the River Surinam with the principal object of 'watching for the arrival of ships and warning them with one or two guns, in case they were not sure of their position'.† From this point, one had to be especially careful, or else 'one would undoubtedly be carried past the entrance and be unable to return, on account of the rapidity of the current',† without making a wide sweep out to sea.

Stedman's ship successfully negotiated these various dangers and at last 'having doubled Braam's Point with a light breeze, under top and top-gallant sails, we finally entered the beautiful river Surinam'. It was the dry season. The sun shone. Everyone was 'in the highest flow of spirits, seeing himself surrounded by the most delightful verdure', continuing unbroken for a couple of miles, or so, until one came suddenly on two redoubts. These

* Henry Bolingbroke, *A Voyage to the Demerary*, 1809. Surinam, Berbice, Demerara and Essequebo were all administered by the Dutch West India Co. and together comprised Dutch Guiana.
† Philippe Fermin, *Description Générale, Historique et Physique de la Colonie de Surinam*, 1769.

commanded the entrance to the river and were advance posts for Fort Amsterdam, slightly further up, at the junction of the River Commewyne with the Surinam.

'At three o'clock p.m.,' writes Stedman, 'we dropped anchor before the new fortress called Amsterdam.' Begun in 1734 as an improvement of the colony's defences not only in time of war, but also against the many pirates with which the Caribbean swarmed, 'it was not finished until 1747. It is built on a sort of rock, surrounded by large ditches and very well fortified besides. It is well supplied with magazines both for munitions and for food. Six or seven years ago, they even built a windmill to make the garrison's flour. In time of war, the fortress could contain at least three thousand men; but in peace time, there are scarcely more than a hundred.'* If efficiently manned, the two redoubts and the fortress could keep up a devastating cross-fire, enough to prevent a ship reaching the plantations that lined the banks from this point and were otherwise completely undefended.

'The river seemed alive by the many boats and barges passing and re-passing to see us,' Stedman notes, 'while groups of naked boys and girls were promiscuously playing and flouncing, like so many Tritons and Mermaids in the water. The scene was new to all and nothing was heard but music, singing and cheering on deck, as well as in the rigging, from the ideas of happiness which each individual now promised himself in this luxuriant flourishing spot ... How miserably these poor fellows were mistaken in their reckoning shall soon be seen,' he adds gloomily. But all that was in the future. For the moment, the sparkling river seemed like the waters of paradise, the tritons, mermaids and other inhabitants under a spell of universal joy. 'Nothing could equal the delicious sensations with which we seemed intoxicated by the fragrance of the lemons, limes, oranges and flowers wafted over from adjoining plantations.' No one would have thought that the expedition had come to save the colony from extinction by rebellious slaves who, moreover, were reported to have put their masters to death with the most excruciating tortures.

They remained at anchor several days, while news of their arrival was sent to the governor at Paramaribo, the capital, some miles up the river. Meanwhile, they made excursions on shore. Here,

* Fermin.

certain dark signs were observed by Stedman: 'The pleasure I had flattered myself with, from exchanging the confinement of the ship for the liberty of ranging over a delicious country was damped by the first object which presented itself after my landing. This was a young female slave, whose only covering was a rag tied round her loins which, like her skin, was lacerated in several places by the stroke of the whip.' She had also a weight 'of at least a hundred pounds' chained to her ankle.

It appeared that she had been guilty of some quite trivial offence, such as not having the strength to perform her allotted task. But how could one say that this severity was justified even if she had neglected her duty from laziness? Fresh from Holland, Stedman was unable to view the scene as a natural part of everyday life. He sketched her on the spot with great indignation.

Under the circumstances, he was glad to re-embark, especially as the grass round the fort 'afforded a harbour to two species of very disagreeable insects' that settled in crowds all over his body and could only be dislodged by a bath in lime juice. On the whole, it was definitely better to remain on board, sniffing the scents and viewing the country and the river, which more and more resembled a carnival: 'We received a visit from several officers of the Society, or West India Company's troops . . . to welcome our arrival in the colony . . . They came in very elegant barges, or tent boats, adorned with flags and attended by small bands of music.'

The tent boat was characteristic of Guiana. 'This boat,' says Fermin, 'which is rowed by six or eight negroes, serves to transport the Master from his Plantation to Town, as there is no road overland; the settlements are all along the banks of the rivers.' There were about 800 plantations. Each owned a tent boat which took its name from the little cabin, rather like a tent, constructed in the stern for the master to recline in out of the sun. 'They are generally from twenty to thirty feet long,' adds Henry Bolingbroke, 'and wide in proportion; they are built very sharp for the purpose of sailing or rowing fast . . . A cockpit is behind for the cockswain to steer in . . . The negroes while pulling . . . appeared quite merry and sung all the way.'

As they were not much beaten, in order not to spoil their

lovely skin – they wore nothing except the smallest possible loincloth – they were also cheerful as they hurried up and down the gangway, carrying 'the large quantity of excellent fruits and other refreshments' brought by the visitors as presents. 'This scene was, however, contrasted by the arrival of two canoes filled with emaciated, starving wretches, who clamorously solicited relief from the soldiers and were ready to fight for the possession of a bone.'

While they waited for word from Paramaribo, Colonel Fourgeoud, the commander of the expedition, mysteriously visited the town incognito. During his previous connection with Guiana, he had made both friends and enemies. He was not, as it turned out later, on particularly good terms with the governor. Perhaps he took with him some of the surviving dainties which had been intended for his officers during the voyage and which he had denied them on the grounds that they must get used to hard tack.

At last the orders came. The ships weighed with the tide and 'sail'd up the river Surinam with drums beating, colours flying and a guard of marines drawn up on the quarter deck of each vessel'. In some ways, they were reminded of home: 'The land in Dutch Guiana, for the distance of near fifty miles from the sea is everywhere flat and level, without a single hill; and so low that, during the rainy seasons, it is usually covered with water near two feet in height.'* This was no new problem to emigrants from Holland. It was necessary merely to dig proper Dutch dykes and canals to enjoy a 'soil more fertile than that of any other part of the globe'.*

On the right, it was a little dull, certainly. One saw 'only forest, which stretches as far as the Town of Paramaribo'.† But on the left, almost immediately on leaving Fort Amsterdam, 'the coffee Plantations begin and form the most beautiful view in the world'.† The leaves were always so green and set off to such advantage 'clusters of little cottages, some detached buildings, the better sort of house of two, three and four storeys high, painted white; and the red boarded roofs made many an interesting group and gave to every plantation the air of a separate village. The passing and

* Edward Bancroft, *An Essay on the Natural History of Guiana*, 1769.
† Fermin.

re-passing of schooners and other colony-boats considerably enlivened the landscape.'*

The hour's journey soon passed and, rounding a bend, they found themselves abreast of Fort Zeelandia, immediately outside Paramaribo, 'receiving a salute of eleven guns . . . which was returned by all the ships of our small fleet'. The governor of Surinam had his headquarters just outside this citadel which was 'extremely crowded by different buildings, such as the Arsenal, several Barracks and various Magazines',† not to speak of the town prison. 'It has no parapets; but the walls are about five feet high and six feet thick.'† Most notably, it contained 'a bell hanging under a roof, to which a soldier climbes by a little ladder every hour, day and night, in order to strike the hour; and there is no other clock for the Town'.†

The ships came to anchor 'within pistol-shot of the shore', on which the whole of the inhabitants of Paramaribo were jostling each other with excitement. The greater part were Negroes and mulattoes. There were also many German and Portuguese Jews for, as in Holland, religious toleration was part of the constitution. 'The jew, the catholic, the protestant, the deist, the heathen visit, or neglect, at pleasure, their respective opportunities of worship,' Bolingbroke remarks with admiring envy. 'Paramaribo is the Buenos Ayres of Guyana,' he continues, 'the residence of all the native wealth and the storehouse of what is most curious and precious among the productions of Europe.'

For all that, it was a long way from the centres of civilization and amusement. The European community was small and its members only too well acquainted with each other. A comfortable income, combined with heat and quantities of slaves to wait on them hand and foot, predisposed the colonists to a somewhat idle and dissipated life. The arrival 'of nearly five hundred young men . . . the oldest of whom was scarcely more than thirty and the whole party neatly cloathed in their new uniforms, and in caps ornamented with twigs of orange-blossom' caused a particular eagerness, not altogether to be explained by the fact that they came as saviours from the terrible runaway slaves.

But nothing seemed further from reality than campaigns,

* Bolingbroke.
† Fermin.

hardships, slaughter, or any kind of serious military duties at this moment. 'After being confined nearly the whole of sixty-three days within the limits of a small vessel ... it would not be easy to describe the pleasure we experienced,' writes Stedman, remembering again those wide streets lined with orange trees, the scent of which hung in the air perpetually. 'The town appeared uncommonly neat and pleasing, the shipping extremely beautiful, the adjacent woods adorned with the most luxuriant verdure, the air perfumed with the utmost fragrance, and the whole scene gilded by the rays of an unclouded sun.' There was, at that moment, no trace of those sinister aspects of the country he had found so oppressive at Fort Amsterdam.

They disembarked, 'all the ships in the roads being in full dress and the guns keeping up an incessant fire' until everyone was on shore. 'We paraded on a large green plain between the town and the citadel, opposite to the Governor's palace; during the course of which ceremonies several soldiers fainted' from heat and the tightness of their uniforms; but, fortunately, not in sufficient numbers to mar the general rejoicing.

For there were various reasons to welcome five hundred young stalwarts. Not only had they sixty-three days' chastity behind them, but also an accumulation of pay.'It spread like wildfire that we were from one of the vessels just arrived,' writes Bolingbroke of his landfall in Guiana, 'and our captain was soon surrounded by the whole band of hucksters and pedlars belonging to the town. Here were blacks, yellows and tawnies, bawling and vociferating ... each trying to hitch himself closer than his neighbour.'

Everyone in Paramaribo felt cheerful, the richer inhabitants making plans for a wonderful round of parties and other amusements; the more impecunious for improving their situation. Celebrations began at once. After the parade 'the troops then marched into quarters prepared for their reception; whilst the officers were regaled with a dinner by the Governor, which would have derived a considerable relish from its succeeding the salt provisions to which we had so long been confined, had any contrast been necessary to heighten our opinion of its elegance. But the choicest delicacies of America and Europe were served up on silver.'

Society in Dutch Guiana was cosmopolitan, since anyone ready to abide by the laws of Holland and the West India Company could settle there. In Demerara, the foreign planters outnumbered the Dutch by the end of the eighteenth century. The dinners reflected this state of affairs. 'There was soup to begin with, as in France,' writes Bolingbroke appreciatively, 'and salted ling to begin with, as in Holland: there was an English huge joint of beef and a couple of Muscovy ducks; there was an Italian desert of Bologna sausages and salad, anchovies and olives; there was fruit of all kinds, pine-apples, guavas, oranges, shaddocks and avoiras. Wine was taken during the repast and porter between the courses, for a *bonne-bouche*.'

This was an ordinary dinner. We must imagine Stedman and his companions gorging from the silver plates more elaborately and variously than that. They were, moreover, 'attended by a considerable number of extremely handsome negro and mulatto maids, all naked from the waist upwards, according to the custom of the country; but the other parts of their persons arrayed in the finest India chintzes and the whole adorned with golden chains, medals, beads, bracelets and sweet-smelling flowers'. One might almost have strayed into the fabled city of El Dorado.

'After partaking of this superb entertainment', Stedman set off for the address of Mr Lolkens, a planter who, in the hospitable manner of Surinam, had sent a message saying he was to use the house as his own until proper quarters were ready for him. Lolkens might not be at home, but the servants would make him comfortable.

Yet, the maids of Paramaribo, in spite of their good nature and training in the domestic arts, were still disconcertingly African, as Stedman now discovered. 'On knocking at the door, it was opened by a young female negro of masculine appearance, whose whole dress consisted of a single petticoat and who held a lighted tobacco pipe in one hand and a burning candle in the other, which she brought close to my face, in order to reconnoitre me.'

He enquired for his host, but could not understand her reply, given in the *lingua franca* used by the slaves. So he then said, 'Lolkens,' loudly and firmly. This caused her to scream with laughter, throwing back her head and 'displaying two rows of very beautiful teeth; and at the same time, laying hold of the breast-buttons of my coat, she made me a signal to follow her. I was much at a loss how to act, but went in,' Stedman continues, never having had the experience of an African welcome before.

She led him to 'a very neat apartment' and produced a bottle of Madeira and some fruit. Though hardly inclined for more refreshments, Stedman took a little from politeness and also poured her out a glass of wine. This horrified her, as it was out of the question for a slave to drink with a European. However, at last, from kindness and pity for his ignorance, she accepted it, meanwhile giving him to understand somehow that Mr Lolkens had gone to his plantation for a short time.

The continual excitements of the day, the crowd of new impressions, the banquet, the drink, combined now to overwhelm Stedman with weariness. 'I longed for some rest and made a signal to my attendant that I wanted sleep: but my motion was strangely misconstrued; for she immediately seized me by the neck and imprinted on my lips a most ardent kiss.' To her surprise, he threw her off in a rage. For this, too, was merely a custom of the country, as he subsequently found out. There was no need whatever to refuse her advances as an insult, just because of her ugliness. She made them only in accordance with the usual rules of hospitality.

Determined to do the honours of the house in a way her master would approve, she pursued her quarry into the bedroom and began undressing him. It was not that she intended to jump in with him, as he feared, 'but this is an office commonly performed by the slaves in Surinam to all ranks and sexes without exception'. He was too tired and flurried to think of a bath, though it might have relaxed him. 'I got into an upright square tub, or cistern,' relates the more experienced Bolingbroke calmly, 'and a negress watered me like a transplanted cucumber.' It was very refreshing after the heat of the day.

When she had got him comfortably into bed, the black girl felt that she could do no more. Evidently this difficult guest came from some strange, barbarian part of the world where they had no notion of how to behave. What sort of ridiculous scene would he make if she performed the last duty of polite households? For this was to take off her only garment and run round the room flapping it in order to drive out the insects before settling the mosquito-net. She therefore retired, with pipe and candle, leaving him to be eaten alive.

'Feb 10,' wrote Stedman mournfully in his *Journal* next day. 'Am spotted like a leopard by the mosquitoes.'

IX

THE SITUATION IN SURINAM

The colony of Surinam had originally been founded as an English settlement in the seventeenth century, many of the planters coming from the West Indies where the soil was not so fertile as in Guiana. This phase, however, lasted less than twenty years. In the Anglo-Dutch War, which began in 1666, Surinam was captured by the Dutch. At the Treaty of Breda, concluded in 1667, it was agreed that each side should keep the conquests made in America. Thus the Dutch kept Surinam and the English New Amsterdam, re-named New York.

Most of the English planters left Surinam for Jamaica with their slaves, yet some remained and there was always a certain English contingent that grew larger as time went on and the West Indies became more crowded and the soil exhausted. Space was unlimited in Guiana. One applied to the governor; a rectangle was marked on the map; one went and cleared the forest off it, built a house, planted sugar. One's nationality and religion were matters of indifference under Dutch law. The sole object of the directors of the West India Company, who administered the country, was to make a profit. Anyone with enough capital to set himself up was welcome. Flourishing plantations meant larger dividends.*

Sometimes the opportunity was abused by persons in difficulties. 'We have had an occurrence here which occasioned me the utmost embarrassment and caused very great commotion in the Colony,' wrote Gravesande, governor of Essequebo and Demerara to his employers in 1753. 'One Edward Simons, from the island of Nevis came to Demerara in a barque . . . bringing with him 72 slaves and intending to settle.' Everything seemed in order. He was allotted a plantation. But then news came that he 'had mortgaged his plantation and slaves on the island of Nevis to a certain Mills, an inhabitant of St Christopher, for a large amount' and fled before any payment could be obtained from him. The diffi-

---

* The eighteenth century saw a steady rise in the demand for sugar. In 1700, 10,000 tons were imported into England; in 1800, 150,000 tons.

culty was that he was a kind master. His slaves were devoted to him. All 72 were armed and ready to defend their owner and the new plantation to the death. The garrison at Essequebo consisted of 35 men of doubtful prowess, who had mostly sold their guns and uniforms for drink. Fortunately, however, the resourceful Mr Simons was captured and obliged to order his slaves to desist.

Such dreadful moments of embarrassment were luckily rare. Most people were honestly intent on bettering their fortunes. 'Applicants for land are arriving daily with their slaves,' Gravesande reports later the same year. 'Various materials for mills have already been landed, more are expected and there is every appearance of rapid progress. It is a pleasure to see how cheerful, zealous and industrious the newcomers are.' One might have expected them to miss their friends and the social round of the West Indies, which was more sophisticated than that of Guiana. 'The beginning is difficult, especially for those coming from the islands,' Gravesande continues, 'and who must find it rather strange to live so simply in a wild forest, but, to my great surprise, they are cheerful and content.' Though trade was regulated and prices fixed in favour of the West India Company, it was possible, by assiduity and good management, to make a fortune within a reasonable time.

Special tax concessions were offered to prospective settlers in Demerara and Essequebo. In Surinam these were not necessary. It was the most thickly inhabited, had been established the longest and was the most prosperous part of all Dutch Guiana. The glories of Paramaribo appeared like those of Amsterdam or London, viewed from the swamps of Demerara. The governing authority was called the Chartered Society of Surinam, in which one-third of the shares were held by the West India Company and two-thirds by an association of merchants of Amsterdam. Every department of trade and business was strictly regulated in order to ensure a profit to the shareholders in Amsterdam. The crops had to be sold to the Society at a price which allowed for re-sale in Europe. Manufactured goods had to be imported only in Dutch ships, with certain small exceptions.

Eighteenth-century economic theory held that colonies were strictly an appendage of the mother country and had, indeed, been set up purely as a business speculation. They should be allowed to develop only in directions suitable to their subordinate status. They were to remain perpetually at the agricultural stage, supplying raw materials and food cheaply and providing, in return, a steady market for manufactured goods and luxuries. Thus, it was argued, both sides obtained the maximum benefit. The colonies were guaranteed not only a market for their crops, but also protection against enemies. The parent country was either the producer, or middleman, of nearly all imports into the colony.

This system was not too bad in those cases where, as in the Caribbean, a concentration on agriculture, timber and so on, actually suited the economy. In North America, conditions were such in some parts that true prosperity depended on a balance of agriculture and industry. This was the main cause of the American War of Independence. The southern colonies might be rather tepid about natural law, the rights of man and other democratic conceptions, for they belonged essentially to the aristocratic, slave-owning society of the West Indies. But they could well appreciate that all sorts of goods would be cheaper and better if they were free to trade as they pleased with the world and if industrial products could be made in the northern colonies and sold directly to them.

In Paramaribo, as far as can be ascertained, no one seriously bothered his head with questions which, in Philadelphia and Boston, were rousing patriots to arms. The European population was small and its appetite for machinery, cloth and fancy goods easily satisfied under existing arrangements. The price might be stiff, but that was not a source of grievance since one had the money to pay. 'Luxury reigns. There are several shops and a number of stores, very well stocked with every sort of goods . . . but at a very high price because there are no manufactories and everything is imported.'*

Another factor which added to the cost of things was a general lack of skilled labour. Very few of the Negroes or mulattoes had been trained as carpenters, builders, cooks, tailors and so on. Any slave who had these qualifications was his master's especial treasure and, if sold, fetched an extraordinary sum. Free Negroes, of which there were a certain number in Paramaribo, could obtain almost any wage they liked to ask, if proficient in these trades. This made

* Fermin.

houses very expensive and rents, as Stedman found, extremely high. Although the country was covered with wood, 'the principal material used is North American lumber . . . the demand (for which) indeed exceeds the quantity imported . . . Lime is a vast expence, being brought to us from Europe: surely a little search in the interior would discover lime-stone rocks among the mountains,' exclaims Bolingbroke with reasonable exasperation.

But the colonists had no taste for saving money, though sharp enough in business deals. They liked to prove their worth by spending what they had been clever enough to earn. 'Their carriages and dress are truly magnificent,' writes Stedman, 'silk embroidery, Genoa velvets, diamonds, gold and silver lace being daily worn and even the masters of trading ships appear with buttons and buckles of solid gold. They are equally expensive at their tables, where everything that can be called delicate is produced at any price; and served up in plate and china of the newest fashion and most exquisite workmanship. But nothing displays the luxury of the inhabitants of Surinam more than the number of slaves by whom they are attended, often twenty or thirty on one family.' These were simply the domestic servants and altogether apart from the gangs on the plantations. 'No one goes out into the streets without a Negro to hold a parasol over his head, men as well as women,' adds Fermin. 'The latter usually have several other attendants also.'

'All the streets, which are perfectly straight, are lined with orange, shaddock, tamarind, and lemon-trees, which appear in everlasting bloom,' Stedman continues, 'while at the same time, their branches are weighed down with the richest clusters of odoriferous fruit', a fitting canopy above the splendid citizens who were gems amongst a variegated crowd of 'sailors, soldiers, Jews, Indians and Negroes, while the river is covered with canoes, barges, etc., constantly passing and re-passing like the wherries on the Thames, often accompanied with bands of music; the shipping also in the road adorned with their different flags, guns firing, etc; not to mention the many groupes of boys and girls playing in the water'. It was possible, at such moments, to disregard the dark side of life in Guiana and be filled simply with happiness and a sense of one's good fortune in having been sent to this paradise in the course of one's employment.

For the rebellion seemed to have died down and it was possible that the troops might be sent home quite soon without any fighting, since they were an expense to the colony. During the last forty years, at least, there had been these alarms at intervals. The trouble was due not so much to risings against harsh masters on plantations as to the gradual accumulation of runaway slaves in the forests who had formed, in course of time, a series of African tribes in the hinterland. They lived in villages under chiefs and had firearms, stolen during raids on the plantations. Their mere existence meant that any slave who found his present captivity worse than that he had experienced in Africa could regain his former freedom.

One might think, under these circumstances, that there would not be a slave in the place, particularly on those estates where severe beatings were common. But the fact was that those who had been slaves in Africa, and therefore took bad treatment as a part of everyday life, felt that to have a European master was a step up in one's career. They regarded newly arrived slaves as mere savages, knowing nothing of the superior white world, the prospect of rising from field labour to domestic service; even babbling some incomprehensible lingo, instead of the proper language of slaves in the Caribbean, which was a special African-English, interlarded, in the case of Guiana, with certain Dutch words that were felt to give an extra smartness to one's discourse. Such people were not inclined, unless driven to desperation, to return to what they regarded as an uncivilized life, especially if they had been born in Surinam and were therefore unhaunted by memories of home in a village in a forest, peopled by the ghosts of their ancestors and spirits whose ways they understood.

For those who had originally been warriors, however, the temptation to abscond was great. The woods were so handy. Often they had a contempt for the overseer, perceiving that he was a low-class fellow and a bully into the bargain. Agriculture was properly women's work. A man should be hunting and fighting. There were many humiliations to be avenged. The present was intolerable. Being spirited young men, they found it almost impossible to keep out of trouble.

By 1730, forty years before the arrival of Stedman and his companions, the fugitives were so many as to be a continual worry to the planters. For the next nineteen years they struggled to hold them at bay. But, as suddenly as they emerged from the trees, in search of arms, food, or just an orgy of destruction, so they would vanish into the undergrowth. No one knew exactly where their villages were, or how many of them existed. The colonists, 'no longer being able to support the expences and fatigues of sallying out against them . . . at last resolved to treat for peace', thus publicly recognizing them as a separate nation on equal terms. 'A treaty of peace consisting of ten or twelve articles was actually concluded between the different parties in the year 1749.'

Unfortunately, the chief rebel captain had not entire authority over certain others who considered themselves insulted, especially as they had not been given proper presents. The treaty was soon broken and, in 1751, an expedition had to be sent out from Holland. The troops scoured the forest, as Stedman himself was to do. The enemy remained unconquered, but appeared acquiescent. A *status quo* might, perhaps, have been reached had owners and overseers resolved to reform the treatment of slaves; or had laws been passed, and strictly enforced, for their protection. But this proved impossible. Slaves were not fully human. They were savages. They needed discipline. If they were enabled to sue through the courts for assault, anarchy and ruin would be the result. More rigour, rather than less, was required.

It is not altogether surprising that 'in 1757 the aspect of affairs becoming daily worse . . . a new revolt broke out amongst the negroes, owing to the treatment which they received from their masters'. Again the colonists, unable to subdue their foes, were obliged to sue for peace. They asked for a parley, which was graciously accorded them. The Negroes said that they must have a yearly tribute of arms and ammunition as well as a number of other European goods, 'as specified in a long list, expressed in broken English', drawn up by a certain Captain Boston.

There was nothing for it but to agree to these demands, though some thought it might be possible to pacify the savages with a few trinkets, instead of giving them regular supplies of guns which, everyone could see, meant their perpetual independence. When the commissioners came again, having consulted the governor at Paramaribo, 'they were introduced to a very handsome negro called Araby, who was their chief and born in the forest'.

He had the manners of a king, receiving them 'very politely and, taking them by the hand, desired they would sit down by his side on the green' and assured them that their safety was absolute.

The commissioners then unpacked the first instalment of tribute which consisted of 'knives, scissors, combs and small looking glasses'. The effect was not as they had hoped. When Captain Boston saw these ridiculous objects instead of 'the principal articles in question, viz. gunpowder, fire-arms and ammunition, he . . . demanded in a thundering voice whether the Europeans imagined that the negroes could live on combs and looking-glasses; adding that one of each was quite sufficient for them all to see their faces'. With this answer, the commissioners returned to Paramaribo.

Long discussions followed among the principal settlers of Surinam. One thing seemed plain: Captains Araby, Boston and their friends could not be resisted and therefore must be placated. They must be turned into allies and induced to look on their former masters as benevolently as they could. For these terrible blacks were fully aware of their power. They had even lectured the commissioners, telling them what fools the planters were to employ so frequently 'drunken managers and overseers who, by wrongfully and severely chastising the negroes, debauching their wives and children, neglecting the sick, etc. . . . wilfully drive to the woods such numbers of stout active people who, by their sweat earn your subsistence, without whose hands your colony must drop to nothing; and to whom at last,' the speaker cried contemptuously, 'in this disgraceful manner you are glad to come and sue for friendship.'

It was worse than useless to go on pretending that such men could be put off with a handful of beads. The commissioners were sent back to Captain Araby with orders to agree to everything. On his side, Araby was to swear never to break the peace, to keep his people in their villages and not to allow more than six of them to visit Paramaribo at any one time.

The blacks now became very genial, insisting 'that each of the commissioners should, during their remaining stay in the rebel camp, take for his constant companion one of their handsomest young women. They treated them also liberally with game, fish, fruit and the choicest productions of the forest and entertained them, without intermission, with music, dancing and repeated volleys.'

The treaty was first ratified in the European manner, sixteen of Araby's captains carefully making their mark on it. Next, there was an African ceremony: for they did not feel that the promised gunpowder and muskets would materialize, unless very special oaths were taken, the gods invoked and curses laid on all defaulters. Each signatory let a few drops of his blood 'into a callibash or cup of clear spring water, in which were also mixed a few particles of dry earth; and of this all present were obliged to drink without exception'. Then the witch doctor 'with up-cast eyes and outstretched arms took heaven and earth to witness and with a' frightful yell pronounced the treaty sealed and anyone who broke it cursed 'from that moment forward to all eternity. To this solemn imprecation the multitude answered, Da so! which signifies in their language, Amen.' These events took place in 1761.

A tremendous feeling of release now spread among the white inhabitants of Paramaribo. It was true that the bush Negroes, as they were called, could be seen in the streets walking up and down in a proud and haughty manner, 'brandishing the silver-headed canes' with which the more important of them had been presented as a distinguishing mark and using the authority thus conferred to obtain from the shopkeepers 'liquors and very often money and reminding them how cruelly their ancestors had murdered their parents and their husbands'. No Jew, mulatto, or free Negro felt it worth his while to stand up to this.

Those who did not keep shops preferred to avert their eyes from such scenes. After all 'the colony now seemed in a prosperous and flourishing state . . . and everything exhibited an aspect of peace and good order', if one did not examine too closely. The citizens 'believed their persons and effects in perfect security, so that nothing was thought of but mirth and dissipation . . . Surinam resembled, indeed, a large and beautiful garden . . . All the luxuries, as well as the necessaries of life abounded; every sense was apparently intoxicated by enjoyment.' What could be done beyond hoping that the bush Negroes would keep their word so long as they were supplied with regular gunpowder?

Yet, the signs were plain to anyone who cared to look: the

total number of bush Negroes had been computed at 20,000; and they were thought to be increasing steadily. 'Should the peace ever be broken,' remarks Stedman in this connection, 'these new allies will become the most dreadful foes that ever the colony of Surinam can have to contend with.' It was true that the various captains were great rivals and not inclined to combine under one leader. They were also very strict in the observance of an oath taken in their own manner and sanctified by the gods. But who knew what mysterious new factors might arise in the forest, connected, perhaps, as much with ghosts and oracles as with ordinary grievances.

The burghers of Paramaribo had lived a long time with this threat and still survived. Obviously, it was better to enjoy oneself than to give way to gloomy prognostications. Why remember that the governor had been obliged to ride in his state carriage with the victorious ex-slaves and to entertain them to a dinner party, as if they were not only human, but even his honoured guests? It was more sensible to put on one's velvet and jewels, to go to a party, a ball, a dinner, the theatre; to have as many lovers as possible – though this was not so easy to arrange as it ought to have been, because the European men were mostly rather enfeebled by their activities with the black girls.

An amusing life necessitated residence in Paramaribo, with only occasional visits to the plantations, which were terribly boring places, from the social point of view. One was usually half an hour's row from one's neighbours. One therefore had an overseer to manage the daily business of getting the slaves to work as hard as they could, in order to raise a really profitable crop; for the gay life was expensive. The overseer was paid a bonus on the cash value of the crop. Anything he saved on the slaves' ration allowances or medical attendance was not particularly enquired into. Driving people to the limit of their strength was a career which attracted men of a sadistic turn of mind. Too frequently, the overseers liked watching men, and especially women, being beaten. The absolute power they enjoyed and the pleasures to be derived therefrom fully compensated them for the loneliness and isolation of their employment.

But why worry one's head unnecessarily? Bad times might come again. On the other hand, they might not. The bush Negroes had sworn to keep the peace and the plantation slaves knew what would happen to them if they tried to make trouble. Those favouring harsh discipline and those who thought kindness better and those who didn't care what happened so long as the money came in, united in a belief that everything would turn out for the best if one didn't think too much.

Thus, ten years passed. Suddenly, in 1772, the gay life was extinguished, as by a thunderclap. 'Plantations were once more seen, some blazing in flames and others laid in ashes; while the reeking and mangled bodies of their inhabitants were scattered along the banks of the river Cottica with their throats cut.' Every slave in the region 'fled to the woods, men, women and children without exception'. Every planter who happened to be visiting his property jumped into his tent boat and rowed for Paramaribo, for fear the rebellion would spread to all parts of the country.

The rebels were led by a formidable black called Captain Baron. He had previously belonged to a Swede 'who, on account of his abilities, had advanced him to the rank of favourite, had taught him to read and write and bred him a mason'. He had also taken him on a visit to Holland and promised him his freedom on their return to Surinam. Unfortunately, Baron was now worth a great deal of money, on account of his intelligence and accomplishments. The Swede succumbed to temptation. Instead of giving him the promised freedom, he sold him to a Jew. In the fury of his disappointment, Baron refused to work. The Jew was much put out by this behaviour, naturally enough. He had not paid a fortune in order to have a great idle fellow sulking his time away. He therefore beat Baron who immediately afterwards took to the forest, breathing murder, particularly against the Swede, saying, 'that he should never die in peace until he had washed his hands in the tyrant's blood'.

Paramaribo trembled; for it was quite defenceless. The permanent garrison was supposed to be twelve hundred men. But some died on the passage out from Holland and more of the yellow fever on arrival. They were, besides, recruited from 'the outcasts of all nations: they are of all ages, shapes and sizes and seem by chance wafted together from all the different corners of the globe'. Yet, they could do surprisingly well if properly led. But there were not enough, and they had not the stamina, to engage a furious horde of slaves; to seek them in the forests and among the swamps; to surprise them in their strongholds and cut them down. The only people in Surinam capable of such prodigious feats were the Negroes.

Since death and destruction were the only alternatives, it was decided to raise a black force, at least until reinforcements could arrive from Holland. Any slave joining and taking the oath obtained his freedom immediately. Instead of being obliged to live in the woods in order to attain the status of a human being, he could enjoy it, here and now, in the middle of civilization. This proved an attractive offer. Three hundred suitable warriors were soon enrolled and given trousers, scarlet caps, firelocks, sabres and a short training. They were apt pupils. 'Of both these weapons,' Stedman remarks, 'they understand the management in the most masterly manner.' They understood jungle warfare also, by instinct. The change of occupation from labouring in the fields exhilarated them. It would have been difficult to find keener or more resourceful fighting men anywhere.

It remained only to send them after Captain Baron in conjunction with the regular forces. They were given the password, Orange, 'to prevent disagreeable mistakes' during battles. There was also supposed to be a force of militia, but it consisted of 'so strange a collection of ill-disciplined rabble' as to be worse than useless, even for holding the forts. The black rangers and those of the garrison who were of a suitable shape and size and whose health was sufficient to permit long marches set off into the forest. One could only hope that the rangers would resist the temptation to join the rebels for, in that case, the whole of Dutch Guiana would probably be laid low before help from Europe could arrive. Some pessimists even suggested that bloodhounds would be safer, more reliable, less inclined to turn on their masters. However, as there were not any, and their training, when obtained would have taken too long even had persons competent to undertake such a task been available, the idea was dropped.

To the general surprise and relief, the black rangers turned out superbly. Their skill and pertinacity resulted in the dreaded Captain Baron being flushed out of two impregnable strongholds in the swamps which could only be approached along certain submerged paths. Many rebels were killed in savage hand to hand fighting and their leader fled further into the forest, a defeated man, accompanied by a mere remnant of his forces.

The celebrations were tremendous. With incurable optimism, the settlers once more felt perfectly safe. There were plenty of slaves, after all. You just enrolled a sufficient number to protect you against the enemy and that was that. Why worry? Paramaribo returned thankfully to the usual round of amusements.

X

FESTIVITIES

It was at this particular point in the history of the revolt that Stedman and his friends arrived and were welcomed like guests to a party. It was not thought that they would stay long. The danger was over. Their rations and pay were a burden the colony did not wish to bear unless it was absolutely necessary. But there was no reason why a good time should not be had by all during the interval before they re-embarked. On this point the ladies were especially firm.

Whatever their other shortcomings, the Dutch of Guiana were famous for hospitality. 'I had a general invitation to visit . . . in more than twenty respectable families,' Stedman notes. There were two or three inns at Paramaribo, but they were not suitable for gentlemen to live at, 'wherefore a merchant's house is more like an inn than anything else', writes Bolingbroke from his own experience. Strangers have only to introduce themselves and 'a knife and fork is laid for them and a hammock prepared, which they occupy as long as suits their convenience'. For hammocks, with mosquito nets hung over them like tents, were the most usual kind of bed in Guiana.

Every day Stedman had invitations to breakfast and dinner and seldom went near the officers' mess, the provision of which was more or less superfluous in the circumstances. He did, however, move into his own quarters: a small unfurnished house, infested with rats. These presented a problem he was unable to solve; but the question of furniture and provisions was not a difficult one. 'The ladies supplied me with tables, chairs, glasses and even plate and china in great abundance; and the gentlemen loaded me with presents of wine, porter, cyder, rum and sugar, besides a quantity of most exquisite fruits.' He was offered a carriage to ride out in and a black boy to carry an umbrella over him.

Solicitude for his welfare extended even further: 'an elderly negro woman with a black girl about fourteen' appeared one morning in his bedroom. It was usual, she explained, for a white man to have a temporary wife to look after him and his household arrangements. The girl was not bad but, he notes in his *Journal*, 'we don't agree about the price'. It was not necessary to be out of pocket, as far as sex was concerned, at any rate. There were coloured girls at all prices, some even free, if they took sufficient fancy to you.

The white women were also rather pressing. As it was not decent for them to have a black lover and as their husbands were usually at a low ebb from gin, fever and too many mistresses, they were inclined to show, even 'in public the most unequivocal marks of preference towards those gentlemen who newly arrive from Europe'. It was quite embarrassing for a man unaccustomed to local ways. Besides, they were much less attractive than the Negroes and mulattoes as their health did not stand the climate nearly so well. 'They are languid,' remarks Stedman unsympathetically, 'their complexions are sallow and the skin, even of the young ladies is frequently shrivelled.' In spite of this, however, they lasted very much better than their husbands, whose freedom was the death of them: 'I have frequently known wives who have buried four husbands, but never a man in this country who had survived two wives.'

Under these circumstances, domestic life in Surinam was often stormy. Jealous scenes were only too common. The wife would knock her husband's favourites about, go out of her way to humiliate them, beat them in a perverted manner. Even murder was not unknown, since white people were seldom charged with the death of a Negro. The less violent found an outlet in their conversation which was extremely frank. One sometimes met a woman who talked as elegantly as any hostess in the drawing rooms of Amsterdam; but, in general, they spoke of sex, with complete lack of inhibition, comparing husbands in peculiar detail and describing every sort of situation without circumlocution.

It was a little startling until one got used to it. They were such amiable people really. 'Balls, concerts, card-assemblies and every species of amusement in their power were constantly contrived for our entertainment.' The day began at six o'clock in the morning, 'by which time coffee and often chocolate is prepared'.*

* Bolingbroke.

Breakfast was not until ten, so that there were four clear hours for attending to business, or household duties. 'Their rooms generally undergo a thorough scrubbing with lemons every morning, which diffuses a beautiful odour, in opposition to the no less regular fumes of tobacco'* and gin. The maids sang a special scrubbing song as they worked. Breakfast, when it came, was a good, hearty meal, as Stedman found in the course of numerous invitations. There was 'ham, or a joint of salted or smoked meat, or young pigeons, accompanied by butter, cheese, cassava and good strong beer, or else Madeira and water'.† At least a dozen servants waited at table and it was remarkable how agile they were, never running into each other at the doorways with the plates, or getting confused over the courses.

In other respects, the arrangements struck the European visitor as primitive, or careless, considering that there was plenty of money to pay for every convenience. Neither bells nor hand basins were provided in the houses, 'even where there are white females'.* If you wanted anything, you blew a strong blast on an ivory whistle. The servants came running in a crowd. If you then announced that you wanted to wash, a jug of water was produced and poured over that part you declared to be dirty. What didn't run off was wiped into a towel. Thus, as Bolingbroke observed, you were generally a rather grubby ornament to the beautifully scrubbed, lemon-scented rooms.

After breakfast, one attended to the rest of one's business until the siesta time. Then the day's entertainment properly began. If a ball or concert had not been arranged, one could have billiards, chess, cards, drink and gossip at the coffee house. One could promenade the waterfront with the ladies. Dinner was elaborate and heavy. There was an amateur theatre and sometimes companies of strolling Americans appeared to give renderings of the classics which were much appreciated throughout the West Indies.

'The company consisted of but four or five persons,' writes Bolingbroke of one such occasion. 'They had chartered a vessel at New York; they had embarked a cargo of canvass palaces and painted forests, of crowns and daggers, sceptres, chains, of the

* Bolingbroke.
† Fermin.

purple attire of majesty and the motley foppery of folly.' Crowd scenes had to be cut out or left to the imagination. Otherwise, they were superb. 'At Grenada and Barbados they had unpacked their portable theatre and had been received with an applause which was re-echoed from the continent' of South America. If audiences were keen enough, they might stay as long as three months in one place, giving performances in which 'the simplicity of the ancient drama was restored'* by force of circumstances, a development quite congenial to eighteenth-century taste.

'The spirit of conviviality next reached on board the men-of-war,' writes Stedman, 'where we entertained the ladies with cold supper and dancing upon the quarter deck, under an awning, till six in the morning' when the night ended with a carriage drive in the dawn, that was felt to be very reviving after so much activity. 'This constant routine of dissipation, rendered still more pernicious by an intensely hot climate', proved too much of a strain for some of the officers. Several were so undermined that they developed fevers from which it was feared they might not recover.

Even Stedman's constitution began to show signs of wear and tear. Since it was not his intention to die yet, if it could be avoided, he pulled himself up: 'Warned by their example, I retired from all public companies, sensible that by such means could I alone preserve my health in a country which has such a tendency to debilitate the human frame.' At least, that was his intention.

'It was during this period of leisure and uncertainty that I seriously thought of employing myself in writing' a proper book, instead of a mere journal. As well as the record of his travels, he would have a history of the colony, a precise description of the government, social customs, inhabitants of all colours, shrubs, trees, animals; the whole illustrated by drawings made on the spot. With this great object in view, he had every incentive to cut down on dancing and drinking, quite apart from simple prudence, a quality, in any case, foreign to his nature.

It was necessary to hurry if he was not to lose this unique chance of furthering those aspirations he had always had for the intellectual and artistic life. Colonel Fourgeoud was on the worst

* Bolingbroke.

possible terms with the governor of Surinam whom he had insulted at the moment of disembarkation by drawing up his troops on the parade ground in front of the palace with their backs to His Excellency. The conventions of rank and the proper treatment of superiors were matters that assumed an enormous importance in a small community. 'The everlasting disputes and animosities . . . concerning pre-eminence and precedence . . . reaches further than is imagined,' wrote Gravesande of Essequebo wearily, 'and is of evil consequences, especially in time of war or disturbance, when it is almost impossible to get the necessary order issued, or being issued, put into execution.'

This was exactly the situation between the colonel and the governor, 'who were both of them our commanders, but totally independent of each other'. Insults and subterfuges of extraordinary subtlety proliferated as each strove to prove himself the stronger, which 'could not but make our stay at Paramaribo extremely disagreeable to all the officers in our regiment, as well as those of the Society corps', the resident garrison. Finally, the governor could stand it no longer, although the redoubtable Captain Baron and his friends were still loose in the woods, presumably making arrangements to avenge their defeat. He decided 'to acquaint Colonel Fourgeoud that as the rebel negroes seemed no further disposed to disturb the tranquillity of the settlement, its own troops and the corps of black rangers were deemed sufficient for its defence'. That would show the fellow who was master. 'Colonel Fourgeoud with his marines no longer being wanted,' the message concluded grandly, 'was at liberty to return to Europe whenever he thought proper.'

Fourgeoud was obliged to admit that he was not, in all respects, the governor's equal. In the last resort, power was vested in the civil authority. Orders were given to provision the ships for the return journey. 'Various were the feelings of pleasure and reluctance with which our gentlemen received this news.' The idea of having to fight in the jungles and swamps was not particularly appealing. But, on the other hand, routine duty in Bergen op Zoom, or some such place, seemed amazingly unattractive after life *en fête* at Paramaribo.

The ladies of Surinam, however, had not yet had nearly enough of the company of these five hundred new young men. A mere handful had, as yet, been incapacitated by their duties as escorts, lovers and dancing partners. The rest were still, more or less, in prime condition, fresh from the vigorous climate of northern Europe, infinitely superior to anything available among Guiana residents. They, therefore, 'clamorously insisted on our staying'. The governor was obliged to accede to their request, temporarily, at any rate. Perhaps he thought, on further consideration, that it would look bad if he dismissed the help sent from Holland in response to his own appeals before it was reasonably certain that the rebellion had really subsided. It was too soon to say definitely whether Captain Baron had given up, or was recruiting himself for a tremendous blow in the forest. It would be prudent to bow to the ladies' wishes, even though some might say he had been worsted by Colonel Fourgeoud in the second round.

'The wooding and watering of the vessels was provisionally stopped, but the ships still kept in commission', as a face-saving compromise. Stedman now realized that if he was really to collect material for his book, he must devote himself to the task. Who could say when he might suddenly be shipped back to Holland and the opportunity of a lifetime be missed through indolence, gin and late nights?

The governor was very excited when Stedman confided his plan to him. He liked this young officer and thought highly of his abilities. Entering on the project with enthusiasm, he advised on writers to be consulted and lent him 'several manuscripts'. Perhaps he had himself aspired to authorship before the climate and the triviality of life in Paramaribo had enervated him too much; for it seems he had made some study of the country at one time, though he was hampered by a fundamental lack of education. Not only did he place his library at Stedman's disposal, 'but daily furnished me with such a succession of animals, shrubs, etc., as I was desirous of being acquainted with'.

To hobnob with the governor was to get into the bad books of Colonel Fourgeoud. It was a tricky situation. Promotion depended on good reports from the colonel; a partial escape from the military treadmill on the governor's benevolence. In this dilemma, 'I made it my earnest study and endeavour, if possible, to keep friends with both parties; and, independent of that duty which I owed to Colonel Fourgeoud, as my commander-in-chief, to treat the governor of the colony with that respect which I thought was due to his dignity, his rank and his conduct.'

It was no easy matter to strike so delicate a balance. There were some who despised the colonel for his obsessive self-importance and these supported Stedman. Others were convinced followers of Fourgeoud, or thought it best to cultivate his good opinion; or took exception to Stedman on various grounds, such as his interest in reading and drawing, or his having insulted them in other ways.

Although he had made resolutions to devote himself to intellectual pursuits, as had happened so often before, Stedman was only able to keep them in a rather fragmentary manner. He did a certain amount of reading and drew a number of plants, but his *Journal* shows that he continued to breakfast and dine with the hospitable planters daily. At one party, he met a rich widow who took a strong fancy for him. He was advised, by friends having his interest at heart, to marry her and set himself up in comfort for life. It was the sensible thing to do, he could see that. But when he looked at her, his romantic soul recoiled. Why did he hesitate, they asked? She might not be beauty personified, but think of her money, her plantation, her slave girls, every one of whom he would have the right to enjoy. Was he not for ever complaining of the military life and trying to think of decent alternatives? Surely, this proposal contained a more certain fortune than his famous projected book? These things were true enough, yet he would not even consider the proposition. With characteristic optimism, he preferred to trust the future.

A few days later, while breakfasting with a Mr Demelly, he himself received the same sort of powerful impression as had the disappointed widow. As he settled down to ham and beer and fruit, his eye was suddenly arrested by 'the beautiful mulatto maid, Joanna'. Though an habitué of the house, he had not happened to see her before. He stared at her with the greatest excitement. 'She was possessed of the most elegant shape that nature can exhibit,' he wrote afterwards. 'Her face was full of native modesty and the most distinguished sweetness; her eyes, as black as ebony, were large and full of expression . . . with cheeks through which glowed, in spite of the darkness of her complexion, a beautiful tinge of vermilion, when gazed upon.'

Continuing his inspection, he found her nose rather small and the lips prominent, as in all Negro features. Her black-brown ringlets were decorated with gold spangles and flowers. 'Round her neck, her arms, her ancles, she wore gold chains, rings and medals: while a shawl of India muslin, the end of which was negligently thrown over her polished shoulders, gracefully covered part of her lovely bosom.' A chintz skirt and a beaver hat, trimmed with silver, which she carried in her hand, completed the dress of this striking girl. He had noticed many handsome maids during his stay in Surinam, but none with such close attention. She seemed to be about fifteen.

As soon as she had left the room, he turned to his hostess, demanding details. How could so wonderful a young woman, with such an air of assurance, be a mere slave? Why, she had quite a substantial sum fastened on to her in spangles, medals, bracelets, chains and necklaces. 'She is, Sir,' replied Mrs Demelly succinctly, 'the daughter of a respectable gentleman, named Kruythoff; who had, besides this girl, four children by a black woman called Cery, the property of a Mr D.B. on his estate called Fauconberg, in the upper part of the river Commewyne.'

Mr D.B. was a notorious brute and Kruythoff, unable to endure the thought of his beautiful children subjected to whippings, tortures and repulsive embraces, tried to buy their freedom. But Mr D.B. only laughed spitefully, even when offered 'above one thousand pounds sterling'. The dismal fate of his sons and daughters so preyed on Kruythoff that he gradually went off his head, 'and died in that melancholy state soon after', having pressed on Cery the golden ornaments, now worn by Joanna, in a short fit of lucidity, 'just before he expired'.

What an extraordinary story. Yet, more was to come. Mr D.B.'s behaviour was so outrageous that all his best slaves took to the woods, among them Joanna's uncle, 'Jolycoeur, and he is now the first of Baron's captains, whom you may have a chance of meeting in the rebel camp, breathing revenge against the Christians,' said Mrs Demelly.

As in all the best tales, the villain came to a bad end. Since every decent workman had fled from his estate, he soon found himself beginning to go down hill. For, though it was possible to replace them with new slaves, these were not much use until trained. In short, everything collapsed, 'he was ruined and obliged to fly the colony and leave his estate and stock to the disposal of his creditors'. His unfortunate wife was then arrested for debt, being held in Surinam until the plantation could be sold. She was not, however, in prison, but lodging with Mrs Demelly. Joanna was her personal maid.

This relation of wickedness receiving its due reward had one awkward consequence: Joanna would be sold with the rest of the effects at Fauconberg by the creditors. She had always been protected and kindly treated by Mrs D.B., one could see that. Nor had she ever had to work in the fields. There was nothing to prevent her new master putting her into a gang; or having her tied to a post and beaten till she was covered with blood because she could not perform the unaccustomed labour; or because she did not welcome his amorous advances. Or, if she submitted with a good grace, her mistress might be driven by jealousy to extremities. The body of a coloured girl floating down the river was one of those objects from which one averted one's eyes in Surinam. The possibilities and permutations were endless.

'I could not help execrating the barbarity of Mr D.B. for having withheld her from a fond parent, who by bestowing on her a decent education and some accomplishments, would probably have produced in this foresaken plant, now exposed to every rude blast without protection, an ornament to civilized society,' Stedman noted. 'I became melancholy with these reflections.' As a boy, he had saved innumerable soldiers from floggings by running to his father. As a young man, he had never unjustly punished the people who happened to be in his power except when mad drunk, a state of mind his victims had understood and forgiven, especially as he was always visibly filled with remorse afterwards. But now he was quite unable even to mitigate hardships which might come to this charming, gentle girl, skipping about so innocently in medals and bracelets, twirling her beaver hat.

His hatred of cruelty had not been dulled by years of the brutalities of army life and, indeed, life in general in the eighteenth century where apprentices and servants were in a position little better than slaves; emigrants died in hundreds from overcrowding in the ships to America; the poor fell down dead in the streets from starvation if there happened to be a trade recession and they could not get work; prisoners were hanged for small thefts. He was not devoted to high philosophic principles like his uncle Dr Stedman in Scotland; or carried away by crusading fervour, like the abolitionists in England. It was just that violence, committed in cold blood and with the carelessness of habit, enraged him.

Stedman's approach to the problem of slavery was strictly practical. He did not see anything wrong with it in principle and never, in his book, discusses it from the theoretical, or political, point of view. It was his opinion that, under a kind master, a slave was better provided for than a workman in Europe. He had always enough to eat and a cottage of his own for his wife and children. On a well conducted plantation, the hours of work were regular and not impossibly long. He had a little plot of land and could sell the produce of it on his own account. There were even cases of slaves who were permitted to set up shop in Paramaribo, paying their master a percentage of the profits. Such men might become quite comfortably off and have slaves of their own. They might buy their freedom; or not bother to run to that expense, if present arrangements satisfied them. Others might be given their freedom in their master's will, together with a small sum of money.

Everything depended on the vagaries of the master's character. If he was a miserable fellow who had bought an estate cheap because it was in debt, in the hope of making a quick fortune, the outlook was poor. If he lived in Holland on money remitted by his overseer, coming to his property perhaps once in a lifetime anything could happen to a girl like Joanna and she would have no redress. For a slave's word was not accepted in a court of law against that of a European. It was only necessary for the master to deny the charge for the whole case to collapse.

Stedman thought that the absence of legal rights was the source of all the evils of slavery. The good master was a blessing above anything experienced by the wage earners of Amsterdam; and the wicked one a curse which could be removed quite simply by passing laws curbing his power to injure those for whose well-being he was morally responsible. But the planters of Paramaribo showed not the smallest intention of effecting this profound revolution. They were vastly outnumbered by their slaves. How could one dare encourage them to be uppish? The bush Negroes showed how difficult and dangerous a black man could become when not kept under proper control.

Brooding on these questions, Stedman 'began to take more delight in the prattling of my poor Negro boy Quaco, than in all the fashionable conversation of the polite inhabitants of this colony', though it was possible, he admitted, that this spirit of retreat was accentuated by the onset of a bad attack of prickly heat, accompanied by fever. In his distress, he was very grateful for an anonymous present of 'a few preserved tamarinds and a basket of fine oranges'. He discovered later that Joanna had sent them.

'My parents lived by hunting and fishing,' Quaco chattered beside his bed. 'I was stolen from them very young whilst playing on the sands with two little brothers; I was put in a sack and carried for several miles. I afterwards became the slave of a king on the coast of Guinea, with several hundreds more. When our master died, the principal part of his slaves were beheaded and buried along with him; I, with some other children of my age, were bestowed as presents on the different captains of his army, and the master of a Dutch ship afterwards had me, in exchange for a musket and some gun-powder.'

In a week or so, Stedman was well enough to accept an invitation to recuperate at a coffee plantation belonging to a certain Captain Macneal.

XI

PLANTATIONS

'We now set out from Paramaribo . . . in a tent boat, or barge, rowed by eight of Captain Macneal's best negroes,' Stedman notes. His spirits rose, for the fever had left him and Guiana again seemed a wonderful country. The slaves sang as they pulled the oars; the plantations glided past. 'The general neatness and formal regularity of a Dutch estate has a peculiar mien,' says Bolingbroke. 'The houses, buildings, bridges, gates are carefully painted white, which is the favourite colour of the Hollanders. Roads regularly serpentine lead to their dwellings: and little square clusters, or straight alleys of cocoa nuts and limes, indicate the measuring, methodical taste of the continental gardners.'

English estates were less elaborately laid out and also more profitably worked, since labour was not diverted from cultivating cash crops to keeping up this almost suburban neatness. 'All the land is so rich,' Bolingbroke continues, 'that it requires little or no attention after being planted, except weeding three or four times within the year. Naturally, therefore, the more ground is planted the greater the produce.' Yet, judging from their usual standard of comfort, the Dutch of Surinam seem not to have suffered very severely from the diversion of some part of the profits to making their plantations attractive to the eye.

A tent boat was especially built for speed and its rowers selected for strength, but, even so, journeys took time, if one's destination was beyond those settlements adjoining Paramaribo itself. The rivers wound backwards and forwards over the flat ground. The boat covered many miles without necessarily advancing very far. One might have to pass down one river and then up another, finally entering a narrow creek, the mouth of which seemed a mere dark hole among the trees. One might be obliged to spend a night on the way. In that case, one disembarked at whatever plantation one had reached at dusk, for there were no inns. According to the custom of the country, the owner, or overseer, came at once to welcome the unexpected guests. The house and every possible convenience were put at the travellers' disposal. A strange face, a new voice, the latest news were welcome additions to an evening otherwise diversified only by gin, draughts and cards with persons only too familiar. Dutch hospitality, however, surpassed the mere necessities of loneliness and boredom. It was renowned throughout the West Indies.

Captain Macneal's estate seems not to have been remotely situated, for they reached it easily within the day. 'The buildings on a coffee estate,' Stedman notes methodically, 'are, first, the dwelling house which is usually situated for pleasure near the banks of a river' and flanked by large flower-beds. In front of it was the landing stage with a sentry box on either side. Behind and more or less concealed by a grove of orange trees, were ranged the overseer's house, offices, barns, sheds, pigsties, slave quarters, hospital, guard house, boat house and a couple of paddocks for the few horses, sheep and cows that managed to survive in a climate totally unsuited to their constitution.

This area was surrounded not only by a large drainage ditch, but also by a navigable canal on three sides. The fields of coffee trees, or sugar, as the case might be, were reached by a single drawbridge over the canal. The settlement was like a village protected by a moat, which gave some defence against surprise incursions by bush Negroes. There was also a system of sentries and night watchmen, whose fires could be seen twinkling and whose regular shouts be heard at intervals until the dawn. These precautions depended for their efficacy, however, on satisfied and loyal slaves.

Captain Macneal was one of the good masters. On landing from his barge, he was informed that the overseer had, during his absence, 'by bad usage and cruelty, caused the death of three or four negroes'. Having satisfied himself that the complaint was justified, he instantly sacked the overseer, 'ordering him to depart from the plantation in an inferior boat, called a ponkee*, to Paramaribo, or wherever he thought proper'. Everyone was much elated by the signal act of justice. How many masters would simply have dismissed the story as a slander and had the complainants flogged to teach them better respect?

This paragon of a planter went even further: 'The overseer's

* A flat-bottomed boat, something like a large punt, but rowed by four or six oars.

sentence was the more ignominious and galling as at the time of receiving it a negro foot-boy who was buckling his shoes was ordered back and he was desired to buckle them himself.' All present felt that the death of three, or four, had been amply punished by the dismissal of the murderer without references in a boat on which it was beneath his dignity to embark and having had to put on his own shoes in public. The slaves were full of joy and praise of their owner, especially as a day's holiday was proclaimed on the spot, 'which was spent in festivity, by dancing and clapping hands on a green before the dwelling-house windows'. Jugs of a special raw sort of rum, called killdevil, were always provided on such occasions.

For the Africans, in spite of their enormous labours, never cared to spend a holiday resting: 'One of the greatest passions of this people is the dance; no one in the world is more attached to it. There are even some who can dance a minuet as well as a White; but it does not amuse them very much. What they really like is to make all sorts of indecent movements and gestures, during which, nevertheless, the rhythm is strictly observed; for they have a wonderful ear.'* It was marvellous to watch their leaps and pirouettes, advancing and retreating, continue unabated hour after hour. 'One would have to be born with suppleness like theirs, in order to imitate them.'*

Their improvisations were extraordinary. Each performer did something different and yet kept time to the drums, guitars, handclaps and singing. The leader sang a line 'on some subject which seems to him apposite and the refrain is repeated by all the spectators'* who formed a circle round the dance and consisted of those temporarily exhausted, or too young or too old to take part. On this occasion, one must suppose, the song described the downfall of the hated overseer, the lucky arrival of the sainted master and his honoured guest; with every possible variation, history and apocryphal adventure, since it lasted all day long.

Although such an entertainment was very far from the sedate figures admired in the eighteenth century, there was something impressive and exhilarating about it, when one got used to the strangeness. The slave captains on the Guinea coast of Africa found it noisy, savage and boring. Only the necessities of trade
* Fermin.

made them sit patiently beside the local king, watching his subjects yelling, jumping and banging on their drums for hours on end. Yet, on those who spent their lives among the slaves of Surinam, a spell was often cast and they could not help exclaiming that the Negroes had, supremely, 'the art of the dance'.*

Stedman spent about a week on this estate and had his sensibilities not been sharpened by the thought of Joanna, he might have continued to admire his friend Macneal as a benevolent man, ready to send a murderer about his business without a moment's hesitation, refusing to listen to excuses. The strong impression Joanna had made on him and the conviction that she was not only fully human, but even deserving of as much respect as any other decent girl, made him look critically at 'a handsome young negro' who was hobbling about 'while the others were capering and dancing'. In answer to his question, the captain readily replied that the boy 'having repeatedly run away from his work, he had been obliged to hamstring him'. This, too, was an instance of humanity on his part, though Stedman did not quite realize it at the time: a usual punishment for attempting to take to the woods was to have a leg cut off.

As so often happened in Guiana, a shade was suddenly cast over the life devoted to comfort and pleasure. One could only avert one's eyes and have another gin to help the moment pass. For, in general, the days were full of interest to one fresh out from Holland and imbued with an unflagging curiosity. Stedman visited a number of plantations during this period of military inaction. He noted carefully the habits of good masters and bad; of overseers and Negroes.

Sometimes he was startled by the careless barbarity, or indecency, of what he saw. On other occasions, he felt the anti-slavery party had not given the planters sufficient credit, or allowed for the plain fact that black men, too, can have a cruel and disagreeable character. I claim 'no other merit whatever throughout these pages,' he writes passionately at the end of his book, 'than that of having spoke the *simple truth*; which, if I wilfully have violated, may these volumes perish and be forgotten with their author!'

With this stern object, he scouted round, his eyes wide open

* Fermin.

and Joanna at the back of his mind. The day began at six in the morning with coffee on the verandah, served 'by half a dozen of the finest young slaves, both male and female'. Having sniffed the air and woken fully, a planter was ready for 'his pipe, tobacco and flask of gin',* with which he relaxed until the overseer made his appearance to report 'what work was done the day before; what negroes deserted, died, fell sick, recovered, were bought or born; and, above all things, which of them neglected their work, affected sickness, or had been drunk or absent, etc.' The master then decided how to punish the defaulters: whether to let them off with a caution, or to have them tied up and beaten on the spot. It depended on his mood and general amiability.

Some relied on lecturing, either on account of a kind heart, or else because they found that ill-treatment only put the slaves into a bad frame of mind; and also made them physically less able to cope with the work, which reduced the profits. Others considered that you had to make an example of wrong-doers, unless you wanted to be taken for a soft character, easily imposed on by sham illnesses or the many ingenious excuses that poured so readily from African tongues. The worst sort flogged everyone 'men, women or children, without exception', walking up and down in front of the victims, gin in hand, enjoying the blood and screams.

Whatever the planter wished was done at once, without the smallest protest being offered. 'Dutch overseers treat their principals with the utmost respect; as they approach Mynheer within half a dozen yards, the hat is immediately doffed as a token of their inferiority and is placed under the arm while receiving his orders, to all of which the answer is, Yes, great and honoured Sir.'*

'Next makes her appearance a superannuated matron, with all the young negro children of the estate, over whom she is governess; these, being clean washed in the river, clap their hands and cheer in chorus', being rewarded thereafter with breakfast consisting of 'a large platter of rice and plantains; and the levee ends with a low bow from the overseer, as it began'.

The day's work on the plantation now started under the overseer's eye. Nobody was a more great and honoured sir than he when the master was out of sight. The amount of cringing and

* Bolingbroke.

grovelling he exacted were in excess of the obeisances he had to give to his superior, the punishments he dealt out more severe. If they resulted in death, sometimes, there were many explanations that could be given. Who would dare to contradict him? It required energy, as well as a sense of justice, to go into matters as Captain Macneal had done. Apart from the tedious business of listening to complaints and deciding where the truth lay, it might not be so easy to find a replacement, a zealous man who could be relied on to produce a satisfactory balance sheet at the end of the year. A planter, says Stedman, 'seldom weighs above eight or ten stone, being generally exhausted by the climate and dissipation'. In such a state of health, even the best were predisposed to let things slide; to take the money and ask no inconvenient questions.

The order of the day having been settled, the master and his guests, if any, sat down to a good Dutch breakfast. 'A soup flavoured with the juice of the bitter cassava and made pungent with red and green pepper is a constant concomitant. Madeira wine and water and malt liquor are substituted for tea; they are considered more strengthening.'* As always, a great number of servants waited at table. They might be dressed in pretty skirts, like Joanna. Or, they might not have a stitch on, as Stedman once found to his astonishment, though no one of the party except himself seemed to see anything eccentric in this arrangement. The mistress merely remarked that it was done with the slaves' consent. They had their own black reasons for approving of a custom which was, perhaps, a little bizarre to a newcomer whose prejudices had been formed in Amsterdam.

Sometimes the atmosphere had a paternal tinge: the room was full of mulatto children. 'I have seen eight, or ten, round their master's chair at breakfast, or dinner, having their platters filled,' remarks Bolingbroke, with reference to a planter whose hospitality he much appreciated. 'There are generally some pets of the kind on every estate; but this proprietor was particularly fond of the children and used to enjoy their antic nakedness. Their sports agreeably recall the basso-relievos of antiquity.'

During the early part of the day, the master wore 'his morning dress, which consists of a pair of the finest Holland trowsers, white silk stockings and red or yellow Morocco slippers; the neck

* Bolingbroke.

of his shirt open and nothing over it, a loose flowing nightgown of the finest India chintz excepted. On his head is a cotton night-cap as thin as a cobweb and, over that, an enormous beaver hat.' For the tour of inspection, a little later, he might become more dressy, putting on a wig, shoes, silk breeches. In all these operations, he was plentifully assisted by his slaves, one of whom was deputed to shave him, while another vigorously waved a fan to keep off mosquitoes. He then sallied out on foot, or horseback, attended by a slave holding an umbrella over him, a boy with 'a pouch of sigars and a stick of fire',* a girl with a decanter of wine and a glass.

Everyone he passed saluted him with the deepest respect and, if asked, expressed the greatest enthusiasm for his person, character and the arrangements made for the general welfare. Thus, people anxious to prove that slavery was congenial to the African personality, had no difficulty in collecting opinions to support their contention. 'During my residence in Demerary,' says Bolingbroke, 'I made it a regular question of enquiry among plantation-negroes . . . whether they preferred their own country to this; and I hereby make a solemn asservation . . . that of several hundred negroes to whom I put the question at different periods, they have all given the preference to their present situations.' No doubt they were speaking the truth in some cases. It depended on the overseer.

It was quite possible to take a rosy view of slavery, provided one was careful where one looked. 'Often have I contemplated, with inexpressible pleasure, a grey-headed negro and his wife sitting at the door of their cottage, fondly protecting and enjoying the active sports of their grandchildren,' Bolingbroke continues, his eyes swimming with sentimental tears.

'Is it not indeed hard, Your Honours,' wrote Gravesande, governor of Essequebo and Demerara, giving the other side of the picture in 1760, 'that these old people (whose number is fairly large) having spent their younger years working for the Honble. Co., should when they have grown old and weak be driven, like old horses, naked and uncared for from pillar to post? Of rations, too, they have no share and are obliged to live upon the mercy of their children and friends, who have not too much themselves.'

* Bolingbroke.

127

Far from it. 'The expence of maintaining the Slaves in this climate is very trifling,' wrote Dr Edward Bancroft in 1766. 'The first year that a slave is purchased, he is supplied with food by his master, and is assigned a piece of ground which, on Sundays, he clears.' Once his yams, cassava and bananas were established, he provided his own food, 'receiving however from his master a weekly allowance of dried fish, to the amount of a pound and a half'. Nor were his clothes a severe charge on the plantation, being 'scarce sufficient to answer the demands of modesty' except in the case of household servants. While a young man, his wife and one or two children might live comfortably off their garden and even have something over to sell, it was not so easy to support a large family and grandparents, unless the plot was generous.

Some owners even tried to get rid of old slaves at a cheap rate to people who would certainly be the death of them in a short time. Apart from the obvious cruelty of this, as Gravesande pointed out in 1769, it would cause great indignation and unrest among the younger slaves, their relatives. 'Besides, who would bid a farthing for such slaves that are naught else than a burden?' he urges his employers, the West India Company in faraway Holland. 'Personally, I would not have them as a gift, except perhaps about four, like my old cook Claertje who was the first slave I possessed and who is a very good midwife.'

Claertje, then, at least, fulfilled Bolingbroke's vision of the happy old slave, sitting in the sun at his cottage door, minding the babies. These so-called cottages were really huts, 'eight or nine feet high ... the only opening being a small, low door ... and their furniture consists only of one, or two, beds for the whole family ... a few earthenware pots ... and a few oddments of little value.'* As the nights were chilly and damp during the wet season, they would shut the door tightly and light a fire, 'without worrying about the smoke, by which they are practically suffocated',* and more or less kippered: they were inclined to smell of smoke, especially during the heat of the day.

Yet, under a master such as Captain Macneal, these slum conditions were not considered intolerable. 'In sickness and in health, in his young and old age (the slave) is alike treated, maintained, clothed and lodged,' declares Bolingbroke. 'All the old settled

* Fermin.

128

estates can boast of having reared negroes of three and four generations.' It was simple good business, as well as the expression of humanitarian feelings, to take care for the happiness and natural increase of one's slaves. Why buy, at great expense, in the market when a little forethought provided a continuous supply of free young slaves? One of Bolingbroke's acquaintance, not having enough women on his estate, took his unmarried men 'to a sale-room, where a cargo of negroes was just landed', invited them to choose those they fancied and paid for the girls himself.

'As a couple, they generally live happy and are very tenacious of decorum,' adds Bolingbroke. Even more, they were as jealous as Italians, in Fermin's experience. It was madness for an owner, or overseer, to debauch a black man's wife. Nothing but trouble came of it. The Negroes were adept in the old African craft of poisoning. They had studied the trees and plants of Guiana with this end in view and could distil potions which it was impossible to detect, even in water.

As Stedman remarked over and over again, it was lunacy to treat the slaves so badly that even those of low intelligence and lethargic disposition began to see that they were, in actual fact, the masters of Guiana. By sheer numbers and the essential nature of their services, they controlled their owners' fate. But it was easy to prevent such dangerous thoughts. One need only to treat them to regular holidays with dancing and drink; to be free with the rations and allow time and opportunity for making a modest private income either from a vegetable plot of generous size, or some other form of trade; to respect their personal relationships, not selling a son, or daughter, without first consulting the parents; above all, to administer justice tempered with mercy. Under such reasonable conditions, the slaves were not only contented, but extremely loyal, never troubling their heads with questions of natural rights, government by consent, the equality of man and similar abstractions of awkward practical consequence.

As Stedman sadly noted, these self-evident truths were not apparent to many planters who, from conceit, dissipation, an idea of making quick money and general low character, had sunk to a condition where they were not even able to realize where their true pecuniary advantage lay. It was useless to argue. They could take nothing in. On these estates the slaves did not increase for various reasons. The infants were not properly looked after and quickly died of fever and wrong feeding. Or the mothers had to work too hard while pregnant. Or there was not a large enough proportion of women among the slaves. But 'the true cause of their want of increase,' in Dr Bancroft's opinion, after many years observation in the country, 'results from the intercourse of the Whites with the young wenches, who derive no inconsiderable emolument therefrom; and as child-bearing would put an end to this commerce, they solicitously use every precaution to avoid conception; and if these prove ineffectual, they ever procure repeated abortions, which incapacitate them from child-bearing in a more advanced age when they are abandoned by the Whites.' It would require an extraordinary revolution of opinion and custom to solve this problem in eighteenth-century Surinam.

Stedman eagerly examined every aspect of plantation life during the short period of military inaction. He drew the plants and watched the mills at work, processing the sugar. Putting the canes through the rollers in order to squeeze out the juice was a job for skilled men. It had to be done very neatly or the fingers were trapped. Since it was impossible to stop the mill quickly, the only way of preventing the whole body going through the mangle was to cut off the arm. For this purpose, a sharp hatchet was kept handy.

He looked into the vats of molasses and saw the furnace used in the distillation of killdevil, the fiery spirit guaranteed to rot a man's guts in due course. Here, he had an unexpected shock on one estate. The owners had been so hospitable, had laid themselves out to entertain him with the utmost kindness. Yet chained to the furnace was a slave 'in the intense heat of a perpetual fire night and day, being blistered all over, until he should expire'. No attempt was made to prevent Stedman conversing with the prisoner. It appeared that, having been sentenced to what he considered an unjust beating, he had first tried to knife the overseer and then himself. 'He shewed me his wounds with a smile of contempt, which I returned with a sigh and a small donation', being powerless to do more than express an inadequate sympathy and pass on, hoping to forget.

Everything else was so gay and genial, 'but these Elysian fields could not dissipate the gloom which the infernal furnace had left upon my mind'. He brooded, therefore, as the slaves who had kept out of trouble went about their tasks, singing the various working songs, dancing on the banks and bathing in the river when the evening came, hurrying to the market place on the news that an itinerant trader had arrived. These were either Jews, or free coloured women, or their slaves. Travelling perpetually up and down the many rivers and creeks, they did business with planters, overseers, Negroes, Indians, anyone with goods for sale, or barter if money was scarce.

'The hucksters expose for sale articles of European manufacture . . . in addition to salt beef, pork, fish, bread, cheese, pipes, to-bacco . . . They are provided with such an assortment as to be able to supply the negro with a coarse check, or the manager with a fine cambric for his shirts. Coloured women of all descriptions are extravagantly fond of dress and . . . feel a lively sensation of joy and pleasure at the sight of a huckster.'* They would buy a Negro's garden produce for resale in Paramaribo, or at one of the military forts. From the Indians they obtained a few slaves, hammocks, baskets and large earthenware pots used for storing drinking water.

Some traders were successful and came to 'possess ten, fifteen and twenty negroes, all of whom they employ in this traffic. It is by no means an uncommon thing for negroes in this line to be travelling about the country for several weeks together, sometimes with an attendant, having trunks of goods to a considerable amount, say £200.'* These were the big bosses in the business with a flair for avoiding bad debts and for finding and training competent slaves.

More usual was the type of person described by Gravesande in a moment of irritation: 'Not a single example can be adduced of any itinerant trader ever having acquired a competency, let alone riches,' he says roundly, determined to put the worst face on things because he desired permission from his employers to forbid them the upper reaches of the Essequebo, on account of the nui-sance they caused there. 'On the contrary, they are always poor and laden with debts. Nor can this be otherwise since for every journey they have to buy the necessary trading wares at a high price and on credit and, frequently not bringing back sufficient to pay what they owe, have to hand over their slaves, or other goods,

* Bolingbroke.

cheaply and in this fashion never get clear but always remain poor and in debt. Moreover, the blessing of the Lord can never be expected to rest on that trade, on account of the godless life those itinerant traders lead.'

Many of them were not Christians, in any case, or, at the best, only partially so. In the French and Spanish possessions, all the slaves were baptized and obliged to attend mass punctually, to confess their transgressions and revere the priests in a suitable manner. But in the English and Dutch West Indies conversion was not encouraged. It was felt that the protestant religion contained ideas, especially among the more extreme sects, which might give the slaves notions above their proper place in life. It would be inconvenient to have them pondering such texts as, 'The last shall be first and the first shall be last'. These cautious feelings accorded very well with the Dutch policy that everyone should be free to practise his own religion as he pleased.

Only an emancipated slave was obliged to embrace the white man's god. For the rest, the Negroes retained their African beliefs. As they came of many tribes and from different parts of Guinea, their divinities were numerous and the rituals confused, either from imperfect remembrance, or lack of qualified witch doctors and the correct sacrificial ingredients to perform the rites. Many thought it only sensible to incorporate Christ and God into their pantheon. For these were powerful spirits, full of dangerous magic. It would be stupid to neglect them, particularly as one was living in their country where their influence was at its strongest. Under these circumstances, and with this background, one feels that the protestantism of the free Negroes and mulattoes of Surinam was of an exotic tinge, helplessly deprecated by their pastors.

During his peregrinations round the various estates he visited, Stedman was also struck by the wasteful manner in which the labour force was deployed. Out of every 100 slaves, he calculated, no less than 75 were house boys, maids, cooks, extra servants standing about for show, gardeners, odd job men, grooms, cow-men, pigmen, oarsmen, nurses and so on, leaving a mere 25 to cultivate the fields where the only real work was done. There were, according to his information, about 80,000 slaves alto-gether. Thus, 'while full 30,000 live better than the common people of England, and near 30,000 are kept in idleness and do no work in the fields; the remaining 20,000 may be classed (that is in general) among the most miserable wretches on earth; and are worked and starved and flogged to death, without being so much as allowed to complain for redress'. Could anything be more impolitic in present circumstances?

Yet, the planters continued serenely, as though under a spell, to employ overseers who, during their absence at Paramaribo, caused the death of three, or four, and the illness of an unstated number. One sacked the man, of course, if one was a benevolent master, but another had to take his place. How was it possible to tell what the newcomer was really like until one had given him a trial? They all made such tremendous protestations and one could not always be watching over them. The heat was too great for such exertions; and the life too dull to be supported by anyone with enough money to escape.

After a tour round the plantation, what could one do to pass the empty hours, unless, by some good fortune, guests arrived? There were books, chess, billiards, cards, music, drink, tobacco with which to fill in the time until the siesta. After this, thank heaven, dinner came on, 'where nothing is wanting that the world can afford in a western climate of meat, fowls, venison, fish, vegetables, fruits, etc., and the most exquisite wines are often squandered in profusion . . . while the cringing overseer sits at the farther end, keeping his proper distance'.

An account of the day's work was then given and any faults requiring punishment dealt with. 'Sometimes it is the wish of the proprietor that the negroes, after leaving work, should come and receive their daily allowance of rum before his door, where he sits in state smoking his pipe, sullenly receiving the reiterated thanks of the negroes in broken English and Dutch.'* The problem now was to fill up the evening until bedtime. Usually, one was reduced to sending for the overseer 'to play cards or draughts with him, which is considered a great mark of favour',* the employee humbly losing all the games or, at least, as many as he thought necessary.

As one might indeed expect, 'his worship generally begins to yawn about ten or eleven o'clock, when he withdraws and is undressed by his sooty pages. He then retires to rest, where he

* Bolingbroke.

passes the night in the arms of one or other of his sable sultanas, for he always keeps a seraglio'. So did the overseer. Nor was a guest neglected in this respect.

It is hardly surprising that, after a few days devoted to business, the planter began to feel that he had had enough, had done his duty, exerted his authority and rights sufficiently for the time being. What was the use of having money unless one could buy enjoyment? At Paramaribo, there were parties and dinners every night. One was continually hurrying from one entertainment to another, instead of sitting here with a rascally overseer in the middle of vast forests and swamps, half an hour's row, at least, from the nearest house, even supposing the inhabitants should be in residence. Such penance was not to be endured longer than was absolutely necessary. Let the tent boat be ready at half past six tomorrow morning.

XII

JOANNA'S WEDDING

Arriving in Paramaribo once more, Stedman found the future of the expedition still undecided. The rebels were quiescent. The planters murmured about the expense of supporting unnecessary troops. The army was being depleted at a rate hardly less than if they had been engaged in active service. 'Our common soldiers fell the victims of idleness and licentiousness, and died frequently six or seven a day.' Yellow fever swept them off after their health had been undermined by too strenuous amusement. This illness was so usual among newcomers to the West Indies, as to be called locally, 'the seasoning'.

Colonel Fourgeoud and the governor had patched up their quarrel sufficiently to observe a frigid politeness towards each other. As the colonel left in his barge to survey the rivers Surinam and Cottica, in case action should ever be necessary, he was 'saluted by the guns from Fort Zeelandia . . . This compliment I acknowledge astonished me,' writes Stedman. But it represented only a sort of armed truce. The two men could never be friends. They had insulted each other too deeply and were, besides, both persons very mindful of their dignity. 'Governor Nepveu was said to be rather a man of sense than of learning and was wholly indebted to his art and address for having risen to his present dignity from sweeping the hall of the court house.' These same gifts had enabled him to make a fortune. Though vain and insecure, as so often with self-made men, he was tough and could control himself if it seemed that he must. He felt that he had to put up with Fourgeoud until it could definitely be said that the danger was over. If he stuck it out for a couple of months, that would surely be enough.

Fourgeoud, on the other hand, conspicuously lacked self-control, tact, calmness, sophistication and all those qualities which help life to glide more smoothly over difficult places. Though 'a most indefatigable man in bearing hardships and in braving dangers not exceeded by Columbus himself', it had to be admitted that 'he was impetuous, passionate, self-sufficient and revengeful'.

It could not be said that he was directly cruel to his men, but since he was ready to endure forced marches, starvation rations and all other dramatic misfortunes, his subordinates were obliged to follow suit, even in situations where such extreme measures seemed totally unnecessary. It was also difficult to get him to disgorge one's pay. He had read a certain amount, which enabled him to put on intellectual airs, but as he 'had no education to assist him in digesting' his studies, discussion was unprofitable. Yet, in his more balanced moments, he knew, as well as the governor, that the danger was not over. Therefore, he cruised up and down the main rivers, keeping his eyes open and laying his plans.

While his colonel thus attended to duty, Stedman resumed his previous round of entertainments, breakfasting and dining in a hospitable circle and making love to a rather lively friend of Joanna's. 'I was once more as happy as Paramaribo could make me.' For, though he desired Joanna extremely, she hesitated and he was obliged to content himself with the role of protector. This was something she stood in need of. Mrs D.B., her owner, had managed to flee the country, secretly boarding the *Boreas*, with the captain's connivance, when the ship returned to Holland after having escorted Stedman and his companions to Guiana. Joanna was staying with her aunt, a free woman of Paramaribo, expecting 'hourly to be sent up to the estate Fauconberg, friendless and at the mercy of some unprincipled overseer appointed by the creditors, who had now taken possession of the plantation and stock till the whole should be sold' in settlement of Mr D.B.'s debts.

Recent observations and experiences crowded his mind. He must somehow find the money to buy her. She should be educated, taken to Holland, pampered, saved, anything rather than partake of such scenes as he had witnessed on the estates.

The life of a servant in Paramaribo was quite degrading enough. Arrangements at the house of his particular friend Lolkens illustrated the point to perfection. This was a most good-natured man, the same at whose door Stedman had received such a strange and warm welcome on his first night in the town. Dining there one day, as was his frequent custom, 'I was an eye witness of the unpardonable contempt with which negro slaves are treated in this colony. His son, a boy not more than ten years old, when sitting at table, gave a slap in the face to a grey-headed black woman who, by accident, touched his powdered hair', as she leaned forward to offer a dish. No one admonished the child for bad manners, Lolkens merely answering his guest's protest with an easy smile, saying that his son 'should no longer offend me, as he was next day to sail for Holland, for education . . . At the same moment a sailor passing by broke the head of a negro with a bludgeon for not having saluted him with his hat'.

Not that he blamed the sailors for being a little short-tempered. It seemed to him that they were 'actually used worse than the negroes in this scorching climate where, besides rowing large flat-bottomed barges up and down the rivers day and night for sugar, coffee, etc., and besides stowing the above commodities in a hold as hot as an oven, they are obliged to row every upstart planter to his estate at a call', because it was cheaper than using slaves who had to be fed and rested, if they were to stand such exertions regularly. It was nobody's business to look after sailors. They received no tips and had to beg water and bananas from the slaves when they felt faint. The planters used them also to drag loads to the warehouses, clean windows, mend gates and attend to any other little handyman's jobs that required to be done. Under these conditions, the sailors died off at the rate of 'five or six' a day, almost as fast as the soldiers, though from an opposite cause. Their captains were, naturally, anxious to save them for the return voyage, but, in many cases, dared not for fear of 'incurring the displeasure of the planters and seeing their ships rot in the harbour without a loading'.

It was as if there was an evil spell over this country, corrupting the inhabitants of what could otherwise be called almost a paradise. Quite distracted by his feeling of helplessness before this malign influence, 'I next ran to the house of my friend Lolkens who happened to be the administrator of Fauconberg estate'. He might not be perfect, but he was amiable. He must save Joanna, cried Stedman urgently. He must buy her, take her to Holland and have her turned into a lady. Lolkens must see to the legal arrangements. The planter was much astonished by all this hullaballoo over a slave girl. 'Having recovered from his surprise, after gazing at me silently for some time', he suggested that they had better put the proposal to Joanna and hear what she said.

A messenger was at once sent and shortly returned with 'the beauteous slave' and her aunt. Stedman was now in a great state of excitement. He explained, as well as he could, his marvellous plans for rescue, education and everlasting happiness. It was, on the face of it, a dazzling offer to a girl with Joanna's prospects. Yet, she again hesitated. The whole question must have been discussed in her family circle. To have a white lover was of the greatest advantage to a slave girl. Was it prudent to take up with one who would most probably be leaving the country in a few weeks' time? There may, indeed, have been other suitors, not, perhaps, so young and attractive as the captain, but more likely to last. As for all the stuff about going to Holland, marriage, education, what person of sense would believe such a story?

So she replied that it would be a mistake for them to start an affair because he was certainly going to be recalled almost immediately. Everyone thought so. In that case, either she would be left behind to console herself as best she could or else he would take her to a country where he would soon find that her colour, upbringing, habits and tastes would not fit into the scheme of things. She would be a drag on him and the adventure would end miserably. However, she thanked him very much for his kind intentions. The aunt concurred in these sentiments. No further arguments moved either of them. They withdrew.

Stedman was much cast down by his rejection. 'I could only intreat of Mr Lolkens his generous protection for her, and that she might at least for some time be separated from the other slaves and continue at Paramaribo.' Mr Lolkens said he would see to it. His thoughts on this unusual occasion have not been recorded.

Upset, worry and frustration always had the same effect on Stedman. 'Notwithstanding my former resolution of living retired', of seizing the opportunity to write a book and rise into circles to which he often felt himself attuned, 'I became a member of a drinking club. I partook of all polite and impolite amusements and plunged into every extravagance without exception.' Soon, he was down with yellow fever. 'I lay in my hammock with only a soldier and my black boy to attend me.' No one from the regiment visited or enquired after him. Most were in the same straits. But, the ladies of Surinam had a regular drill for such emergencies. 'These philanthropists not only supply the sick with a variety of cordials at the same time, but crowd their apartments with innumerable condolers, who from morning to night continue prescribing, insisting, bewailing and lamenting, friend and stranger without exception; and this lasts until the patient becomes delirious and expires.'

The noise, the fever, the conflicting mixtures and the general atmosphere of waiting for the worst, so wore him down that he was certain the end was near. Suddenly, he saw Joanna entering the room 'to my unspeakable joy and surprize, accompanied by one of her sisters'. From that moment, he began to pick up. She cleared out the mourners and nursed him tenderly. In a few days, he was well enough to renew 'my wild proposals of purchasing, educating and transporting her to Europe; which, though offered with the most perfect sincerity, were by her rejected once more'. These things were simply impossible, she said. However, she would live with him while he was in Surinam, if he still wanted it.

In a few days, he was able to take an airing in a carriage lent by a friend. He came home with 'presents to the value of twenty guineas'. Though touched by his generosity, Joanna thought this a great waste of good money and at once 'carried every article back to the merchants who cheerfully returned her' the price. Perhaps she explained to them that his fever had come on again and these expenses had been incurred in a delirious moment, now regretted.

The arrangement into which she had entered with Stedman was perfectly conventional. 'When a European arrives in the West Indies and gets settled or set down for any length of time, he finds it necessary to provide himself with a housekeeper, or mistress,' writes Bolingbroke. It was obviously best to buy her, if one could and there were regular agencies to which one could apply, run by coloured women. 'Some of them are so much educated as to be able to read and write,' Bolingbroke continues. 'They are tasty and extravagant in their dress; but when once an attachment takes place, it is inviolable. The strictest scrutiny of their conduct in general cannot glean one particle of impropriety by which their fidelity or constancy can be brought into question. They embrace all the duties of a wife, except presiding at table.' The only objections Joanna's relations can have had to Stedman were his inability to buy her from the creditors of the Fauconberg estate and his inevitable departure within a short time.

For his part, Stedman swore that he would never leave her and would perform every one of the promises he had made. She would see that it had not been just seductive talk. The first thing was to get married. She might be satisfied with the position of lover, but he was not. He must prove that he respected her more than any women he had met. So he went to Mrs Demelly, at whose house he had first seen Joanna, and asked her to arrange a proper wedding, with parson and reception. Mrs Demelly thought it a most amusing idea, as did a number of her friends. What an impulsive simpleton poor Stedman was. One couldn't help liking him. Everyone felt gay. The ceremony went with a swing. 'I was as happy as any bridegroom ever was.'

Joanna made a charming bride, although she considered the marriage a mere eccentricity. How could it be otherwise when a slave had no rights at law? Besides, she was due to be sold in the near future to someone who might take her away to a distant plantation. Her husband swore that he would save, or beg, or borrow, her purchase price. If recalled, he would raise the money in Holland and send for her. She did not believe things would turn out like that. Equally, she did not anticipate trouble until trouble came. They set up house very contentedly together.

Meanwhile, the expeditionary force melted away at a great rate. It was better to die of a surfeit of pleasure than of active service, yet it had a bad effect on morale. Soldiers were buried in the common cemetery, which was also the execution ground, and officers at Fort Zeelandia, immediately outside the town. Here, the interment, though classy, seemed really less decent. The fort contained the prison and the captives were to be seen clanking about in their chains and lighting fires on convenient tombstones in order to cook their dinner. On these occasions, various ideas for allegorical pictures in the eighteenth-century fashion presented themselves to Stedman, such as, 'a number of diabolical fiends in the shape of African slaves, tormenting the souls of their European persecutors'. He had rather a taste for fancy subjects, often accompanied by explanatory stanzas, somewhat in the manner of Pope.

The perennial question was: should they go, or should they stay

Stedman's boa constrictor

Marching through a swamp. Preceded by a slave, to test for depth, Colonel
Fourgeoud leads his men. Stedman is directly behind him. Rebel snipers perch
in two palm trees on the left.

View of the estate L'Esperance

View of the estate Clarenbeek

A slave family

Camping in the forest

The cottage at L'Esperance. In the foreground, Stedman, Joanna and Johnny

The toucan and the fly-catcher

An Indian family

The celebrated Graman Quacy. The old magician wears the outfit presented to
him by the Prince of Orange for services to the community.

a little longer to be quite sure the danger was over? It was now May 1773. They had been a four months' expense to no purpose. The governor did not think his nerves would stand much more of the colonel, for the feud between them had broken out more violently than ever. They now insulted each other on all possible occasions, though not actually resorting to blows. A transport with supplies for the troops unexpectedly arrived from Holland and on May 24th, it was definitely settled that they should leave within a fortnight. The governor felt that four and a half months of Colonel Fourgeoud, during which nothing whatever alarming had happened, was as much as any human being could be asked to bear. The colonel was unable to think of an effective answer to this. Orders were given for the ships to be got ready and the new provisions loaded into them. Captain and Mrs Stedman had been married less than three weeks.

The worst had happened. 'I must say nothing of what I felt on this occasion.' To have Joanna's relations proved right so soon was a hard fate. But, by great good fortune, the rebels suddenly raided a plantation, burnt the houses and murdered the overseer. This splendid news arrived next day. The governor was obliged to ask Colonel Fourgeoud to unload the ships and get his men ready for service. The colonel, thereupon, became extremely uppish, refusing even to treat 'the governor with that civility which he might have evinced without lessening his own consequence'.

Paramaribo was divided into two camps. Those afraid of being suddenly murdered 'acknowledged us to be the bulwark of the settlement, by keeping the rebels in awe'. The less nervous, or prudent, pointed out that isolated attacks on plantations were by no means uncommon. Why assume that this particular incident was going to lead to a general conflagration? The mere fact that everything had been so quiet for months on end proved the contrary. The support of a crowd of idle and licentious soldiers was totally unnecessary. They 'hesitated not to call us the locusts of Egypt, who were come to devour the fruits of the colony'. Many of them had been personally insulted by Fourgeoud.

The governor was much inclined to listen to this last opinion, the logic of which was powerfully reinforced by the treatment he daily received. A fortnight passed without alarm in any part of the country. The governor allowed himself to be persuaded either that the danger was actually over; or else that he could not be censured by his employers for saying it was and thus getting rid of an enemy who harassed him far more than the thought of a few runaway slaves skulking in the forest. On 7th June, 1773, 'we were for the third time officially acquainted that things seeming quiet and presuming that tranquillity was at last re-established, the colony of Surinam had no further occasion for our services.'

Although Fourgeoud rallied his supporters to such an extent that there were one or two fights in the street, he could not prevail. The stores that had just been laboriously carried from the ships to a warehouse on the quays, began the return journey. Stedman and Joanna renewed their agonized farewells. 'Give her a gold medal to remember me, which my father gave my mother the night that I was born,' he noted in his *Journal* mournfully. Days passed without another murder to give hope. The ships were to sail 'with all possible expedition'. Joanna believed that she would never see him again. Now that he had come face to face with the appalling problem of carrying out his reiterated promises to her, he was almost of the same opinion.

At this time bad omens were observed which could be interpreted either as presaging the end of personal happiness, or the collapse of the social order, depending on the direction of one's fears. People were struck by lightning and such claps of thunder were heard that it seemed as if the world were blowing up. It was reported that the entire city of Guatemala, in Mexico, 'was swallowed up by an earthquake, by which eight thousand families are said to have instantly perished'.

The next news from the interior was no surprise to persons accustomed to study signs and portents. A lieutenant of the West India Company's troops, stationed at a small post up river, sallied out with a detachment to attack a rebel village which, he was informed, had been discovered not far off in the forest. At a certain point, it was necessary to cross a marsh. 'No sooner had the unfortunate men got into the swamp and up to their armpits, than their black enemies rushed out from under cover and shot them dead in the water.'

There was panic in Paramaribo. 'The whole town was in a tumult; some parties were so vehement that they were ready to tear the governor and council to pieces for having dismissed

142

Colonel Fourgeoud.' Others, invincibly optimistic, or too cynical to face reality, or blinded by sympathy for the governor's sufferings, 'declared that if we were intended for no further use than we had hitherto been, our company might without regret be dispensed with'. Lampoons and slanders on the governor were secretly printed and scattered about the town. In spite of an enormous reward, the authors could not be found. The governor could scarcely bear the humiliation of having to implore Colonel Fourgeoud a third time to stay and save him. But he had no option. 'To this petition we once more condescended to listen.'

Joanna had studied the auguries as eagerly as anyone and had come to the conclusion that she was fated to lose her husband, either by his eventual return to his own country, or else from his death in the forest. There was, however, a short reprieve for some reason so difficult to understand as to seem supernatural. 'We still continued doing nothing to the unspeakable surprize of every person concerned.' Stedman occupied this unexpected leisure by carefully observing the habits and drawing the portraits of 'the Toucan and the Fly-catcher'.

XIII

THE FIRST CAMPAIGN

This time, Fourgeoud had resolved on a campaign and the
governor was obliged to acquiesce. At least it would get his
enemy out of Paramaribo. With average luck, he would soon die
of disease and over-exertion as he hacked his way through the
undergrowth of the forests. He was about sixty and it was now the
wet season, the most unhealthy time of the year.

The general plan was that some detachments should cruise the
rivers Cottica, Commewyne and adjacent creeks, the area which
had been the centre of unrest and where the chief murders had
been committed and plantations devastated. Others would patrol
the hinterland, searching for camps and villages of runaway
slaves and, in particular, for the headquarters of Captain Baron,
their redoubtable leader. There were no paths in the forest, nor
any way of knowing one's direction except by compass. But the
enemy was perfectly acquainted with the terrain and could unexpectedly appear at whatever point he found convenient.

It was not considered likely by the local inhabitants that the
rebel slaves would be altogether defeated, much less exterminated.
The most that could be hoped for was that they might be harried
into moving further up country and eventually consent to become
another tribe of bush Negroes, bound to peace by treaty as an
independent nation. But first, they had to be convinced that this
was their best course. It must be properly demonstrated that the
Europeans were ready and able to defend their property. Captain
Baron's idea that the white men could be rooted out of Surinam
and an African kingdom be substituted for a Dutch colony must
be proved, conclusively, to be impractical.

Once the decision to start the campaign had been taken, all was
hurry and bustle. 'The officers and men were ordered to be ready
at a minute's warning to set out on actual service.' It was found
that about a quarter of the original 'corps of the finest, healthiest
young men that ever sailed from Europe, with blooming fresh
complexions' were either dead or in the hospital which was

'crouded by invalids of every kind'. The survivors, one and all 'the sallow colour of a drumhead', were mustered and the ranks filled with anyone who could be induced to enrol himself. In this emergency, a certain number of extremely undesirable persons got into the force.

There were, for instance, 'two desperadoes who had both been rebel captains in the colony of Berbice' during the revolt of 1762. They had obtained pardon by changing sides at the right moment. It was said they had been guilty of the most abominable murders. Something about their impudence, subservience, dishonesty and reckless bravery – they had no regard for human life – appealed to Colonel Fourgeoud. They became his 'greatest favourites' amongst the private soldiers. Perhaps he had more reason than Stedman was prepared to allow. These two knew the forest and how to read its signs. They could interpret the talking drums, signalling from one camp to another. They could read the smoke of bonfires and, from the ashes of a sacrificial feast, foretell possible future manoeuvres. With such special qualifications, they might turn out valuable members of the expedition, if well treated and made to feel at home in the army; and if a decent veil was drawn over their past.

For the river patrols, a fleet 'of half a dozen crazy old sugar barges' was collected, 'such as are used by the colliers in the Thames, being only roofed over with boards, which gave them the appearance of so many coffins'. Stedman was to take two of these far up the Cottica, beyond the last settlement, 'where absolutely no kind of refreshment was to be had, being surrounded by the most horrid and impenetrable woods, beyond the hearing of a cannon-shot from any port or plantation whatever'. His company would have to exist entirely on the official rations of salt beef, pork and dried peas. 'This was not the case with the other barges, who were stationed in the midst of peace and plenty, being within view of the most beautiful estates.'

Already the joys of Paramaribo, by which he had felt sated, began to seem like a dream of better life. He wondered at himself for having chafed at six months' enforced gaiety and idleness. As for Joanna, she was 'in a flood of tears'. Her husband was leaving all his belongings in her care, but what if she should be sold before he came back? What if he died of some horrible disease in the forest with no one to look after him? He could not even buy a store of supplementary rations to vary the official issue on account of Colonel Fourgeoud's financial gifts. It was the accepted thing for a commander to make ten per cent on the pay and commissariat arrangements. No one knew what Fourgeoud got, such were his dexterity with paper money versus silver coin and his insistence that the full mess bill be paid, whether one ate there or not. All one could say was that none of his men ever had a halfpenny to spare.

Fortunately, the ladies of Paramaribo came to the rescue. Stedman would not languish on the upper Cottica if they could help it. Obviously in a place like that what one needed most was plenty of drink. Without delay, they loaded on to his barge two gallons each of brandy, coffee and lemon juice; two dozen claret; four dozen Madeira, port, cider and rum; six bottles of sweet wine; hams, tongues and mustard; and, since he was fond of reading, '6 dozen of spermacetti candles'. 'If some of the inhabitants of the colony of Surinam shew themselves the disgrace of creation by their cruelties and brutality, others by their hospitality and social feelings prove themselves an ornament to the human species,' Stedman remarks thoughtfully.

It was now the first week of July 1773 and four o'clock in the morning. 'I bade farewell to my Joanna', begging her mother and aunt to take good care of her and to see that she attended the regular lessons on reading and writing he had arranged. He then stepped into his flagship, already crammed with twenty three soldiers, ten slaves to row and his black servant Quaco. He named her the *Charon* and she was 'armed with swivels, blunderbusses, etc., and provided with allowance for one month'.

As Joanna mopped her eyes and who knows what ceremonial African wails were raised by her mother and aunt, they 'cast off from their moorings and, with the ebb tide rowed down as far as' Fort Amsterdam, at the junction of the rivers Surinam and Commewyne. The Cottica was a tributary of the Commewyne.

Next morning, on the flood, they began to ascend the Commewyne, rowing past estates and amongst other boats, halting for a short rest, 'before Elizabeth's Hope, a beautiful coffee plantation'. The owner happened to be in residence and invited them ashore at once. Though hospitable and kind, he proved a gloomy

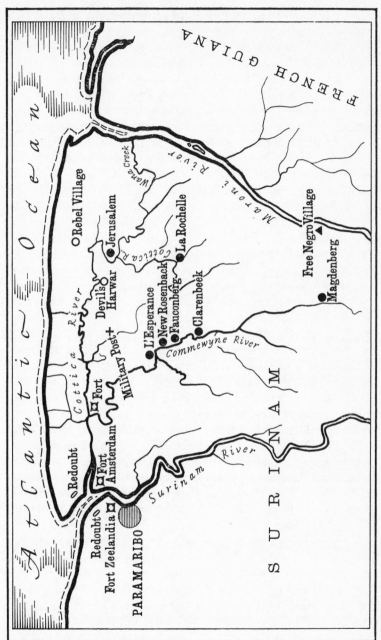

East Surinam

brute. 'He told us that he pitied our situation from his heart and foretold the miseries we were going to encounter.' His prophesies proved only too accurate in the sequel, but it was discouraging to hear them on the first day of the adventure.

'As for the enemy,' he said lugubriously, 'you may depend on not seeing one single soul of them; they know better than to make their appearance openly while they may have a chance of seeing you from under cover: thus, Sir, take care to be upon your guard – but the climate, the climate will murder you all.' In the wet season, especially, it was impossible for anyone to preserve his health. 'However,' he added, trying to look on the bright side of things and cheer his listeners up a bit, 'this shews the zeal of your commander, who will rather see you killed, than see you eat the bread of idleness at Paramaribo.' 'This pleasant harangue he accompanied with a squeeze by the hand', while his slaves loaded the 'barge with refreshing fruits, vegetables, etc'. As they said goodbye and rowed on upstream, his daughter, a most beautiful woman, stood on the jetty, weeping for their fate.

That evening, they entered the Cottica which wound backwards and forwards in a series of loops, the general direction being parallel with the coast and towards the frontier with Cayenne, French Guiana. For five days they journeyed on. The plantations gradually were fewer, some being in ruins. The river became narrower, the forest omnipresent. The rain was very heavy most of the time. It proved almost impossible to cook the salt beef without setting the barge on fire.

On the fifth morning, they anchored off one of the inland forts maintained by the West India Company. All the plantations above this point had been burnt, or abandoned. It was a melancholy spot called 'Slans Welveren, which signifies the welfare of the nation' in an effort to give it some sort of an attractive glow. The popular name, however, was 'Devil's Harwar, on account of its intolerable unhealthiness'.

A substantial part of the garrison was in the hospital, 'where I beheld such a spectacle of misery and wretchedness as baffles all imagination'. Not only fevers, but every sort of ulcer, skin disease and septic poisoning flourished in these tropical damps, the effects made worse by lazy habits, such as never bathing or changing the clothes. Neither the eternal salt beef, nor the standard of doctoring helped to combat these conditions. Often, 'the medical staff . . . was very numerous,' writes Bolingbroke who had watched the progress of an epidemic among Dutch troops, 'but consisted principally of inexperienced young men and boys of sixteen or seventeen as mates, who, from all appearance, had been taken out of apothecaries' shops in Holland.' Stedman was himself to undergo their ministrations and almost be killed in the process.

It was with some relief that they weighed anchor, even though the fort represented the last trace of civilization in an intimidating country. Beyond, all was hostile, unexplored, unmapped. 'I cannot but lament the unpardonable indolence and inattention of the civilized inhabitants of this country, few of whom have ever penetrated the woods beyond the confined limits of their planta-tions,' writes Dr Edward Bancroft, an enthusiastic naturalist, in 1769. The forest seemed to him a mysterious and beautiful region, 'cloathed in perpetual verdure and adorned with lofty trees, whose elevated summits' sometimes disappeared into the clouds during the rainy season.

As Stedman's Negroes rowed on, his spirits sank. 'Here we saw nothing but water, wood and clouds, no trace of humanity, and consequently the place had a most dismal, solitary, appearance.' Sickness had already attacked his men. Three had had to be aban-doned in the hospital at Devil's Harwar. Paramaribo, Joanna, the drinking club, the dinner parties, dances and cold suppers seemed like a dream from another life, an echo of a legendary golden age.

One could try and distract one's thoughts by examining the mangroves with which the banks were lined. But it required the scientific passion of a Bancroft actually to enjoy the occupation. 'The properties of that vast multitude of plants and herbs, with which the earth is everywhere covered, remain almost wholly unknown,' he cries. The Indians distilled from barks, leaves, roots, extraordinary medicines, poisons, dyes and inks that became invisible after a few days and were much in demand by swindlers making false contracts.

Carried away by visions of fame and riches, as so often happened in Guiana, the doctor embarked on a series of impetuous experi-ments: 'I have spent many days in a dangerous and almost fruitless endeavour to investigate the nature and qualities of these plants;

and by handling, smelling, tasting, etc., I have frequently found . . . almost all the several senses and their organs either disordered or violently affected, without being able to determine to which of the many subjects of my examination I ought to attribute these uncommon effects.' Were his symptoms due to his having chewed a certain soporific gum 'having a sweet and graceful smell' and guaranteed to remove the most obstinate headache? Or to drinking Indian mixtures calculated to heal wounds, cure diarrhoea, promote virility, empty the stomach of undigested matter? Who could say which of the various ointments, powders and juices he sampled had caused him to sleep for hours, or stay awake for days, to have dizzy turns, or swelling of the feet?

All one could aver with certainty was that here were medicines enough to cure the ills and invalids of Devil's Harwar, if properly applied. But those of a less intellectual nature were inclined to sink under the everyday hardships of life in the wonderful forests of Guiana. 'The elements now seemed to unite in opposing us,' wrote Stedman from his barge. 'The water pouring down like a deluge, the heavy rains forced themselves fore and aft into the vessel where they set everything afloat; the air was infested with myriads of mosquitoes which . . . left us in the morning besmeared all over with blood and full of blotches. The smoak of the fire and tobacco which we burnt to annoy them was enough to choak us; and not a footstep of land could we find where we might cook our salt provisions in safety.'

Days passed with nothing to break the monotony except an occasional alligator, monkey, strange bird, or patterned snake. Fights broke out between the soldiers and the slaves. The mosquitoes increased by the hundred thousand. By clapping my two hands together, I have actually killed to the number of thirty-eight at one stroke,' noted Stedman, having passed the idle minutes counting corpses. 'The multitude and variety of insects is incredible in Guiana,' says Dr Bancroft happily, 'where the warmth and humidity . . . of climate facilitate their production and where their longevity is unimpaired by winter or their activity chilled into a torpid lethargy for one half of the year.' Most of them bit and stung in a highly individual and interesting manner.

The only distractions they had were short patrols up and down their stretch of river and the odd canoe coming up from Devil's

Harwar with letters from friends in Paramaribo. The men were now beginning to fall rapidly sick and several had to be sent down to the fort hospital. Guiana was famous for the variety and virulence of its fevers, blood disorders, skin diseases, worms which infected not only the intestines but settled themselves horribly under the surface of the skin. 'They are of a whitish colour,' writes Bancroft industriously, 'several feet in length and in thickness equal to the large string of a violin.' The best way to get rid of them was to catch the head as it peeped out through the ulcer and carefully wind the body on to a stick.

'What methods do you take to preserve your health?' demanded Stedman of an elderly Negro, perfectly fit like most of his slave companions. 'Swim every day twice, or thrice, Sir,' said he, 'in the river.' This ensured cleanliness and also sufficient exercise: for it was necessary to keep kicking and splashing on account of alligators and a certain savage kind of fish, peculiar to these waters, which had been known to bite off a woman's breast or a man's genitals in one mouthful. Stuffy European clothes were a mistake, continued the old slave, encouraged by a glass of rum, handed to him by a thoughtful Stedman at this point. A loose, thin shirt and trousers were as much as one should wear in these hot and wet conditions. Let the master also harden his feet by going barefoot. The day would come when his shoes and stockings disintegrated 'in the midst of thorns and briars'. Then he would be glad of a good horny sole to his foot. 'Our feet were all made alike,' the slave remarked, flourishing his own. 'Do so as I advise you and, in the end, you will thank old Caramaca.'

'From that moment,' says Stedman, convinced by such concentrated practical sense, 'I followed his counsels, to which, besides being cleanly and cool, I in great measure ascribe the preservation of my life.' He was unable to convert his men to these new habits which seemed to them totally unnecessary and also to smack of going native.

They had now been three weeks at their station without the slightest sign of the enemy. Sometimes rustling was heard on the banks, but it turned out to be monkeys. Once or twice they thought they saw small lights on the river at night, as if people with lighted pipes were paddling stealthily across. The Negroes, however, declared these to be fireflies and investigation seemed to prove them right. On appointed days, they fired their cannon and blunderbusses, by previous arrangement with the commander at Devil's Harwar. They never heard any answer to their signals, though listening keenly. The only result of these exercises was that Stedman, not being accustomed to such an antiquated weapon as a blunderbuss, was thrown 'backward over a large hogshead of beef' by the unexpected recoil and had his shoulder somewhat damaged.

It was an agreeable diversion, therefore, to receive an urgent message from the other boat under Stedman's command, which was moored some distance up an adjacent creek: they were, they said, surrounded by prowling enemies in the woods. They had not actually seen them, but knew definitely that they were there, planning a sudden assault. Having hurried to their assistance, Stedman found it was a false alarm. Not a soul was to be seen in that terrible dripping forest except his own soldiers, trembling with fever and covered with running ulcers.

Yet, there were omens. On the way back to their station, they fell in with a witch. Stedman believed her story that she was a poor useless slave abandoned in the wilds by a hard master in order to save money. He gave her 'a piece of salt beef, some barley and a bottle of rum'. In return, she tried to present him with one of her cats. He would have accepted – the rats were a scourge – but his Negroes would by no means permit him. This was not a cat at all, they said. It was an evil spirit. Only a madman, or one bewitched, would receive it as a travelling companion.

Shortly afterwards, a black woman with a baby in her arms appeared, saying she had escaped from the rebel camp. They had carried her off by force about a month before. Campaigns were being planned in the depths of the forest. People were gathering together and marching in different directions. A stray Jew who turned up at the same time confirmed her story. They began now to hear drums reverberating faintly up country.

Nothing definite happened to relieve the tension. The men began to murmur that they had not signed on for this sort of life. What was the use of it? Their 'cloaths and hammocks were rotting from day to day, not only from their being almost constantly wet, but being also composed of the very worst materials sent from Holland'. The salt provisions disagreed with them violently.

Fourgeoud had a fixed idea that fresh food would be the death of them and so provided none. The occasional boxes of oranges which came from Joanna were too few and small to alleviate the general distress. Why die here instead of at Paramaribo where their girl friends were waiting? Only fifteen men out of the original complement were fit for a fight if these mysterious enemies ever should be found. They began to whisper of seizing the *Charon* and returning to civilization forthwith.

Stedman did not know how best to soothe them. He sent down to Devil's Harwar, in case any tasty provisions should have arrived; but they had not. Though shaky with fever, he staggered along the banks and shot several monkeys to provide at least one decent dinner. He himself would almost rather continue with salt beef: a baked monkey reminded him so horribly of a human infant, 'especially their little hands and their heads'.

They had now been six weeks on the river. The men began to die at an increasing rate. The medicines were all finished. Stedman became so ill that he could not even sit up in his hammock. A mutiny could hardly have been prevented had not orders suddenly come from Fourgeoud to take over at Devil's Harwar, as the garrison was transferred to an even more remote post in the forest. Everyone's spirits revived wonderfully. The fort, which had appalled them as newcomers from Paramaribo, now seemed a perfect haven of comfort and luxury. It was never under water, for instance. There were houses in which one could keep out of the rain, 'proper kitchens, a bake-house, etc., beside a well with fresh water'. One could lie down in the hospital until one's fever abated. Special sheep, pigs and chickens were reserved for invalid meals. Some people even had small gardens of vegetables and fruit. What if it was infested with sand fleas and mosquitoes? What if the cemetery contained hundreds of graves?

They began rowing down the river very cheerfully, the sentinels keeping a sharp look-out for snipers on the banks. Suddenly one 'called to me that he had seen and challenged something black and moving in the brushwood on the beach, which gave no answer'. This must be a spy who, if caught, could be obliged to give them certain information of the enemy, his plans and position, so that this terrifying campaign could be quickly concluded and everyone return, if not to Holland, at least to Paramaribo. They dropped anchor and jumped into the canoe. No one listened to the slaves who said the sentinel had seen a passing boa constrictor.

'We all stepped ashore to reconnoitre', search the bushes and examine the ground for footprints. Nothing was to be seen except recent tracks that might well have been made by a small boa constrictor, say twenty feet long. The slaves became very keen to hunt the boa. The master ought to have a souvenir of his time in the woods. They would skin it for him. Also, there was twenty feet of 'exceedingly good and wholesome' eating to be had, they said. 'To this however,' Stedman disappointingly replied, 'I had not the least inclination, from the uncommon size of the creature, from my weakness and the difficulty of getting through the thicket.'

The slaves urged him not to miss the chance of sport. One did not happen on a boa every day. They were harmless animals, really, provided one kept a proper distance. They would make an easy path through the undergrowth. So he was persuaded. But it turned out quite as tiring an adventure for an invalid as he had feared. They found the snake coiled in a nest of leaves, looking round and flicking its tongue in and out. The first ball only wounded it and the animal writhed 'with such astonishing force as to cut away all the underwood around him with the facility of a scythe mowing grass'. The hunters fled into their canoe.

Stedman would have liked to give up at this point, but the slaves insisted that he must go back. Eventually, it was killed. Skinning took no time. Nor did cutting up the carcass in slices and lighting a fire. The Negroes were bent on a banquet, with singing, dancing and all appropriate celebrations. They would mime the hunt and recite the master's prowess in dispatching this enormous monster single-handed. Active service, rebels, spies and similar inconveniences were forgotten at the prospect of a wonderful party. They were surprised and crestfallen when Stedman ordered them on board at once to continue the journey to Devil's Harwar. It was now August 1773 and they had 'been on board the *Charon* exactly fifty-six days'.

The fort required a garrison of about 300 men effectively to defend the perimeter. On reviewing his force, Stedman found he had 'left out of five officers but two, who were both sick, the three others being dead; I had also only one serjeant, two corporals and fifteen privates'. It was true that there was quite a substantial army in the hospital, some of whom might recover sufficiently to bear arms in an emergency. Also, the outgoing commander said he would leave 20 of his men behind.

When mustered after his departure, 'they proved to be the refuse of the whole part with agues, wounds, ruptures and rotten limbs and most of them next day were obliged to enter the hospital', where there was not much hope of treatment as all the doctors and most of the orderlies had taken the opportunity, during the change of command, to escape down the river to Paramaribo. There were, however, one or two surgeon's mates who could 'occasionally draw blood and cut off a beard, or a corn'. In any case, the medicines were finished.

Everywhere he looked, Stedman found the same hopeless situation. Though scarcely able to stand, he was among the fittest of his company. The only thing to do was to go to bed and hope the enemy would not attack just yet. He sank into his hammock. After about ten minutes of delightful sleep, he was woken by an express messenger, who handed him a letter. 'This is to acquaint you,' it said, 'that the rebels have burnt three estates by your side . . . the ruins of which are still smoking; and that they have cut the throats of all the white inhabitants that fell in their way. As on their retreat they must pass close by where you are posted, be on your guard. I am in haste.'

There was no need to spread the alarm, as everyone had heard the news the moment the messenger stepped out of his canoe. 'Not only the few soldiers who were well, but the whole hospital burst out; and several of them, in spite of my opposition, crawling on their hands and feet to their arms, dropped dead upon the spot.'

The remainder manned the walls, augmented by as many slaves as Stedman dared to arm. 'I pressed the messenger to stay, in order to add one to our miserable number, being determined to sell our lives as dearly as possible.' Nothing was heard all night except water dripping and trickling and the screech of nocturnal animals.

In the morning, several of the soldiers were found to be dead. Merely to keep awake had been too great an exertion in their weakened state. The remainder were on the verge of mutiny, cursing Fourgeoud with as much vigour as they could command for not having sent up reinforcements, though he knew the state they were in; for not even having taken the trouble to dispatch regular supplies of food, ammunition and medicines. They would no doubt, have fled to Paramaribo, as the hospital staff had sensibly done, but there were no boats, not even a canoe. Stedman had seen to that. The suspense lasted four days and nights. It seemed incredible that the rebels should neglect to call in as they were passing and cut their throats. It would be such an easy job. Yet they did not. 'At length, being persuaded that the rebels must have passed . . . I determined to let the remaining few watch no longer, but permit them to die a natural death.' There were only seven left who were suffering from nothing worse than swelled feet, caused by insect bites.

In his own difficult way, Fourgeoud was surprisingly efficient. On receipt of the reports from Stedman and others, he began collecting reinforcements, provisions, medicine, doctors, ammunition and loading them on to barges. The first of these arrived a few days after the latest alarm, together with orders that a patrol should be made through the woods in an effort to discover the local rebel headquarters.

Everyone was tremendously cheered by the new arrivals. The feeling of having been abandoned to die in the swamps while others made merry at Paramaribo disappeared. 'I prepared to march myself, having recovered a little strength,' writes Stedman, who longed for action, a chance to distinguish himself and gain promotion after all the weary days of waiting. This whole adventure had been undertaken with the object of bettering himself and if he did not succeed, his sufferings were a perfect waste of time. It would have been more sensible to remain among the salubrious comforts of Bergen op Zoom.

Within a few days, a party of forty-five set out, with eight slaves to carry the luggage and cut a path through the undergrowth. They proceeded slowly and in single file which made them practically defenceless against an ambush. Their objective was a military post on another frightful river winding through the trees, some ten or fifteen miles in the direction of Paramaribo. On the way, they would traverse the country over which the rebels must have passed during their recent depredations. It was thought that they might stumble on a village, or hideout.

So they pressed on as fast as the Negroes could hack down the thorns and the vines, some eighteen inches thick, that could be seen, 'communicating from tree to tree to a great distance, in oblique, horizontal and perpendicular directions, like the rigging of a ship.' Some had poisonous juices, interesting to a naturalist, 'so active and fatal that many of the Indians are afraid even to cut them'.* The trees from which these vines hung were of many varieties unknown in other parts of the world. They were covered with exciting flowers and fruits, the leaves were strange, the trunks enormous and the wood of every gradation from the soft and pithy to the hard and close-grained that took a wonderful polish when made up into furniture.

But what the soldiers chiefly noticed were the briars that tore their clothes to shreds and covered them with blood; the bees emerging from their hives in hollow trees, 'pitching always by instinct on the eyes, lips and hair whence they cannot easily be dislodged; their stings generally cause a fever and swell the parts so very much that they occasion blindness for several hours'; the ants, 'very numerous, various and troublesome . . . In the day time, they almost cover the trunks and branches of fruit trees and their bite is extremely painful . . . In the woods, they frequently inhabit large round nests . . . many feet in circumference and each containing millions of these insects.'*

All day they stumbled on, sometimes 'through water and mire above our hips'; sometimes climbing 'over heaps of fallen trees'; or squeezing 'underneath on our bellies'. Ten men succumbed to fever, fatigue, bees, swelled feet and had to be left by the wayside to be picked up on the return journey. They did, however, discover certain footprints in the mud, broken bottles and banana skins that must have been left by the rebels.

The last two hours of the march were performed 'in total darkness, holding each other by the hand'. No one was capable of more next day than lying in his hammock with his eyes shut. Their host very kindly sent out a party to collect the invalids from the bushes where they lay at intervals along the path. By some merciful dispensation of providence, the rebels seemed to have vanished entirely from this part of the country.

After a day in bed, they felt ready for the march back. Every-

* Bancroft.

157

one was now barefoot, shoes and stockings having been ripped to pieces, sucked off in swamps, eaten by insects, or simply disintegrated. It was the very situation foretold by the old slave Caramaca on the *Charon*. Stedman blessed his perspicacity as he staggered along, shaking with fever and exhaustion, but having a good, tough pair of feet under him. No one else was so well equipped. Again the enemy kept his distance and spared their lives, the only trace of him being the old footprints, bits of glass and banana skins.

At Devil's Harwar, they found a new colonel had come to take the command, which Stedman was happy to relinquish. The next morning, a second barge arrived with more reinforcements, provisions, and a letter and fifteen bottles of rum from Joanna. These were very welcome. It appeared that Stedman's trunks had been removed from her care by Fourgeoud's order, otherwise she would have sent shirts. Some said Fourgeoud wanted to safeguard Stedman's belongings against his return; others that he expected him to die and had taken possession of his property prematurely. In his reduced state of nerves and general health, Stedman firmly believed the latter, especially as his application for leave to go to Paramaribo was refused and his quarters in the town had been given to someone else.

His reaction was to open the fifteen bottles thoughtfully provided by his wife, 'get mortally drunk', shout obscenities against Fourgeoud and rush aimlessly into the woods. Soon, he was raving to such an extent that the doctors declared this could not be a mere fever: he must be clean off his head. Far from being an officer who could not be spared, he had become a liability. The best treatment would be to humour him by putting him into a canoe for Paramaribo. He would certainly die if his persecution mania was exacerbated by his being kept in the hospital at Devil's Harwar.

So they put him into a boat, together with a bag of mail for the capital, in the care of a reliable slave. News of more murders had just come through.

XIV

JOANNA SOLD

The journey to Paramaribo was accomplished at great speed, even allowing for the fact that it was downstream. They travelled day and night with hardly a break. The Negroes were capable of extraordinary exertions, particularly when their destination was the capital with all its pleasures and excitements, which embraced even the slave state.

This phenomenon was observed also by a Dr George Pinckard, who happened to be coming down the River Demerara in a hurry in 1796.* For days at a time, they could row for twelve or fourteen hours with only the shortest possible intervals of rest and refreshment. Finally, 'observing that they rowed with langour and that we made but little progress,' he writes, 'the cockswain was desired to exchange the helm for an oar and to encourage his comrades with a song . . . This operated with magic effect. Every slave was inspired and, forgetting all sense of fatigue, they again pulled with unwearied vigour.'

The ballad, entirely extempore, consisted of short stanzas in the African manner, each concluding with a rousing chorus, during which the boat shot ahead. 'The names of the slaves, their wives, their food, drink and all their pleasures were introduced . . . and tuned to the pulling of the oar.' Many of the verses were certainly indelicate, though Pinckard draws a veil over this aspect of African art. The coxswain's composition included the names of each of the party whom they were rowing, their professions, qualities and occupations. Here, nothing doubtful, or mean, was suggested and the subject of tips was introduced and much enlarged on; the song lasted for hours and could be heard far and wide, if there were any ears in that deserted forest to hear. Pinckard was struck by the darkness and silence of the woods. In a day's walk, 'two wild hogs, some parrots and parroquets' were the only signs of life he saw. The path wound between trees 'usually perpendicular in their growth; and their wood is heavy and of uncommonly hard

* See, George Pinckard, *Notes on the West Indies*, 1806.

texture, approaching in some instances to the solidity, weight and even the sound of metallic substances . . . Their thick foliage forms a canopy which is not easily penetrated by the sun or the rain.'

Through these lonely scenes he had come to know too well, Stedman's Negroes rowed without intermission, until, at two o'clock in the morning of the third day, they reached Paramaribo, mooring in front of the house of a merchant of his acquaintance, Mr La Marre, the owner and lover of Joanna's sister. Despite the hour, this amiable person came to the door himself, embraced his emaciated, trembling guest and called him brother-in-law. The best room in the house should be his, the finest medicine and nursing that Paramaribo afforded. Joanna was sent for at dawn.

The horrors of the River Cottica began to seem like a dream: 'I found myself in an elegant and well-furnished apartment, encouraged by the hopes given by the physician, caressed by my friends and supported by the care and attention of my incomparable Mulatto.' He got hold of the luggage seized by Colonel Fourgeoud, but on opening the trunks found that the cockroaches had feasted on the contents to such an extent that 'most of my shirts, books, etc., were gnawed to dust'. He especially regretted twelve new pairs of shoes, bought in Holland before leaving.

However, Joanna proved an excellent needlewoman and soon he was decently fitted out once more, except in the feet. 'None can conceive the comfort I felt in being properly dressed and shifted; my mental faculties were recruiting apace and I felt with gratitude the blessing of a strong constitution.' His fever abated, though the boils with which he was covered and the multitude of worms living inside him proved difficult to dislodge. But rest and the constant ministrations of his wife and friends worked wonders. Within a few days, he was able to attend to some of the duties of commandant at Paramaribo, a post that was temporarily vacant as Fourgeoud and everyone well enough to stand had departed up river in the hope of catching the rebels.

'The colours, regiment's cash, etc., were transmitted to my own lodging and a sentinel placed before my door,' he notes with satisfaction. For this gave him the opportunity of countermanding the colonel's order of cheap sour wine at a bargain price, for distribution to sick officers, and substituting a decent quality claret. He would have liked also to vary the meals at the hospital by garnishing the eternal salt pork and beef with fresh fruit and vegetables. It was not possible to do this because Fourgeoud had left the most strict injunctions to the contrary. It was his fixed belief that troops should be fed on salt provisions, whatever their state of health. Anything else rendered them unfit for the rigours of military service in a tropical climate. He was a man of experience and knew what he was talking about.

'Perhaps it were easier to overturn the Alps, than do away with the prejudices of the Hollanders, whose inflexible attachment to custom and to ceremony reigns paramount in all their proceedings,' writes Dr Pinckard from a large experience of Dutch medical arrangements. He particularly objected to elaborate funerals on psychological grounds, believing that many might have been saved had they not heard, several times a day, 'the dead march sounding at the very door of the hospital', as a man's comrades came in procession to collect his corpse with proper gravity. Of course, one could not help being pleased to observe such attention to higher things, but the low spirits which descended on the severely ill at the blowing of yet another last post were often fatal.

Yet, one could argue that it did not matter whether the soldiers died of unsuitable food and treatment in the hospital, rather than after falling down in the forest and having to be abandoned in the undergrowth because nobody was strong enough to carry them to the journey's end. Stedman was never inclined to look on the dark side of things for long. His wife was due to be sold any day and to someone unknown and he would have no power to save her from ill-treatment, for lack of the money to buy her with. Why surrender to depression on this or any other account, when here was a friend's carriage waiting to take one for an airing along the quays, fully manned with slaves to hold umbrellas, wave fans, pour drinks and light pipes as one went along?

He even felt sufficiently vigorous to accept invitations to dinner, though the extraordinary sumptuousness of West Indian meals seems hardly calculated to tempt a semi-invalid. It was usual 'to put on table three or four substantial puddings of different kinds and four or five dishes of the same sort of meat, differently dressed . . . An English eye, on looking into the dining room is surprized at the continuation of mutton, mutton, mutton, pudding, pudding, pudding, from one end of the table to the other'.* But then, Stedman was only half English.

There were other things, too, that might be thought distasteful to one not in perfect health, even though the eighteenth century was less genteel in such matters than we have now become. Certainly, the occasion was convivial. Besides the diners and the huge crowd of slaves belonging to the house, each guest usually brought his own attendant to stand behind his chair in case he should be needed. Mutton, pudding and a great variety of other courses steamed upon the table. The temperature was over ninety and everyone sweated frightfully.

In a well regulated house, the slaves were very keen on their job. The master and his friends should not wait a moment before a dirty plate was whipped away and a fresh one put down. They were in the habit, therefore, 'of taking a plate from the sideboard before it is wanted and standing with it under the arm . . . closely pressed to certainly not the sweetest part of the naked skin'.* Stedman records no objection to this habit. On the contrary, he continually emphasizes the cleanliness of the Negroes: how they were always washing themselves in the river; how the mere fact that they were unencumbered with soiled coats, shirts, trousers, socks, raised them above the white inhabitants of Surinam, from the sanitary point of view.

With Joanna and her approaching sale in mind, he brooded on the subject of slaves during the daily outings the doctor had ordered. One day, bowling along the quays in a borrowed chaise, he saw a ship from the Guinea coast at anchor. Half the cargo was coming ashore. The other half was dancing and singing indefatigably all over the decks to celebrate the end of a terrifying voyage: they had not been eaten by the captain and his officers in order to propitiate the white gods; though much reduced, they had survived the fevers, fluxes, melancholies and unfortunate accidents of different sorts which had carried off too many of their fellows. They felt beautiful, having been 'dressed over three or four times with a compound of gunpowder, limejuice and oil'* calculated to give them a glossy sleekness, most attractive to prospective purchasers. The captain had generously handed out lengths of cotton 'to serve as fig leaves, arm bands, beads' and any

* Pinckard.

other ornament that pleased them. He had provided also a number of broken bottles with which they had shaved their wool in curious shapes signifying good fortune, as well as a playful fancy.

Those who were landing seemed equally cheerful. 'I perceived not one single downcast look among them,' says Stedman, observing them with the greatest attention. There were about sixty of them. In front, walked a sailor, to lead the way 'and another followed behind with a bamboo rattan' to prevent any straggling. For these, too, were continually breaking into song and dance, which impeded progress towards the saleroom. The sailors seemed to share in the general good humour, flicking their charges with the bamboo 'with the utmost moderation'.

Crowds always gathered when a Guinea ship docked. 'On arriving at the town,' says Dr Pinckard, speaking of Berbice, the Dutch colony adjoining Surinam, 'we were surprized to find it quite a holyday, or a kind of public fair. The sale seemed to have excited general attention and to have brought together all the inhabitants of the colony. The planters came down from the estates all arrayed in their gayest apparel: the belles and the beaux appeared in their Sunday suits: even the children were in full dress; and their slaves decked out in holyday clothes.'

The auction room was crowded with buyers and people come to see the fun. 'Good negroes are generally valued at from fifty to a hundred pounds each. Amongst these, should a woman chance to be pregnant, her price is augmented accordingly.' There were captains who saw to it that most of their female cargo was in this desirable condition.

The actual sale was not particularly alarming for the Negroes, as they had been through the same procedure in Africa, where they had in some cases changed hands more than once before being finally embarked. There was no difficulty in getting them to stand on a chair, or table, and 'make all the different gestures with arms and legs of a Merry-Andrew upon the stage to prove their soundness, or unsoundness'. They may not have enjoyed having their mouths looked into, their limbs pinched and their persons examined for signs of venereal disease, but in general they submitted quietly enough.

Sometimes, they entered into the spirit of the thing like the natural clowns they often were. Or they might refuse to move at all unless their wives and relations were sold together with them in the same lot. Planters could often be prevailed upon to purchase a whole family, especially if a reduction were offered on account of some members being not quite up to standard. Besides, it was better business to buy a contented slave, one feeling himself under an obligation to the new master and who, moreover, could be counted on to increase the plantation stock regularly and free of charge.

Others, however, were not successful in their pleading. They were being bought by a planter who had definitely decided on a certain number and was not to be moved by sentimental appeals, particularly from sub-human blacks. Or the buyer might only be an agent for an absentee landowner, without authority to spend more than a certain sum. But what about Joanna? This was Stedman's constant preoccupation. Her turn to stand up naked on the chair before the crowd was coming very shortly. He would have to watch his wife 'exposed to public vendue even as the herds of sheep and oxen in Smithfield market,'* because he had no money, as usual. He would have to see her knocked down to a new owner and branded with his initials 'as we mark furniture or anything else to authenticate them properly', though it was true, 'these hot letters which are about the size of a sixpence occasion not that pain which may be imagined and the blisters being rubbed directly with a little fresh butter, are perfectly well in the space of two or three days'.

She could be expected to fetch a high price, far more than these rough women straight from the forests of Africa. For, besides being young, handsome, healthy and semi-white, she was trained in all the household arts and could now read and write a little. He could not obtain deferred terms or raise the necessary loan because he was not properly resident in the country, nor even expected to remain in this world very long, considering his conditions of employment.

He felt as helpless as the slaves he saw being authenticated with their master's initials. 'No sooner is this ceremony over and a new name given to the newly bought slave, than he or she is delivered to an old one of the same sex and sent to the estate.' They were allowed six weeks to settle into the new environment, feed up,

* Pinckard.

164

learn the rudiments of the slave dialect and the sort of behaviour expected of them under a white owner in a civilized country.

Some aspects of this unknown society into which they had been pitchforked they found alarming; some so surprising that they screamed with laughter in the African manner. In general, they adjusted themselves well, 'becoming plump and fat with a beautiful clean skin', lovely, glossy creatures with none 'of those languid pale sickly-looking countenances so common' among the Europeans. A Negro had to be very ill indeed before he turned a 'disagreeable sallow olive' colour.

There was much to remind them of Africa, never to be seen again, except as spirits. Only after death could they hope to revisit the land of their ancestors. True, the tribes were all jumbled up on the plantations and one had to associate familiarly with people who, in the old country, were not highly thought of in one's village; or who were in deadly enmity with one's king and liable to cast spells. For witch doctors and priestesses practised their art in Guiana as powerfully, though less openly, as in Africa. They conducted the sacrifices to all necessary gods and sold amulets, love potions, lucky charms. They could interpret dreams, foretell the future and divine secrets unknown to ordinary men.

The priestesses were also able to sing such songs that snakes came down from trees and sat before them. They knew how to perform dances during which they whirled round and round with increasing rapidity until they fell down in convulsions, possessed by a god who then spoke in a strange voice. 'Whatever the prophetess orders to be done during this paroxism is most sacredly performed by the surrounding multitude; which renders these meetings extremely dangerous.'

The ceremony was only performed in times of great emergency, when it was essential to have supernatural guidance as to whether or not certain irrevocable steps should be taken. Thus, it happened that 'she frequently enjoins them to murder their masters, or desert to the woods; upon which account this scene of excessive fanaticism is forbidden by law in the colony of Surinam, upon pain of the most rigorous punishment: yet it is often practised in private places'. Nothing so fundamental to African religious life could be suppressed by the martyrdom of the few mediums caught in the act of communication with their god.

No slave would sit down to a meal, however meagre, without setting aside a libation to the spirits. This done, the rules of hospitality took over. 'The poorest negro, having only an egg, scorns to eat it alone; but were a dozen present, and every one a stranger, he would cut, or break, it into just as many shares.' For everything became a party with the African. Even funerals ended up with dancing, singing and drinking for hours, once the corpse was decently buried and the departed wafted back across the ocean with an appropriate hymn.

They were essentially a gay and sociable people. One did not find them sitting alone brooding on the nature of existence, unless circumstances were extraordinarily adverse. But, if they should fall into melancholy, it was almost impossible to keep them alive. This was a trait recognized and dreaded by the slave captains of Guinea. They would refuse to eat; or dose themselves with earth, and other poisonous substances which made them gradually waste away; or suddenly throw back their heads in a particular manner that choked them to death in a second. Suppose Joanna were driven to one of these alternatives, after her coming sale?

In the forest, recollections of Paramaribo had seemed like a vision of a better world, a simulacrum of the fabled city of El Dorado. The streets were not actually paved with gold, indeed; yet the brocaded and bejewelled inhabitants, strolling under the scented trees in peace and the perpetual sunshine of the dry season, surely belonged to memories of a golden age. Sundays shone especially. For, not only was the entire white population even more at leisure than usual, but every square, or green, or wide part of the road contained an African dance in full swing. All day, and most of the night, they danced, dressed in their best. The air vibrated with their drumming, clapping, stamping and the rhythms of their song.

Now, these Elysian scenes suggested more a thin disguise over appalling obscenities. Stedman's legs were covered with huge boils he could not get rid of. 'Oct. 8, 1773,' he wrote in his *Journal*. 'Crawl out and see the selling of my dear Joanna and the whole plantation' to an agent of a merchant of Amsterdam at a very reasonable price, on account of the rebel situation. He was reduced almost to hysterics: 'I fancied I saw her tortured, insulted, and bowing under the weight of her chains, calling aloud, but in vain, for my assistance.'

As it turned out, however, he had taken too extreme a view. His friend Lolkens, up to this a sort of trustee for the creditors of Mr D.B. the last owner, was appointed administrator of the estate for the new proprietor. Let his friend Stedman keep calm, he said. Joanna could stay in Paramaribo as long as he liked. No one was going to put her into a field gang. What use would she be there, anyway, being totally inexperienced in that kind of labour? He had the power to hire her to Stedman for the duration of the emergency and he would do so, cheap.

Stedman was cheered by these assurances. All his worries vanished in an instant and the boils abated. Soon, he was dining and dancing with avidity. His duties as commandant at Paramaribo did not interrupt him much, being mostly confined to sending up the rivers boatloads of those foods and comforts for which he knew, from hard experience, his comrades in the forest longed. But this could not go on. If he was ever to gain promotion and the money to buy Joanna with, he must rejoin Fourgeoud on active service.

Some of his acquaintance thought this excessive zeal. Why insist on going to his death? Having once miraculously survived a campaign, surely it was asking too much of providence to return. The governor himself pronounced, with all the authority of an old resident and participator at innumerable military funerals 'that what I was now going to suffer would surpass what I had already undergone'. Let him stay in town with Joanna and enjoy himself at the parties where he was in such great demand, on account of his good spirits, activity in the ballroom and capacity for gin. This sort of life was strenuous enough; many had found that to their cost. As for money, something would turn up. Opportunities would occur. It would be all right in the end.

'I nevertheless persisted in wishing to go,' he writes. For these seemed to him dishonourable counsels.

XV

WITH FOURGEOUD ON THE MARCH

On the 25th of October, 1773, he was ready on the quay with his luggage, complacently awaiting the arrival of a tent boat which, he had been assured, would be provided by the authorities to row him to the Wana Creek, a station further up the Cottica River, where he had been before. But, instead of the expected craft, 'I found a greasy yawl, with a few drunken Dutch sailors' who were going part of the way, they said. He would have to make his own arrangements after that. It appeared that the magistrates had decided to save the thirty shillings a tent boat would have cost.

Stedman flew into one of his rages. Were these the sort of skin-flints for whom he was to risk his life and certainly ruin his health! Nothing would induce him to get into this yawl. Many of the bystanders, who had come out of an adjacent public house on hearing the argument, took his side. A fight developed, during which 'hats, wigs, bottles and glasses flew out' of the tavern windows. The riot continued for hours to the great delight of all. Everyone concerned was able to pay off private scores. The black women loved this kind of disturbance and always actively assisted. The taverns of Guiana were also brothels.

In the end the problem was solved by four American captains, by good fortune anchored in the river. They offered to provide a boat and sailors, free of charge, the whole way to the Wana Creek. Stedman accepted gratefully. 'I can aver,' he remarks, 'that, notwithstanding the threatening rupture between Great Britain and her Colonies which seemed then upon the eve of breaking out into open violence, nothing could surpass the warm and cordial friendship which these gentlemen possessed not only for me, but for every individual that bore a British name, or had any connexion with that island; professing that they still retained the greatest regard for everything in Britain but its administration.' They were ready to start next day with the tide.

Everything now went swimmingly. A letter arrived to say that a friend on the River Commewyne, about half way to his destination, would lend a tent boat and slaves to transport him from that point. A large crowd assembled to see him embark outside the tavern. 'I shook hands with my Mulatto' and drank a farewell bowl of punch with the Americans, who had hoisted the colours on their ships and lined up the crews to give three cheers. Altogether, it was a very fine send-off.

Two days' hard rowing brought them to the jetty of the hospitable planter who was to provide the tent boat. With a grand gesture, worthy of his lamented father, he ordered, and paid for, twelve roasted ducks and thirty-six bottles of claret, though he could not afford either item. The oars did not dip with perfect regularity as they glided away on the ebb.

Stedman continued on into the wilderness, passing the three estates which had been burnt while he was at Devil's Harwar. At one, he landed and spoke to the overseer, who related the terrors of that night. The first thing he knew of the attack was that his house was surrounded and set on fire. 'In this dilemma,' he said, 'I fled to the garret, where I laid myself flat on one of the beams', hoping they would move off when the flames had caught hold of the ground floor, so that he could jump out of the window. But they still stood there, yelling and brandishing 'sabres and billhooks'. The moment came when he had to decide whether to be burnt, or hacked, to death.

He jumped and, by a miracle, escaped to the river bank and plunged in. It was well-known that he could not swim. 'They concluded me to be drowned', but he had managed to grasp the roots of a mangrove tree. He lay there, 'just so far above the water with my lips as to continue in a state of respiration. Having killed every other person, the rebels departed and I was taken up by a boat from my very perilous situation.'

There was not time to do more than congratulate the man on his good fortune, before again stepping into the boat and ordering the slaves to pull, but without the benefit of a rowing song. They were now in country where the rebels were known to be prowling about. The river was getting narrower and trees overhung it more closely. At night, they moored under the thickest branches and hoped for the best. Sentinels were posted, silence enjoined and everything went peacefully till three o'clock in the morning, when 'Quaco and myself were both suddenly thrown down from our benches by the boat all at once heeling upon its side'. The slaves immediately jumped overboard to swim for the opposite banks. Stedman cocked his pistol 'positively determined to defend myself to the last extremity' and shouted a challenge. No answer came, but the boat lurched again and he fell flat on his face. A manatee, or sea-cow, which had been having forty winks under the shelter of their hull, swam slowly away.

As soon as dawn broke, they hastened on. It was not safe to linger. Now they had entered a maze of dark and silent creeks. The oars sounded extraordinarily loud in the narrow, sluggish stream. At last, 'we discovered a smoak' which meant camp fire, friends, a clearing in the forest, other Europeans. On landing, they found a large quantity of salt beef, guarded by a few black rangers. Fourgeoud was marching through the woods and had not yet arrived.

During the three days' interval, Stedman carefully examined an armadillo and a porcupine and enquired into their habits, foods and general characteristics with a view to incorporating them in his projected history. 'I was now in excellent health and good spirits.' He also made sensible resolutions. He had, for instance, in the course of his illness, when his nerves were bad, said some very insulting things about his commander-in-chief. Even worse, he had written rude letters. His mother had so often warned him that his temper would be the ruin of him.

Now was the time to remember her advice. 'I determined by my active and affable behaviour, to make him my friend, if possible.' It was to prove uphill work. 'At length, the wished-for hour arrived; and being apprized of Colonel Fourgeoud's approach, I went half a mile from the camp to meet him.' His effusions met with a singularly cold bow.

The expedition settled down to a routine of patrols through the woods and swamps in search of rebel villages, or roving bands. They never met any and succeeded only in exhausting themselves. People began to fall sick. Quarrels arose out of nothing. The men murmured that the rations were not large enough. Stedman fought a duel because he was insulted by a German over a glass of wine. The rains came on, although it was supposed to be still the dry season.

It was decided to make a three day march to a military post

called Jerusalem, on the banks of another creek, in all respects similar to the Wana, except for a different name. Although they had been only three weeks on active service, the troops were sinking under fever, ulcers and malnutrition. Provisions never arrived on time. Medicines were ineffectual. The swamps became deeper and the camp turned into a marsh. It was impossible to keep the ammunition dry.

'I rose from my hammock soaked as in a washtub,' writes Stedman of this desperate journey. Breakfast was a glass of rum and a piece of biscuit so hard that it had to be chopped up with a hatchet. The fragments, on examination, were found to contain 'worms, spiders, gravel and even broken bottles'. But they ate them. The slaves were worse off. Besides carrying all the luggage, existing on half rations and sleeping in the water, as no hammocks were provided for them, they bore the brunt of everyone's exhaustion. Continually kicked and cursed, they staggered on with a most saintly patience. What could have been easier for them than to desert to the rebels? They had only to step aside into the impenetrable bush. Their masters were incapable of following them; incapable of fight, should the enemy appear. Fortunately, none did.

One day, the rangers caught a turkey which was stewed in an immense cauldron, together with everyone's mouldy biscuit. They ate it soaked to the skin and up to their knees in water and it was better than anything tasted at the feasts of Paramaribo, a town situated, it now seemed, in paradise, or else belonging to a dream of long ago. During the daily splashing trudge, people's thoughts had time to wander, to conjure up enticing visions of other days when life had seemed worth living; before one had been such a fool as to embark on this adventure in the hope of bettering one's prospects; days in which music had played a part.

Most of the Guiana birds, though beautiful, had no voice. But now the column was accompanied by two which 'sung so true, so soft and to such proper time that, in any other place, I should have been inclined to believe they were the performance of a human artist on his flute'. Like gay, incongruous spirits of the swamps, they hovered, near and far, all day. 'As I never saw either of those birds but imperfectly and at a distance, I can say nothing more concerning them than that they are frequently heard in marshy situations.'

On reaching their destination, fully half the army was ill and some had to be carried in hammocks by the slaves. Fortunately, the rain cleared off for the time being, as there was no accommodation at the post Jerusalem until the slaves had built some huts. The stores that ought to have awaited them had, for reasons not altogether explained, not arrived. 'Being now almost starving for want of provisions, we were most opportunely supplied by a quantity of fish . . . very plentiful in the marshes, where they were left by the retreating waters.' The ever busy slaves snatched them up in handfuls from the mud.

After five days' rest and boiled fish, during which many died, the indefatigable Fourgeoud, 'as invulnerable as a machine of iron, or brass', decided on a week's exploratory march into the surrounding forest from this point. Appointing Stedman commander of Jerusalem, he set off with the most able-bodied of his soldiers. The Negroes said he was mad. He would kill them all, one by one. It was impossible for the white human frame to stand such exertion.

However, the expedition proved quite a success. They actually made contact with the enemy, having chanced on three rebels armed only with hatchets and engaged in cutting down a cabbage palm. Fourgeoud was much elated by this victory and the return to Jerusalem was like a triumphal procession. The next thing, he said, filled with energy, was to march to the camp at the Wana Creek by a different route. One must be thorough. It was true there was still nothing much to eat, but this did not greatly trouble him. The men must get used to hard tack. That had been his principle from the very beginning. But they noted that he himself had taken the precaution of loading his private slave with a box of nutritious foods: it was essential for the commander-in-chief to remain on his feet, or what would happen to them, to Surinam, to all Guiana, to the great merchants of Amsterdam who depended on him for the preservation of their business interests?

Everyone's nerves were bad and unseemly quarrels, rivalries, jealousies broke out, particularly in the evenings, between the colonel and his officers, the slaves and the soldiers and generally

172

among all ranks. Yet, they trudged on intrepidly in the direction, as they believed, of Wana Creek. Who knew where these black guides were taking them, they thought, peering suspiciously at the few compasses they had. It was now raining again, twenty-four hours a day, and still Fourgeoud meticulously powdered his wig. The only time he seemed really alarmed was on looking up and seeing a snake leaning out of a tree towards him.

Somehow or other, they arrived at last in their camp. The sun came out. A barge appeared from Paramaribo with salt beef, letters and six gallons of rum from Joanna. Stedman presented a good part of the rum to his commander, for hard words had again passed between them and it was known that reports and recommendations for promotions were being compiled for dispatch to Holland. Vacant places in the hierarchy occurred every day as officers were rowed down to Devil's Harwar to enjoy the superior comforts of the hospital.

With rest and good weather, they might have recovered their health, but it was suddenly reported that a party of rebels had crossed the creek, just below the camp. On examination, clear signs of their passage were observed. The question was, in which direction? Most people were of the opinion that they had gone west, towards the coast, and the inhabited part of Surinam. On the contrary, said Fourgeoud, they had gone east, into the interior. He had no convincing evidence to support his view; nor did he bother to seek it. He simply ordered an immediate march eastwards.

They now entered a different sort of country. Passing out of the coastal belt of alluvial swamp, they came to rising ground and open savannah where herds of deer were grazing. It was easy walking and a delightful change after so much hacking through undergrowth. There were even signs of the rebels: a field overgrown with weeds; the ruins of a camp. Though one could scarcely feel one was hot on the enemy tracks, yet it was heartening to see something. The only lack in these delightful surroundings was water. No one took this seriously, as yet. It seemed hardly possible to suffer thirst in a place like Guiana.

They marched three days, the ground becoming drier every mile, until they found themselves in a region of rocks and sand dunes. Fourgeoud thought the only possible course was to go on in the hope of coming to a river, or at least a stream, or damp place where they might dig and find water. 'It was truly affecting to hear the poor soldiers lament for want of drink, but to no purpose.' The slaves were not quite so badly off as they knew of certain cactus plants which collected rain water into a reservoir at the base of the leaves. But there were not nearly enough of these to go round.

The weather continued serene. The heat was terrific and not a tree to cast a patch of shade was to be seen anywhere. 'During all this, some of the soldiers devoured salt pork, while others crept on all fours and licked the scanty drops of dew from the fallen leaves that lay scattered on the ground.' At the noon halt on the fourth day, it became obvious that they could go no further, 'the ground being strewed with distressed objects that appeared to be all of them in raging fevers. Despair now seemed to be impressed even upon Fourgeoud's countenance as he lay prostrate on the earth, with his lips and tongue parched black'. By a merciful dispensation of providence, the enemy continued perfectly invisible.

It seemed impossible that they would ever regain that wonderful haven of dampness and flood, the camp on the Wana Creek. But the thought of it gave them strength. The slaves carried some. Others were dragged by their comrades. Nothing seemed more delightful and comforting than the swamps when, at last, they plunged into them, 'fatigued beyond the power of description with these fruitless sufferings'.

Fourgeoud gave a celebration party to his particular friends with Joanna's rum. He did not invite Stedman, by whom he considered he had been once more grossly insulted. Luckily a boat had called during their absence with more rum, ham and biscuits from the faithful Joanna. There was also a letter from one of his mother's relations in Ceylon, declaring that if he came east a splendid fortune would be his in no time.

The camp was now attacked by dysentery and all military operations had to be suspended. Those who escaped the epidemic were covered with ulcers and skin diseases, made worse by their habit of never washing or changing their clothes until they rotted off them. The slaves tied vines tightly round their waists in an effort to alleviate the pains of hunger. It was not clear why there were never enough provisions for them to be issued with full rations. But so it was. They lived mainly on such 'seeds, roots, wild berries, etc.' as they had leisure to collect during the intervals of their labours. Many of them died during the epidemic.

Stedman escaped with a mild attack and a nasty swollen foot. 'I pass my time making baskets for the girl I love,' he notes in his *Journal*. These were the only presents it was in his power to send her. He also made drawings of plants and insects, some very strange and beautiful. The Negroes collected them for him, having heard of this eccentric habit and knowing he had a store of rum.

It was an austere existence. Everything was lacking: 'I had not so much as a trencher, bason, spoon or fork', let alone any medicine for his foot. It got dark at six in the evening and there were no lamps until he invented one by 'breaking a bottle, in which having melted some pork, it produced a quantity of oil and a slip of my shirt served for a wick'. Such were the commissariat arrangements in eighteenth-century Guiana.

When the dysentery had abated and the survivors were once more staggering about, the question arose as to how best to pursue the campaign against the enemy. Short patrols were resumed, without the least positive result. It began to seem clear that there were no rebels in the region of Wana Creek. Whether this was because they had been frightened off, or whether there never had been any, it was difficult to say with certainty. They had been three months in the woods and the rains were coming on in earnest. Fourgeoud decided to end the season with a march across country to the uppermost reaches of the River Cottica, where there was a small fort called La Rochelle.

'On the 4th of January, 1774, at six o'clock in the morning, all were ready to decamp.' The route lay across savannah and over a ridge of hills which, though not very high, were precipitous. For the next five days, they scrambled up and down, sometimes in deep gullies, at other times clinging to sharp and slippery rocks. Encumbered with the luggage, the slaves had great difficulty in keeping their feet. Illness and privation had weakened them and several fell down slopes and over cliffs. A number of their companions, feeling that this last task was really too much, put down their burdens when no one was looking and quietly melted away. Many of the soldiers must have wished they could follow suit.

It was this belt of country, stretching right across Guiana and marking the end of the coastal flats, which cut off the hinterland. The great rivers were not navigable any further and all beyond was unexplored, mysterious, a legendary place full of gold and silver, jewels, strange rich kings and numerous peoples. The Indians still recounted the stories they had told Sir Walter Raleigh, two hundred years earlier. It was part of their folklore. These dreams, so alluring and so frequently repeated, were difficult to disbelieve even in the eighteenth century, after many expeditions had failed to discover the least substance in them.

In 1714, the West India Company sent secret instructions to the Governor of Essequebo 'to seek exact information, but in as careful and guarded a manner as possible, concerning the nature and location of the towns of Lake Parima and especially also concerning Manoa or Eldorado, or the Golden City . . . and to establish a trade with them, with promises to bring them only such goods as they shall desire . . . The same shall be sold to them, or exchanged for gold or silver; and for no other monies than for gold and silver alone.'

Though nothing further is recorded of this grand project at that time, the vision of great riches, easily acquired, remained in everyone's mind. In 1739, one Horstman, an itinerant trader by profession, was fitted out and sent up the river with instructions to discover everything and prove or disprove the existence of Manoa, once and for all. But for reasons best known to himself, he deserted to the Portuguese in Brazil. It was a sad blow to Dutch hopes.

Yet, no one despaired. In 1746 miners had been sent to prospect among the sandy foothills over which Stedman and his friends were struggling in the wake of their indomitable commander. On their return, they reported that, though prostrated by illness and want, they had examined the mountains and were convinced that another three days' journey inland – that it had been quite impossible to perform – would have brought them to the famous crystal mountain that Sir Walter Raleigh had once glimpsed from afar, 'the top of which is full of brimstone and vitriol and almost covered below with crystals and beautiful veins of silver ore'.*

* Gravesande.

The local Indians had strongly advised them not to go near it as it was inhabited by a very powerful evil spirit.

There were also strange pyramids, extremely difficult of approach on account of devils, hostile Indians, exhaustion, distance and other problems not precisely specified. There was a trader who claimed to have examined one and seen a row of statues at its base. But his drawing of the site and his explanations were both so confused that it was impossible to make anything of them. He swore, however, that it marked the place of gold and silver mines and was full of the most terrible ghosts. He unfortunately died before he could be more fully questioned on the subject.

By 1766 the West India Company were a little sceptical – or, at least, some members were. Let the pyramids be surveyed and mapped, they wrote to Gravesande, 'not because we attach any belief to the stories which you inform us people are wont to relate about them, namely that near them, or under them, gold or silver mines exist, though this is not therefore impossible, but particularly because one might thereby make discoveries of much importance to the whole learned world and especially to all lovers of ancient history and to geographers'.

Gravesande did his best. All traders in touch with the Indian tribes were instructed to find out about the crystal mountain, the mines, pyramids, the unknown nations, cities, lakes, habits and circumstances of the country beyond the rapids and waterfalls. He never received anything except excuses and vagueness, he reported to his employers in 1769, 'at one time that there was high water; at another that the natives were at war; and at yet another something else'.

Perhaps the question would never be definitely answered. All one could say was that odd emeralds, diamonds and bits of crystal had turned up; that gold dust was certainly washed down from somewhere in the mountains; that metals of different sorts were in the rocks. One could detect their presence in the water. 'It was so impregnated with minerals,' said Stedman of one mountain stream from which he drank, 'that it tasted almost like that of Bath, or the German Spa'. For the rest, they discovered nothing more extraordinary than an abandoned camp and 'a very curious piece of candle which the rebels had left behind, composed of bees-wax and the heart of a bulrush'.

At last they reached the military post La Rochelle, 'such a display of meagre, starved, black, burnt and ragged tatterdemalions and mostly without shoes or hats, as I think were never before beheld in any country'. Plain hunger troubled him to such an extent that, seeing a black woman sitting down to some sort of a banana mash, he pressed half a crown into her hand and snatched the plate away.

A good deal revived, he entered the encampment: 'Here we found a set of poor wretches ready to enter the woods which we had just left and destined to undergo in the same manner the severest misery that ever was inflicted on sublunary beings.' It was most cheering to reflect that others were now to endure the 'ringworm, dry gripes, putrid fevers . . . horse-flies, wild bees and bats, besides the thorns, briars and alligators . . . burning hot days, cold and damp nights, heavy rains and short allowance'.

Everyone had surely earned a holiday. It was suggested to Fourgeoud that the regimental funds might provide the soldiers with a change of diet and a suit of clothes. Many, including Stedman, had only half a pair of trousers left. 'But he replied that Hannibal had lost his army at Capua by too much indulgence.' However, a day or two later, some were given leave to go to Paramaribo.

Stedman immediately jumped into a tent boat with five companions. It was like being posted to heaven. There was much to be said for those religions where the hereafter was represented as one long round of feasting, dancing, drinking and love. Only persons well rested and thoroughly gorged could question the standards of Paramaribo, or regard 'the astonishing supper-appetites betrayed by some of the Dutch females',* with anything other than the greatest approbation.

'Scarcely had we taken our seats,' the good Dr Pinckard continues censoriously, 'before my fair neighbour requested me to help her to a glass of claret, of which I found a full bottle standing between us'. She also required him 'to cut her food into small pieces ready for the fork', because she had sprained her wrist. It was, perhaps, fortunate that he was too over-fed to do more than toy with a course or two. Soon, the claret was empty and he had to get her a bottle of Madeira. 'With this her eating was in no

* Pinckard.

degree at varience, for she commenced by forming a solid substratum of two heavy slices of fat ham, after which I helped her to no less than fourteen other dishes', not counting fruits and sweets. Sometimes, it was true, she would bestow a tasty bit on the slave girl standing behind her chair, and some of the sweets went on to a plate under the chair, in case she should feel in need of them later. But, even deducting these items, Pinckard exclaims: 'Such a supper I had not before seen swallowed by man, woman, or anything in human shape!'

To this divinity, the famished Stedman and his friends rowed down the River Cottica as hard as the slaves could be persuaded to pull, 'all night and day, shouting and singing', particularly after they had passed Devil's Harwar. For there they intercepted a barge containing twenty bottles of claret, four gallons of rum, tea, biscuits and a barrel of butter, sent by Joanna and others. The butter and ten bottles of wine, they dispatched to La Rochelle to comfort those left behind.

There was not a drop left two days later as they staggered ashore at Paramaribo, 'a band of such scarecrows as would have disgraced the garden or field of any farmer in England'. News of their coming had preceded them. Friends crowded round to welcome these ghosts from another world. 'I next sent for my inestimable Joanna, who burst into tears the moment she beheld me.' Rumours had reached her that he had died in the swamps.

XVI

THE GOLDEN AGE

Stedman immediately took up the round of feasting, dancing and dining which had been going on without intermission during the whole of his frightful adventure in the woods. Apart from finding shoes most uncomfortable after so long walking barefoot over every sort of ground, he recovered his vigour very rapidly. Continual large meals restored his figure to a proper rotundity. Struck by his air of sleek alertness, 'a certain lady, whose husband had shown me extraordinary civilities, now made me an offer', and was much incensed by his refusal. He was put to a good deal of trouble over this unfortunate incident, as she spread the most abominable stories about him all over the town.

However, the interlude did not last long. The indefatigable Fourgeoud, still scouring the forests of the upper Cottica, had actually made contact with some rebels. There had been a skirmish in which he had rather got the worst of it. This redoubled his martial zeal. The enemy should be exterminated. He would march and counter-march through swamp and desert until not one runaway slave dared show his face in the vicinity of the plantations. More he could not achieve with the forces at his command, that dwindled every day from the innumerable diseases with which they were afflicted. He himself remained indomitable, in spite of his sixty years. It was due to 'a medicine he called *tisan*', invented by himself. Every day he drank an enormous basin of the mixture 'as hot as he could bear it'. The constituents were 'jesuit's bark, cream of tartar and stick-liquorice, boiled together'. The taste was so horrible that no one cared to join him, despite the magical effect it seemed to have on his constitution.

Under these circumstances, every able-bodied man was required on active service. Within three weeks of his arrival at the capital, Stedman was preparing to embark for a plantation called L'Esperance and take command of a camp guarding the River Commewyne. An old hand now at campaigning in the wilds of Guiana, he at once began collecting all those comforts, such as medicine, candles, drink, biscuits, tea, that made the difference between a tolerable life and almost certain death in the forest from misery, undernourishment and general debility.

To be posted to a plantation, moreover, was a great piece of good fortune. One would be in touch with civilization. Food could be regularly got hold of and proper quarters built. Patrols were not nearly so arduous when one had a dry place to return to and a tasty dinner boiling over the fire. It was with a certain cheerfulness, then, that he stepped 'on board a decent tent-boat rowed by six negroes, having once more bid adieu to my dear Joanna', on 17th February, 1774.

Passing up the Commewyne, which wound through much the same area as the Cottica, though slightly westward, he was charmed by the prospect. The estates were beautiful and peaceful. Half way up there was a nice protestant church. He thought it scarcely possible that the future could contain much hardship. On arrival at L'Esperance, things wore a less rosy face, but this was mainly due to lack of organization. The camp had been established at a place where it was inundated completely by the spring tides and marshy at all times. 'The officers were all crowded in one apartment' thatched with palm leaves. The plantation house was vacant, but the overseer would not take it on himself to give permission for the army to use it. The general level of health was rather low.

A little energy and resolution worked wonders. Stedman soon had the slaves building a proper Dutch system of dykes and sluices to control the tides and as many more thatched huts as were necessary to give everyone a room of his own. 'About a cannon-shot higher up the river is the estate Clarenbeek, where I went . . . to examine the state of the hospital.' Here too, conditions were worse than they need have been 'owing chiefly to the amazing number of rats . . . destroying the men's clothes and provisions and running over their faces by dozens as they lay in their hammocks'. The only remedy seemed to be to gather up the enormous quantity of empty bottles lying everywhere and 'string them like beads upon the lashings of each hammock . . . When this was properly done, their polish rendered it impossible for the rats to reach the canvas'. He could not think of any way of preventing the depredations on clothes and food.

Returning thankfully to L'Esperance, 'I became daily more charmed with my situation'. The enemy remained in the outer wilderness where Fourgeoud sometimes saw them clearly enough to take a pot shot; and at other times only heard their voices shouting insults and roaring with sarcastic laughter at his efforts to come to grips with them. The latter tactic was particularly discouraging and difficult to bear. For Stedman, the prospect was very much more pleasing: 'Respected as the prince of the river; caressed by the neighbouring planters, who plentifully supplied me with presents of game, fish, fruit and vegetables', he occupied his time in observing wild life, making drawings and notes for his book. 'I had very few wishes unsatisfied,' he writes.

Even these were reduced quite soon. 'One day . . . I was surprised by the waving of a white handkerchief from a tent-boat that was rowing up the river; when to augment my happiness, it unexpectedly proved to be my Mulatto, accompanied by her aunt,' Lucretia, making for the estate Fauconberg to which they belonged. As this was only four miles above L'Esperance, they had decided to move in there, instead of remaining at Paramaribo.

As he had no pressing duties, Stedman jumped into the boat and went with them. They were welcomed by a host of friends and relations, including Joanna's grandfather, a venerable and blind old slave who presented his grandson-in-law 'with half a dozen fowls'. For the rest, he was not much inclined to converse, merely stating that 'he was born in Africa, where he had once been more respected than any of his Surinam masters ever were in their country'.

The world now seemed a wonderful place to Stedman. He had 'an elegant tent-boat with half a dozen negroes at my command'. His health was good, his leisure long. He spent much time being rowed to Fauconberg, sleeping there almost every night. This was the right way to put down a rebellion. Why kill yourself stumbling through forests with nothing to eat? It was so much more sensible to settle down on an estate and enjoy oneself. It kept the enemy off equally well. It was not as if there was the least hope of defeating them fully, since they refused to engage in a battle. Only one thing marred the delightful days: the overseer at L'Esperance could not be prevented from beating the slaves in the most abominable manner. The fact that his victims could not safely murder him, on account of the presence of the military, encouraged his excesses: one or two died.

Nevertheless, 'upon the whole, I was here so happy and so much respected, that I could almost have engaged never more to change my situation'. Except for the overseer, the hospital full of rats only partially defeated by the ingenious system of suspended bottles, it was like living in a fairy tale with a princess of the woods. Sometimes his friend Lolkens paid visits to Fauconberg, for which he was still responsible to the new owners in Amsterdam. Why did Stedman not have his wife with him at the camp? Let the slaves put up a nice little thatched house for the two of them. Now was the time also to write to Joanna's proprietor and enquire her price. It was necessary under Dutch law to have the written consent of the previous owner if one bought a slave with the object of emancipating her. Lolkens himself would second his friend's request, recommending Joanna as a suitable candidate for freedom.

Everything was quickly arranged. 'Never two people were more completely happy.' Joanna grew more beautiful each day. The sense that they lived on borrowed time, that this enchanted woodland existence could not last, intensified their pleasure. They took walks, noting strange trees and plants. They bathed and ate and made love. Occasionally the war made a brief appearance: several barge loads of soldiers landed one day, on their way downstream 'and behaved so very disorderly as to oblige me and my officers to knock them down by half dozens'. But they went away the same evening and peace descended again. Even the arrival of Fourgeoud and the exhausted remnant of his men was not very disturbing, for they fixed their camp at another plantation, nearer the hospital. It remained 'the golden age of my West Indian expedition'.

He wrote poems in honour of his incomparable mulatto and reflected generally on the mental capabilities of slaves which had, he thought, been underestimated considerably. 'Amongst others' too numerous to mention, there was the famous 'Phillis Wheatley, who was a slave at Boston in New England' and who not only learned Latin, but composed 'thirty eight elegant pieces of poetry on different subjects which were published in 1773'. True, Joanna could not yet emulate these feats, but her conversation was so fascinating that he never tired of listening to it. Then there was that impressive old man her grandfather: what sort of career might he not have had in his own country, had he escaped the misfortune of being sold?

She had a great number of relations, some very interesting to meet. One day, she turned up with her Uncle Cojo, 'a stout black', previously a rebel, on account of the treatment meted out to him by the bankrupt Mr D.B. Now, he wore 'a silver band on which were engraved these words: True to the Europeans'. He was a cheerful person, full of anecdotes about his adventures on the run. In particular, he related the story of an attack on a plantation by Jolycoeur, another relative, 'the first captain belonging to Baron's men and, not without cause, one of the fiercest rebels in the forest'.

This furious slave had descended on the neighbouring estate of New Rosenback, now in ruins. Led by Baron, the raiders suddenly emerged from the woods and seized the overseer, 'one Schults . . . who formerly was the manager of Fauconberg'. Having plundered the house, they then began feasting and dancing, Schults lying on the ground meanwhile, 'only waiting Baron's signal for death'. In this painful situation, he recognized Jolycoeur. 'Remember Mr Schults, who was once your deputy master,' he cried despairingly. 'Remember the dainties I gave you from my own table when you were only a child, my favourite, my darling among so many others . . . and now spare my life.'

Jolycoeur, mad drunk with killdevil, dancing, freedom and revenge, replied that what he chiefly recollected was the rape of his mother by Schults. So saying, 'he severed his head from his body with a hatchet at one blow; with which having played at bowls on the beach, he next cut the skin with a knife from the back, which he spread over one of the cannon to keep the priming dry'. Having related his story with animation, Uncle Cojo departed as agreeably as he had come, leading by the hand a little girl, one of Jolycoeur's daughters, he said.

Fourgeoud's camp was on this very estate of New Rosenback and there he had found, on arrival, the remains of Schults. The troops 'were melted down to a very small number', all more or less ill. It was impossible to continue the campaign actively. After an official visit to Stedman, during which he behaved most genially to Joanna, the redoubtable old colonel sailed for Paramaribo and a well earned holiday.

At first, Stedman's Utopian life seemed to continue as before. But, as so often happened in Guiana, bad omens for the future were observed. Alarm guns were heard in the distance one evening. Next day news of an attack on a plantation came down the river. However, the slaves had proved loyal and the rebels were obliged to retire into the woods after a sharp skirmish. Another boat came up the river with messages to the effect that a number of dissatisfied slaves in Paramaribo had planned to join the rebels, 'after first having massacred all the inhabitants'. Fortunately, 'they were detected and the ringleaders executed'.

The blackest sign of all, as Stedman thought, was a letter announcing the sudden death of Joanna's owner in Amsterdam. This meant that Fauconberg would be sold again. The negotiations for his wife's purchase and manumission would have to start from the beginning once more. Who knew whether the amiable Lolkens would still be in charge of affairs? What sort of hands might she pass into? He feared the worst. In addition, she was pregnant. The idea that his first child was to be born a slave seemed to affect him more strongly than anything. He became very depressed and began drinking, although Joanna did what she could to cheer him, saying they ought to look on the bright side and no doubt their fortune would take a turn for the better. For they had certainly enjoyed good luck so far. It was almost impossible for persons blessed with luck – that intangible magic quality – to come to a bad end. Anyone who had studied the subject of augury and divination would tell him so.

Yet, it preyed on his mind to such an extent that he became a perfect nuisance in the mess. Everyone was sick to death of his gloomy face and grumblings. Why, they said impatiently, each one of them had as many black girls as he fancied. None could swear to the exact number of his offspring. Nor was it necessary. 'If our children are slaves,' they remarked with reasonable exasperation, 'they are provided for; and if they die, what care we should they be d-n'd in the bargain? Therefore keep your sighs in your own belly and your money in your pocket, my boy, that's all.' In the case of any other girl except Joanna Stedman might have agreed with them, downed a gin, given the mother a nice present and forgotten about it.

Perhaps on account of drink, low spirits and a restlessness which made him swim backwards and forwards across the river until fatigued, he developed a fever. It did not seem severe, however, and in a few days he was convalescent, 'sitting with Joanna before my cottage'. One of the doctors attached to the camp appeared and 'after having felt my pulse and examined my tongue, he declared without ceremony that I should be dead before the morrow, unless without further delay I made use of his prescription'. His manner was so abrupt and certain that Stedman meekly swallowed the mixture.

Almost immediately, he fell flat on the ground, as if dead. The doctor was greatly surprised. Joanna called four slaves to pick him up carefully and put him on a mattress. He showed no signs of coming round, even though the doctor 'put blisters on several parts' of his body. The patient must have unfortunately died, he remarked 'and suddenly left the plantation', on his way ordering a grave and coffin to be prepared forthwith. The next day, they came to bury him, but Joanna made such strong protests, insisting that he was not dead at all, that they went away again.

Left to her own devices, Joanna knew what to do. She sent to her Aunt Lucretia at Fauconberg for a supply of the proper remedies for poison. She bathed him in vinegar and prepared a special invalid wine. She prayed fervently to Stedman's God and also, one must assume, to those African divinities whose help was generally found efficacious in these circumstances by the slaves. She had money to pay for the necessary invocations and we cannot suppose that she neglected any proved form of treatment in her desperate straits. Despite all efforts, he remained perfectly motionless until the fourth day when, on opening his eyes, he saw 'poor Joanna sitting by me alone and bathed in tears, who begged of me at that time to ask no questions', for fear of a relapse.

It was a whole month before he could stand. A special chair was constructed and two slaves deputed to carry him out in it for airings. He was not fit for service until seven months later and during most of the time was so feeble that he could not even perform the light duties connected with the camp. The doctor was eventually sacked for incompetence and sent back to Holland in disgrace. It is not recorded how many soldiers he killed before this extreme course was taken.

Stedman's recovery was much impeded by his state of nerves over Joanna. Together with her aunts, uncles, grandfather, sisters, brothers, cousins, a multitude of lesser relations and all the other stock on the estate, Fauconberg had again been sold. The faithful Lolkens did not know the new owners and was not continued as administrator. However, he said, he and Mrs Lolkens would be happy to take Joanna to their house in Paramaribo so that she could have her child in the easiest possible circumstances. They both accepted the kind offer with gratitude and Joanna embarked immediately.

Returning alone to his cottage, the disconsolate Stedman began drinking in earnest. Not that it helped much, as he remarks. For, though considerably cheered up during the intoxicated period, he felt worse than ever afterwards. Everything conspired to make him take a dismal view of this golden country where supreme happiness seemed to hover always just beyond one's grasp. 'A marine drowned himself, in one of those phrenzy fevers which are so common in Guiana. About the same time another soldier was shot by order of court-martial. Thus perished those men who were spared by the climate or the enemy.' The overseer at L'Esperance indulged himself in the joys of flagellation to such an extent that the slaves became desperate, even though the troops were living in the middle of them and they could not hope to escape very far.

He accepted an invitation to join a party at a neighbouring estate, thinking it might distract him. But he could not shake off his melancholy and crept away to sit 'by myself on the small bridge that led to a grove of orange trees, with a settled gloom on my countenance'. In this romantic spot, deliverance came. 'Mr De Graav, the proprietor' found him thus and began the following oration – or so it seemed to Stedman, recollecting the scene in later years as he wrote his book in Devonshire: 'Sir, I am acquainted by Mr Lolkens with the cause of your just distress. Heaven never left a good intention unrewarded.' Continuing in this formal manner, he explained that he was to administer Fauconberg for the new purchaser and that nothing would give him more pleasure than to make himself useful to Stedman and 'the virtuous Joanna, whose deserving character has attracted the attention of so many people, while your laudable conduct redounds to your lasting honour throughout the colony'.

These were his sentiments, whatever his actual mode of expressing them may have been. 'No angel descending from above could have brought me a more welcome message', was his guest's instant reaction. 'The weight of a mill stone was removed from my labouring breast . . . I felt I should yet be happy.' They left the retired bridge amongst the orange trees and rejoined the party, the rest of the 'day being spent in mirth and conviviality . . Nor did we separate or cease feasting up and down the river' for the best part of a week. The amiable 'De Graav having bought some new slaves, gave a holiday to all the negroes on his estate', so that they might welcome the newcomers properly and make them feel easy in their changed life. The strange African rhythms of drum and chant, of clapping and stamping formed an exotic background to the European minuets performed in the planter's drawing-room.

It was more than a background, for it drew the ladies and gentlemen from their ballroom to the slave compound. They came to laugh at barbarism and to enjoy the lascivious movements of the black dancers who, 'instead of being fatigued, become more and more enlivened, and animated, until they are bathed in sweat like post-horses, and their passions wound up to such a degree that, nature being overcome, they are ready to drop into convulsions'. It was impossible to deny the power of such dancing: the civilized variety seemed, by comparison, a sickly imitation of the real thing.

But the Elysian interlude could not last long. In the woods, behind the drums, Fourgeoud continued his strenuous patrols. Sometimes he fell on a stray rebel and killed him; or stumbled into a clearing planted with yams and burnt it; or heard of murders done further up, or down, the river and arrived when all was over, the enemy vanished, as usual into the silent darkness of the forest. News of the outer world came infrequently, percolating thinly by means of the barges loaded with salt beef. The commander still refused to allow any other sort of rations to be issued, on the grounds that his remaining men – about one-fifth of the original force – must not be softened and rendered unfit for harsh campaigning by luxuries such as medicine, back pay, 'the many hogsheads of wine sent from Amsterdam, together with scores of kegs containing preserved vegetables', paid for and shipped by that city in the belief that 'the poor emaciated and languishing troops' would benefit. Some of these provisions went mouldy and no one, except Fourgeoud, knew what happened to the rest.

Yet, in other ways, he discharged his duty superbly. Very few planters had actually been murdered. The great mass of the slaves remained quiescent, whether from fear, indifference, or loyalty. The rebels launched no attack on Paramaribo. Only on isolated estates, far up narrow creeks, was it unsafe to visit. For the rest, the life of the colony went on as usual and this was due to Fourgeoud's incessant activity and alertness. Though he could not defeat the rebels, he drove them to the conclusion that their best course was to retreat further into the hinterland and live there as independent tribes, trading for the European goods of which they felt in need. But a five years' expedition and the death of almost all the volunteers was needed before this bare compromise was reached.

XVII

JOANNA MORTGAGED

In January 1775, reinforcements arrived from Holland. Four-geoud was now encamped at the headwaters of the River Commewyne. From this base, he was determined to launch a new campaign which would finally drive the rebels into the mountains of the interior. So far, he had not made much impression on them, despite intense activity. Raids on plantations were rather more frequent than they had been the previous year. But he was not dismayed. Before all the fresh troops died of exhaustion and disease, he would have performed his task. Grateful colonists would shower him with money and honours. The West India Company, even the Prince of Orange himself, would see that he was suitably rewarded for his immense labours in their service, carried out at very modest expense, when one considered the present and potential value of Surinam – and also of Berbice, Demerara and Essequebo, since these small colonies could not last long if Surinam were overrun.

Inspired by visions of future prosperity as a hero and saviour, he ordered the reinforcements to embark immediately and row up the Commewyne to the post Magdenberg, situated on a narrow creek, under a hill, far from any house, plantation, or cultivated ground. Stedman was now well enough for active service and prepared to accompany the expedition. He had become one of the oldest and most experienced officers by the ruthless process of natural selection.

He set his affairs in order, as well as he could, by writing to his wife's new proprietor, who also owned his son, born at the end of 1774. He had promised his faithful boy Quaco to buy him, too, and give him his freedom. How he was to come by the necessary funds was not yet clear, but he had great hopes that it would become so in the near future. He was making small extra sums by doing portraits. For the rest, he trusted to divine providence and said an affectionate farewell to Joanna, who was bathing the baby in wine and water, provided by Mrs Lolkens; this was considered in Guiana the best preservative against the many illnesses fatal to infants in that climate. There was just time, before the barges sailed, 'to partake of a feast' with the other officers at the house of a hospitable planter, 'by whose command (to crown the banquet) half a dozen negroes continued blowing the trumpet and French horn in the room where we dined, till the company were absolutely deafened by discordancy and noise'.

Now the woods closed round them. 'Magdenberg, which is about a hundred miles from Paramaribo, was formerly an estate, but has now not a vestige of cultivation left, a poor old orange tree excepted.' The ground was not swampy, for they had passed to the fringe of the forest belt. On the contrary, it was dry and sandy, with shells scattered over it. Perhaps here the elusive riches of Guiana might be found: 'I have no doubt but gold and silver mines might be met with if the Dutch would be at the expense and persevere in making the discovery.' Diamonds and agates had sometimes been picked up in these parts, the impecunious Stedman brooded. How many jewels would buy him Joanna and little Johnny?

He never found any. It seemed as if there was a curse of futility over the whole country which drew men down and destroyed them. 'I have as good a master and mistress as I could wish and a family of my own that I much love,' said an elderly Negro, trying to explain how it was that he had been moved to attempt suicide. 'I had slept sound during the whole night till about four o'clock in the morning when awakening, I took my knife to pick my teeth with it, and instantaneously cut my throat, without knowing why.'

The woods were full of magical influences; for there the Indians lived their secret life. They had totally rejected civilization, being unable to see any sense in it. The only work they did was to hunt, fish, build temporary huts, plant a little cassava and bananas, make enough extra baskets and eathenware pots and hammocks to trade for knives, beads, hatchets, looking glasses, rum. When these tasks were done, they lay down to rest, or got drunk. They did not want clothes, preferring to paint themselves red. Wigs, coats, shoes, hats, appeared to them eccentric and unnecessary. They despised the Negroes greatly for labouring in the fields. The sight of soldiers drilling on a parade ground excited their contempt.

Europeans and their way of life filled them with profound in-difference. One could walk round a village, poking, prying and staring and they would behave as though one were invisible. 'We were anxious to see them at their different employments and, therefore, hastened from hut to hut in the idea of coming on them before their occupations were interrupted by the curiosity which we thought it probable might be excited from the unexpected arrival of a party of clothed strangers among them. But on this head we need have had no anxiety. Not an individual suffered any interruption from our presence . . . We passed through their huts and around their persons in a manner unnoticed . . . Whether on their legs, whether seated or lying in their hammocks, so they remained, no observable change being induced by our visit.'*

One could even descend on them at midnight without causing them to do more than partially to open one eye. 'Desirous of witnessing their mode of sleeping in their native dwellings,' the industrious Pinckard continues, 'we . . . without hesitation entered the house and advanced with our light close up to their hammocks.' In one he discovered 'a naked Indian man: over the sides of the other were hanging several legs and arms and two heads . . . We rambled about until 3 o'clock.'

The only person who showed the slightest interest in their arrival was one 'Vandyke, a hardy old Dutch soldier', living among the Indians as a trader. 'Nothing could exceed his sur-prise, on waking at the dead of night and finding a party of officers armed and in scarlet uniform, standing at his bedside . . . It was with difficulty that he gave credit to his senses or believed that he was actually awake.' He had adopted many Indian customs, including polygamy, but their inscrutable calm was beyond him.

Even on visits to the towns, their mysterious gravity did not desert them. Appearing unexpectedly in their canoes, sometimes with live parrots and monkeys for sale, they would land and state their terms of business. Their scale of values was not calculated on any European system. They might insist on a hatchet for some object; or they might take a fish hook. It depended on what they stood in need of at that particular moment. 'We made it a settled experiment,' says Pinckard scientifically, 'to rouse them from that

* Pinckard.

fixed apathy and indifference which form so striking a feature of their character.'

The naked guests willingly entered the house and sat down, the women, 'two upon a chair . . . with their backs towards us'. They did not respond to any sort of conversation, nor evince the slightest curiosity in their surroundings. One 'who appeared to be very old' – but one couldn't be certain – carried a pierced reed, like a flute. Thinking he might be musical, they played Mozartian airs on 'the German flute'. He appeared to listen, somewhat, though evidently considering his own music vastly superior. Drums and bagpipes, even when 'played unexpectedly below the window where they were sitting' had no better effect. They heard the noise, one could tell that much, but did not trouble to get up and look out. 'Rum possessed the only charm,' Pinckard found. 'Of this both men and women drank glass after glass as fast as it was given them.'

As suddenly as they had come, the Indians would get into their canoes and paddle off into the forest. They had no fixed destination, as their villages were only temporary. No one could tell when, or for what reason, they might embark, leaving their huts to fall down. Each family had a boat large enough to contain all its members and their possessions. When they reached a spot which seemed to them appropriate – it was impossible for an outsider to say why – or on which they had determined from the beginning, they would put up a new village in a few hours.

It is not surprising that these mysterious people were credited with secret knowledge and occult powers. People felt that extraordinary and very profitable revelations would follow, if they could only be induced to speak. It was certain that they knew the location of Manoa, of innumerable gold and silver mines, the meaning of the strange pyramids and statues that were sometimes glimpsed in the distance by itinerant traders. They had a fund of legends and stories concerning witches, ghosts, and other spirits with whom their priests had commerce: during certain ceremonies, two distinct voices could be heard conversing while the wizard swung his rattle rhythmically. It was not easy, even for an Indian, to make out what they said and this added greatly to the import of the utterance.

They were dead shots with the bow or blowpipe, and made

such powerful poison for the arrows that the slightest wound caused instant death. Even a drop on the skin was dangerous, 'as I once unluckily experienced', writes Dr Bancroft of one of his numerous experiments in this line. 'When stirring a parcel of human blood poisoned therewith, a drop accidentally fell into my left eye; and tho' I immediately plunged my head into the River Demerary, by the side of which I was standing, it nevertheless excited a painful inflammation, which continued for several days.'

They knew also of narcotics that, sprinkled on the river, caused all the fish in the vicinity to float up to the surface, intoxicated. Their medical reputation was high. As they could not be induced to part with the secret of their mixtures, sick white people were sometimes to be found receiving treatment in their villages. One seldom saw an Indian out of sorts. They appeared to enjoy long life and perfect health, never taking to their hammocks until death was near.

Funerals provided one of the few emotional occasions their sense of fitness allowed. During the whole process of washing the body and preparing it for burial under the floor of the hut 'they never cease uttering the most terrible cries and screams'.* Once the corpse had been safely interred, the evil spirits scattered and the right songs chanted to speed the departed on his journey to the other world, they began dancing and drinking until their strength gave out.

The most macabre experience of the forest was to meet these people assembling for the annual festival of the dead. 'At this time, all who have died since the last solemn feast of that kind are taken out of their graves . . . Some appear dry and withered; others have a sort of parchment upon their bones; some look as if they were baked and smoaked, without any appearance of rottenness; some are just turning towards putrefaction; whilst others are swarming with worms and drowned in corruption.'†

Fully dressed in nose plugs, lip plugs, feathers, paint and beads, the Indians converged from all directions with these corpses on their backs. The ceremonies were long, culminating in the re-interment of the dead, followed by the usual eating and

* Fermin.
† Bolingbroke.

drinking and what seemed to the earnest Bolingbroke to be sports, or games, 'in the spirit of those which the ancient Greeks and Romans celebrated upon similar occasions'.

To these haunted woods repaired Stedman and his commander, determined to kill runaway slaves and thus earn the money for a comfortable retirement to Europe. Fourgeoud swore 'that not a soul should be exempt from duty, provided they could but stand on their legs'. Now was the time to bring the campaign to a successful conclusion, he cried. For the rainy season was upon them and there were no fruits or wild vegetables to be picked in the forest by rebels whose camps and stores had been discovered and burnt.

They began an endless series of patrols, slithering over the spongy ground, taking their direction from the compass. Fourgeoud marched at the head of his dripping column. 'His dress consisted of nothing but a waistcoat, through one of the buttonholes of which he wore his sword; on his head he wore a cotton nightcap, with a white beaver hat above it and in his hand a cane; but he seldom carried his musket, or his pistols. I have seen him all in rags and bare-footed, like the meanest soldier.'

Sometimes they traversed 'deep and dangerous marshes, up to our breasts in water and in very heavy rains', where monkeys amused themselves by pelting them with nuts and 'broke the head of one of our marines'. At other times, they 'passed over very high mountains, by many supposed to be pregnant with treasure'. Though they saw remarkable trees of the most beautiful colour and grain, white squirrels with red eyes, lizards, chamelions and many strange birds, the enemy remained perfectly invisible. The troops sickened and died at a great rate, as they were allowed no relief until too weak to keep upright.

No matter. It was all to the greater glory of the survivors. In return for the loan of fifty pounds with which to buy the slave boy Quaco, Fourgeoud asked Stedman to give him 'various drawings representing himself and his troops struggling with the hardships annexed to the service they were sent on'. These, the old man cunningly said, would 'shew the Prince of Orange and the States a specimen of what he and his marines did undergo in the forests of Guiana', for very poor reward.

Perhaps fortunately, Stedman damaged his ankle and was, for some months, unable to walk. He became commander of the base camp at Magdenberg. The enforced leisure in this comparatively healthy spot restored his strength. As there was nothing much to do, he worked on the notes and drawings for his projected book. If Fourgeoud really managed to drive off the rebels in this campaign, they would soon be returning to Holland. There was not a moment to be lost. He made wax figures of Indians, Negroes and planters and gathered 'a little collection of natural curiosities', with a vague idea of 'exhibiting to the public, if it should be my fate evermore to return to Europe', and of making extra money to pay for Joanna. He had still not heard from her new owners how much she was going to cost, but knew it would be a substantial sum, particularly with young Johnny included.

Occasionally news would come from Paramaribo, winding through the forest on a provision barge: Joanna was well; or not too well; or, the baby was recovering nicely from a touch of fever. Faint echoes of the tremendous arguments then being conducted in North America and, indeed, all over the world, would come floating up the sluggish creeks along with hogsheads of salt beef.

These international problems also turned on the question of money. It was becoming more and more expensive to defend the Americans from the French in Canada and from the Red Indians, with whom they refused to live in amity, though economically urged to do so. The continual increase in the number of Americans meant more judges and other officials whose salaries had to be paid. The large smuggling trade prevented the customs from producing any great increase in revenue. The English government therefore thought itself perfectly justified in introducing extra taxes. Whoever heard of a colony causing the mother country to be out of pocket? The whole colonial idea was intended as a sound business investment, bringing in a proper dividend. Trade and manufacture were regulated solely with this object in view. The tax on tea and the Stamp Act seemed most reasonable in London.

But it was a fatal mistake: 'I can by no calculation justify myself in placing the number (of colonists) below two million ... of our own blood and colour – besides at least 500,000 others,' declared Edmund Burke in Parliament in 1775. 'You ought not in reason to trifle with so large a mass of the interest and feelings of the human race.' It would be much more sensible to give them their financial independence and remain their friends. The American trade was too valuable to throw away for the sake of an outmoded theory. 'Every man now plainly sees that we shall never be able to retain the Americans in due and constitutional Subjection . . . but at such an Expense both of Men and Money as would, in the Event, prove our Ruin,' wrote Josiah Tucker, Dean of Gloucester.

This was the crux of the matter, and the Americans knew it. Not only would they be better off if they had full control of their own money and trading arrangements, but they were strong enough to insist on it. A short study of the philosophers, particularly Locke, showed how justified, in the highest sense, were their feelings of outrage and oppression. The various theories of the noble savage, the rights of man, natural law, the social contract, the inalienable sovereignty of the people in the last resort, were all, they felt, strictly applicable to their situation. If one regarded politics in the strong light of reason, it was plain that George III could by no means substantiate his claim to order American life and business.

The picture of these sturdy artisans and farmers defying the might of a corrupt England in the name of liberty, became immensely popular in Europe, particularly in France. When Benjamin Franklin visited Paris in 1776 in order to persuade the French to enter the war on the American side, he was welcomed as a hero and saint. Medals, snuff-boxes, handkerchiefs, hats, cloaks and bits of china were decorated with his portrait. Innumerable parties were given in his honour. Poems were written and his membership sought by learned societies; for he had invented the lightning conductor.

A very sickly light was cast over the revolutionaries by some enthusiasts: 'They say that in Virginia the members chosen to establish the new government assembled in a peaceful wood, removed from the sight of people, in an enclosure prepared by nature with banks of grass.'* Here, they held elections, guided purely by the light of reason and the spirit of democracy and liberty. Others, more robust, were revolted by such stuff. 'How

* M. R. Hilliard d'Auberteuil, *Essais Historiques et Politiques sur les Anglo-Américains.*

is it,' shouted Dr Johnson in a frightful rage, 'that we hear the loudest yelps for liberty among the drivers of negroes?' The mere mention of America was enough to set him off. 'Upon one occasion,' Boswell relates, 'when in company with some very grave men at Oxford, his toast was: Here's to the next insurrection of the negroes in the West Indies.' It became impossible to discuss the American question with any profit in his presence. If one did, 'the change was great', Boswell noted sorrowfully, 'from the calm philosophical discussion in which we had a little before been pleasingly employed'.

These agitating blasts and counterblasts reverberated only distantly beyond the woods of Surinam, where all one's thoughts were concentrated on the struggle against disease and exhaustion. Fourgeoud would appear among the trees at intervals, a nightmare figure of determination at the head of his remaining men, many of whom were carried on the backs of slaves, like Indian corpses coming to the feasts of the dead. Finding his deputy busy drawing insects, fruits, butterflies, rats and fresh-water fishes, 'he requested me to paint his portrait at full length in his bush equipage'. This also, he would send to his employers in Amsterdam, and he had no doubt that an immense engraving would there be made of it. 'He thought himself now as great a man as the Duke of Cumberland was in England after the battle of Culloden.' Perhaps he was greater. The rule of Bonnie Prince Charlie would surely have proved milder than that of Captain Baron and Jolycoeur.

'I began to delineate this wonderful character in his own hut. While I was now looking full in his face . . . the whole mountain was suddenly shook by a tremendous clap of thunder, while the lightning actually scorched the Colonel's forehead; and, what is very curious, broke all the eggs under a hen that was sitting in a corner of the room where we were engaged.' This was certainly a portent of some sort, but they did not allow themselves to be distracted. 'The hero's features being re-composed, I proceeded, and the picture was completed in a short time after, to his great satisfaction.' He would, he said, use his influence in court circles at The Hague to further his friend's prospects.

Soon afterwards, news came up the river that a party of the West India Company's troops had actually discovered a rebel village near the seaside, a hundred miles from Magdenberg. They had waded through a swamp and thought to demolish the place, but the defenders had sallied out and beaten them off. The camp was galvanized. At last there was a definite objective and they could cease their aimless stumbling through the woods. 'Orders were immediately issued for all the troops that were able to march to keep in readiness. The black rangers were particularly delighted at the prospect of a real fight. Yet, for reasons not easily explained, two months passed before they attacked.

Meanwhile, they moved down river, leaving Stedman behind; for his damaged ankle had mortified and he could not stand. Then he got a fever and was given up for dead, being saved only at the last moment by an old Negress who poured boiled buttermilk down his throat which so far revived him that, next day, they put him on a barge for Paramaribo. Halting at Fauconberg on the way, he intercepted presents of beef, tongue, drink and an attractive pointer dog. There was also a letter from Amsterdam saying he could have Joanna and Johnny for 'near two hundred pounds sterling, a sum I was totally unable to raise', especially as he already owed Fourgeoud fifty pounds for Quaco. But he thought that if he lived on bread and water for two or three years – a regime he contemplated with perfect equanimity – he might be able to save enough.

All Joanna's relations at Fauconberg gathered round the invalid, expressing the greatest sympathy for the low state to which he had been reduced, giving him what small presents they had and recommending courses of treatment. 'Oh, that I could have but found a sum sufficient to purchase every one of their freedoms,' was Stedman's sad thought, as he handed out the beef, the tongues and gallons of assorted drink he had just received.

Once arrived in Paramaribo and taken in hand by the capable Joanna, his health improved rapidly. He became almost entirely recovered after meeting a certain rich Mrs Godefrooy, who had been very much taken by his romantic predicament and the financial complications that threatened to bring it to a sad end. Here was a fine young warrior, very personable in many ways, daily risking his life for the sake of everyone in Surinam, brought into a state of melancholy and despair for lack of a mere two hundred pounds. She would fix it. Heaven should be within his grasp at the flick of her pen. What was the loan of two hundred pounds without security to her? 'Go immediately, Stedman,' she is represented as saying, 'go and redeem innocence, good sense and beauty from the jaws of tyranny, oppression and insult.'

These were her words, or something very similar. 'Seeing me thunderstruck and gazing upon her in a state of stupefaction without the power of speaking,' Stedman records, 'she continued with a divine benignity: Let not your delicacy, my friend, take the alarm and interfere in this business.' He did not. Thanking her as well as he could in his excitement, he rushed home to tell Joanna the news. She was overcome with joy; so were all the aunts, uncles cousins, sisters, nephews and nieces with whom the house was full. It was the unanimous opinion, however, that Stedman would be well advised to make Joanna over to Mrs Godefrooy as security for the debt. He tried to protest that his benefactress had imposed no such conditions on the loan, but they were adamant. They had their reasons, as slaves and black people. 'Thus, I instantly drew up a paper, declaring my Joanna, according to her desire, from this day to be the property of Mrs Godefrooy, till the last farthing of the money she lent me should be repaid.'

The scene at the good lady's house was most affecting. 'Then come here, my Joanna,' she cried with the utmost enthusiasm. 'I have a spirit to accept of you not as my slave, but more as my companion: you shall have a house built in my orange-garden, with my own slaves to attend you, till Providence shall call me away, when you shall be perfectly free.' She rounded off this splendid statement by producing two hundred pounds. Nothing could demonstrate more clearly the sound judgment of Joanna and her dark relations. If Stedman died and the debt was never paid, she would have a benevolent mistress.

He put the money into his hat, which seemed to be the most convenient receptacle and hurried round to Mr de Graav, the administrator of Fauconberg, who, not to be outdone by a mere woman, 'on counting the money, addressed me in the following terms: Stedman, two hundred florins of this sum belong to me as administrator. Permit me also to have a small share in this happy event by not accepting of this dividend.'

It was a miraculous day. Seizing the rebate, he tore back to Mrs Godefrooy. The debt was now only one hundred and eighty pounds. He would certainly redeem his darling in the near future. He felt convinced of it. His luck had turned. Fourgeoud had promised to speak for him to the Prince of Orange. All his illnesses had vanished away. He would rejoin the expedition and take part in the final glorious battle, now imminent, when the rebels would be exterminated, for the major part, and their broken remnants driven into the high wastes where lay the magic Lake Parima.

XVIII

THE LAST CAMPAIGN

Fourgeoud was now on the Cottica, poised for the offensive at the very spot on which Stedman had shot a boa constrictor at the conclusion of his first campaign. He arrived just in time. They were 'ready to start the following day. I never saw the troops in such fine spirits or so eager for service; which proceeded from different motives; . . . some in the hopes of plunder, some from revenge on the rebels and some from a wish to see the war at an end.'

On their side, the rebels were equally excited. They held an all night party and 'continued shouting and hallooing' until dawn. Undisturbed by the noise, a large jaguar padded through the camp. But it did not stay to eat anyone. It was difficult to determine the precise significance of this apparition.

The army started at first light and managed to force a way through the undergrowth for 'about eight miles, which is a great distance in this country'. There was no sign of the enemy, but the mosquitoes were so bad 'that I saw the poor men dig holes with their bayonets in the earth, into which they thrust their heads, stopping the entry and covering their necks with their hammocks, while they lay with their bellies on the ground. To sleep in any other position was absolutely impossible', unless one had sufficient nerve for heights to sling one's hammock at the tops of the trees. A friendly slave advised Stedman to do this. It would be well above the mosquito level and also much more airy, he said.

The march continued thus for about a week. Besides the usual ants, lice, horse flies and so on, they were greatly incommoded by enormous hairy spiders of very hideous appearance and ferocious disposition. Everyone was covered with boils and poisoned sores. They negotiated quicksands where one suddenly sank up to the arms and had to be dragged out with difficulty; and quagmires that swallowed one up in a second, if nobody was close enough to seize one by the hair. The only signs of the enemy's presence were occasional yells of derisive laughter from among the trees.

However, they persevered and eventually came to 'two old cassava fields', an inspiring sight, since it indicated their near approach to the rebel headquarters. Here, the redoubtable mulatto Captain Bonny commanded. He represented an independent army, quite distinct from that of Captain Baron and Jolycoeur. Some of his followers were cannibals. As Fourgeoud and his men emerged from the last swamp on to the beach before the village, they saw the half eaten remains of the West India Company troops who had been defeated.

Passing through these grisly outworks, they came in sight of the village, 'in the form of an amphitheatre, sheltered from the sun by the foliage of a few lofty trees, the whole presenting a *coup-d'oeil* romantic and enchanting beyond conception'. Before it was a large field of rice strewn with tree trunks, behind which the rebels lay, taking careful aim. Fortunately for the troops, they had run short of bullets, being obliged to substitute pebbles, metal buttons and coins. But they were confident that, even so, they would give a good account of themselves. For they had taken steps, by means of spells and incantations and by amulets, to render themselves invulnerable.

A confused fight developed. To the noise of firing was added the shouting and swearing of the troops on the one hand and, on the other, wild yells and invocations and blasts on trumpets. At the end of an hour, the rebels found that their invulnerability had been cancelled out by superior white magic of some sort. 'A rebel captain, wearing a tarnished gold-laced hat and bearing in his hand a torch of flaming straw . . . set the town on fire.' The whole place was instantly in flames. Under cover of the smoke, the rebels fled over the swamp behind by a secret path, the only way of crossing without rafts. Their pursuers were brought up short.

An examination of the ruins showed that all food and other valuables had been taken into the woods when it was known that an attack was imminent. There was no loot except a few stolen spoons and forks and a number of broken plates. This was a disappointment to the soldiers after their labours. The black rangers, however, greatly enjoyed a prolonged game of bowls with the heads of dead rebels. To all protestations they flatly replied that it was 'the custom of their country'.

The enemy seemed not in the least discouraged by defeat. During the night, they began a shouting match with the rangers, the most terrible abuse 'resounding through the woods, which echo seemed to answer with redoubled force'. They let off their guns and 'insulted each other by a kind of war-hoop, sung victorious songs on both sides and sounded their horns as signals of defiance'.

Since it was impossible to sleep, Fourgeoud stood up and made an address. 'He promised them life, liberty, victuals, drink and all they wanted', if they would surrender. This provoked the most tremendous screams of laughter Stedman had ever heard. It was not worth wasting good gunpowder on such scarecrows, they bellowed, 'white slaves hired to be shot at and starved for fourpence a day'. Captain Bonny would soon be governor of Surinam and then things would look up a bit. 'After this, they tinkled their bill-hooks, fired a volley and gave three cheers.' As the sun rose, the forest grew silent again.

Everyone in the camp was exhausted by the night's festivities. What could one do with opponents like these? They behaved as though they had the victory. Fourgeoud was beside himself with rage 'on finding himself thus foiled by a naked negro . . . and swore aloud he would pursue Bonny to the world's end'. Many of his hearers thought this was not far off: there was hardly any food or ammunition left. The furious colonel would listen to no gloomy prognostications. Everyone would go to half rations, while a substantial party went back to the base on the Cottica for supplies. It would not take long, now that a path had been cut through the bushes.

This plan, too, the naked Negroes foiled by means of an ambush, shooting down from tree tops while the men were wading through a swamp. 'Nous sommes perdus!' exclaimed Fourgeoud, on receiving the news. He could not stay where he was with nothing to eat. To walk along a path in single file in woods full of marauding rebels was suicidal. A theatrical gesture seemed the only answer. Snatching up an empty bread box and holding it in front of him as a shield, Fourgeoud plunged into the surrounding swamp at the head of his men. They reached the Cottica without incident.

It was as if they had never won a victory. The supposedly defeated rebels were now cruising about in the woods, descending on plantations here and there as the fancy took them. Usually, they murdered everyone, set the place on fire and carried away as great a weight of valuables as possible. In few places were the slaves inclined to risk their lives in their owners' defence. The old routine of random patrols had to be taken up again.

While the first disastrous battles of the American war reverberated through Europe, Stedman noted: 'Some rebels taken. Discourse on the existence of mermaids. Heavy rains. Disease. Famine. Misery.' On bad mornings he would wake up streaming with blood, having been bitten by vampire bats. On good days, wild boar, or other small animals related to the rabbit family, would blunder into the camp and be instantly cut down, cut up and devoured. Once, Stedman, immersed in a private dream of happier times, found he had wandered from his companions and had not the slightest idea of how to rejoin them. All around, the woods were silent and every direction looked the same in the twilight under the leaves. Quaco burst into tears, certain that they would be eaten by jaguars, boa constrictors, or rebels. Suddenly, however, he recollected that the bark of the south side of the trees was smoother. This enabled them to set a course for the nearest river and so they were saved.

There were nights when darkness caught them in the middle of a huge swamp and they had to sling their hammocks above the water, hooking their guns on to the trees; while the slaves and provisions reposed on improvised rafts. Though the task would have been even more hopeless, they would at least have been more comfortable in the North American war. But the Dutch government refused a request for the return of the Scots Brigade for service against the disobedient colonists. They admired their republican principles too much, they said. Liberty was dear to them. Had they not freed themselves from the Spanish yoke two centuries before? Also, they dared not offend the French who were on the American side with the intention of weakening their real enemies, the English, and obtaining the advantage in as many parts of the world as they might.

'Where we are going, how we are going and what we are going about nobody pretends to conjecture,' wrote a young laird to his wife. 'Our whole force amounts to 2,600 men compleat, with which we can make but little impression on the

Continent of America.'* These were sentiments Stedman had very often experienced in the wastes of Guiana. But the war was being run from the far side of the Atlantic, where one could indulge in pious emotions, without being afflicted by reality. Thus, William Cowper wrote to his friend, the Rev. John Newton, once a prominent slave captain, now a devoted parson: 'The Americans who, if they had contented themselves with a struggle for lawful liberty would have deserved applause, seem to me to have incurred the guilt of parricide, by renouncing their parent, by making her ruin their favourite object and by associating themselves with her worst enemy.'

Or one could put forward all sorts of wrong reasons for opposing American demands, like George III. It was impossible to concede independence, he said, because the West Indies would want it also. 'Ireland would soon follow the same plan and be a separate State . . . and Shoals of Manufacturers would leave this country for the New Empire.'

Or one could permit oneself a plain fury. 'Dr Johnson attacked the Americans with intemperate vehemence of abuse,' Boswell noted sadly. 'Bursting into horrid fire, he breathed out threatenings and slaughter, calling them Rascalls – Robbers; Pirates.' The ladies present were astonished by the display. 'During this tempest I sat in great uneasiness,' says Boswell, fearing actual violence, fits, or even something worse.

These various hot voices shouted down the advocates of peace who pointed out that it was impossible to subdue the Americans, now become a nation and no longer struggling colonists dependent on a mother country. As a result, many men on both sides died needlessly.

In Guiana, too, the enemy was irreducible and fought for freedom from oppression and from tyranny. They had never read the philosophers, for they did not require any theoretical support of their tenets. Everyone knew what they were talking about and the reasons by which they had been driven to hold the opinions they had. The word liberty had an altogether more powerful connotation in their mouths than in those of the North Americans.

* See *The American Revolution Through British Eyes*, ed. Martin Kallich and Andrew MacLeish, 1962.

What was to be done? One could not march for ever round and round between the Cottica, the Commewyne, the Surinam. Special embassies were sent with large presents to the various independent tribes of Negroes, who were supposed to be the allies of the government. These people accepted the gifts very gracefully and made extensive promises of different sorts, but, somehow or other, never made definite moves to implement them. There were many reasons for delay connected with the weather, sickness, harvest, distance and the auguries. Yet, they were always so polite and genial.

The only part of the troops to remain in good spirits was the black rangers. Not only had they been promoted to their former African status of free warriors, but they had also taken steps to render themselves invulnerable by buying amulets from Graman Quacy, the most celebrated magician in Surinam. Born in Africa, now over seventy and slightly leprous, this unique individual early took up the profession of witch doctor, for which he had a vocation. His hypnotic manner was such that most of his spells worked, his prophecies seemed to come true and no thief was able to assert innocence before him. The Europeans began to remember his name. 'No crime of any consequence was committed, especially at the plantations but Graman Quacy . . . was instantly sent for to discover the perpetrators.' He was often well rewarded by grateful planters.

The gradual accumulation of money and a good name enabled him to buy his freedom. He set up in practice in Paramaribo where his services in the detection of crime were even more widely appreciated. He had also a medical reputation, having discovered, and marketed, a certain root, called Quaciae Bitter, that was found efficacious with fevers. But the solid foundation of his prosperity was his power as an African wizard, in touch with the ancestral spirits and gods of Guinea. No one except a fool would go on a journey, or into battle, without first buying one of Quacy's amulets, if he could afford it. The exceptional bravery and dash of the rangers was, in great part, due to his spells.

Even the most powerful incantations that money could buy failed to halt the rebel depredations. Reports were always conflicting. It was said they were starving in the forest and that Captain Bonny was dangerously wounded. Also that a large armed crowd had been sighted 'swimming across the River Cottica'. It seemed certain the supposed Negro allies were supporting them with arms and supplies. Most of the soldiers were delirious with fever and the vampire bats settled on them nightly.

Yet, sometimes, Stedman would be overwhelmed by a feeling that paradise was perhaps really situated in this haunted country. Emerging from the woods 'almost naked as well as starved, with a running ulcer in my left foot,' he found himself gazing over 'immense savannas of the most lovely verdure, interspersed with meandering brooks of water, cool and clear as rock crystal; their borders adorned with flowers of every lively hue and fragrance'. At such moments, 'when universal silence reigned everywhere around, how often have I thought on my *dear friend*, and wished with her to glide through life in these Elysian fields'.

Once, he even went so far as impulsively to ask the governor for a grant of land. Certainly, replied that amiable man. His friend could have 400 acres of forest free at any time. The colony owed it to him for immense services rendered. He drew an oblong on the map and made out the necessary deeds. But when Stedman afterwards reflected on the amount of capital needed to buy slaves, clear trees, plant the ground, build a house, he saw that this way out was not for him.

The matter became pressing. At Paramaribo in January 1776, Colonel Fourgeoud 'received letters from the Hague, with express orders to abandon the expedition immediately, and with his few remaining troops to sail for Holland without delay'. A new corps of free Negroes had been raised and this would have to suffice for the defence of the colony. It would be much cheaper and probably just as effective. Besides, the black constitution stood the climate and conditions infinitely better than men fresh out from Holland.

During his prolonged sufferings in the forest, Stedman's pay had accumulated. He had the fifty pounds owed to Fourgeoud for Quaco's redemption and something small towards the immense debt to Mrs Godefrooy for Joanna and Johnny. She would be quite happy to trust Stedman for the balance, said this wonderful creditor. Let him take his family with him to Holland now and send the rest when he could. But Joanna would not consent to the arrangement, saying that they could not honestly leave the debt unpaid with no security.

These were admirable sentiments and, no doubt, she meant them. Certainly, she was devoted to Stedman and the idea of a parting filled her with grief. There were, however, other substantial considerations. For she had reached an enviable position in the slave world. As a mulatto and the inamorata of a white man, she belonged to one of the top social grades recognized by slaves among themselves. She was now owned by the best kind of mistress; had a lower slave to do menial work in her apartments; was expected to perform only very light duties, such as standing behind Mrs Godefrooy's chair, or holding an umbrella over her during short walks on the quays. This left plenty of opportunity to earn money by trade, sewing, or whatever seemed most lucrative. She could thus, within a reasonable time, buy her own freedom, unless Mrs Godefrooy should die first, when she would be automatically emancipated in accordance with the provisions of that lady's will.

Slaves thus favourably situated were not always so keen on freedom as was expected by persons prejudiced in favour of natural rights, the equality of man and other theories propagated by European philosophers. Dr Pinckard made particular enquiries on this subject during his service in the West Indies in 1796. He found the Negroes, above all, practical. Who would give him food, clothes and medicine, if he were free, said one old man, long past work? He would starve without his master. The girls expressed a desire for freedom, but it turned out, on further questioning, 'that they thought it would enable them to find white lovers more easily. 'I have always discovered,' says Pinckard, disillusioned, that it was not from any just sense of independence; but from the mere desire of becoming the sultana of a white man, and being placed by him above the ordinary slaves of his house.'

To the question whether they would accompany the man who had bought their freedom to Europe, they replied with a decided negative. They would say goodbye to him and find another white lover. On being pressed for reasons, it appeared that the idea of leaving the enormous host of their friends and relations for a distant country where there would not be a black face to be seen except for their own in a mirror, terrified them. They had heard alarming stores of the customs in those far-off parts. Why should any sensible girl wish to leave a place where she was getting on well and making money, too? The moment of farewell would be painful, but such things passed. Everyone knew it.

Joanna never explained matters so frankly to Stedman. His romantic temperament and conception of ideal love made it impossible. She is represented in his narrative, therefore, as an extraordinary paragon of virtue and self-denial, refusing certain happiness from a strictness of principle amounting to inhumanity. Their separation would not be long, she said at last to comfort him. In a couple of years, at the most, their united efforts would find the necessary money to repay Mrs Godefrooy. He could not move her from this and left in a very depressed state.

Hoping to distract his thoughts, he went to a neighbour's house to see a collection of Indian curios. His eye chanced to fall on a bottled rattlesnake which roused the naturalist in him and he at once felt a little better. 'The head is dreadfully deformed, being flat and broad with two large nostrils near the snout,' he noted eagerly, 'and a large scale, or knob like the alligator above his eyes, which are jet black and sparkling.'

The transports now began loading in the river and every survivor of the expeditionary force strong enough to celebrate the end of his trials did so, day and night. 'But, on the 15th of February, by letters from Holland to our chief, our return was again countermanded for six months. My companions were therefore suddenly cast down with disappointment, while I was as suddenly revived, and now determined to save all my pay until Joanna's redemption should be fully accomplished.'

Fourgeoud had also made plans for self-improvement. Stedman's portrait of him and the drawings showing him as a suffering hero in the woods had already been sent to Amsterdam, where engravers had been set to work on them. But he was very much afraid that the governor had included uncomplimentary paragraphs in the official dispatches. Who could better dispel wrong impressions of this sort than the picturesque figure of the chief magician, Graman Quacy? Besides, his merits ought to be recognized. He was the backbone of the army. Fourgeoud arranged a round trip to The Hague and an audience with the Prince of Orange, during which he was instructed to enlarge affably on the colonel's virtues, high moral principles and unsparing exertions in the public service. At the same time, he was to point out that the present situation in the colony need never have arisen, had the governor been capable of efficiently discharging the duties entrusted to him. It is not disclosed what fee the old African required for this particular bit of wizardry.

The visit turned out a great success, as one would expect from an experienced magician. He received 'in a compliment from His Highness a broad gold-laced coat and hat, with a white feather, a large gold medal, a gold-headed cane and silver gilt hanger. The fellow had two chests of wine and all free.'*

Stedman now returned to his old camp at the estate L'Esperance. He had the cottage rebuilt, the sluices and dykes attended to, installed Joanna and Johnny, planted 'carrots, cabbages, onions, cucumbers, etc.', and looked forward to an indefinite period of happiness. The rebel situation was bound to be the same as it was now in six months' time. They might stay for ever. Promotion was certain. Everybody in the original force senior to him had died, except for the indestructible Fourgeoud. The camp 'was now a truly charming habitation, being perfectly dry, even at spring tides and washed by pleasing canals that let in the fresh water every tide; while the hedges surrounding the fields and gardens were neatly cut'. There was plenty to drink and all the men were healthy.

By midsummer 1776, Fourgeoud had had enough of burning odd ricefields and old huts once frequented by rebel gangs. Calculating that the impression made by his sorcerer envoy would be at its height, he wrote to Amsterdam saying he could do no more. The murders had decreased. The enemy appeared to have retreated. In July the answer came that they were to set sail for Holland.

It seemed like the final goodbye. The transports were again prepared and everyone embarked. Stedman took every penny he had to Mrs Godefrooy, who again urged him to take Joanna and Johnny, just recovering from an attack of convulsions. Joanna again refused, apparently from the most saintly motives: 'No persuasion could make the least impression on her, until her redemption should be made complete by the payment of the very last farthing.' The scene was made the more affecting by her

* Stedman's *Journal*.

sincere distress at parting with her lover.

The last presents for the voyage were sent on board, the last farewells said and drinks taken. They were to sail at dawn. All at once, a ship was seen in the mouth of the river. She was straight from Holland with a letter ordering the troops to disembark and re-engage the enemy until relieved by a new regiment. For Surinam was too valuable to be allowed to go to ruin, whatever the expense. It would be better to devote more of the profits to the garrison than to let the whole of Dutch Guiana revert to a wild country, inhabited by tribes of Africans and Indians.

'In the midst of this gloomy scene, the men were ordered to give three cheers' for the Prince of Orange. They refused. Threatened with court-martial and instant death, they remained obdurate. Only when promised twenty gallons of gin by an exultant Stedman would they consent to raise a feeble noise. The sick were allowed to sail. This was, actually, most of the force as only a small proportion had kept in good health at L'Esperance. Stedman took the opportunity to send presents to his mother and friends in Holland: 'a couple of beautiful parrots, two curious monkies, an elegant collection of fine butterflies, three chest of sweetmeats and some pickles'. None reached the recipients as the ship was wrecked off Ushant, and though the people were saved, all the luggage went to the bottom.

At this same time, Graman Quacy arrived back from his visit to Europe. In the new finery, which he now permanently wore, he 'looked, upon the whole, not unlike one of the Dutch generals'. He had cast such a spell upon his highness, he said, as to cause a law to be passed granting freedom to every slave taken to Holland six months after his arrival in the Texel. It was a supernatural achievement and raised his reputation among his countrymen to the heights of a true god. He was rather intoxicated by such concentrated success and became 'very proud and even frequently very saucy'.

It was ungrateful to complain, however. If Stedman could only induce Joanna to accompany him to Holland, she would be free in six months, and Johnny too, whether or not the debt to Mrs Godefrooy was discharged. He was beginning to feel that she would never consent and his anxiety on the subject was great. Wherever he looked, the most diabolical cruelties seemed to be taking place, as though there were some dreadful contamination in the air of Guiana.

From his window, he heard a lady 'give orders that a young black woman should be flogged principally across the breasts, at which she seemed to enjoy a peculiar satisfaction'. It was quite usual to see slaves jumping from top floors. On the parade ground and on the decks of ships, one could watch soldiers and sailors being beaten for being drunk, or impertinent, 'till their backs were black and swelled like a cushion'.

The number of murders was uncountable. Supposing his Johnny should be sold to a sadist when he grew older? There was nothing in the compact with Mrs Godefrooy to prevent it. He had once visited a plantation where the hospitality and entertainment were lavish, even by Surinam standards, but there was always someone beside the front door, tied to a stake and streaming with blood.

Very likely, Johnny would grow into a handsome quadroon youth, tall and strong like his father, beautiful, like his mother. He knew of a woman who had sent such a boy to Fort Zeelandia for specially severe punishment on a trumped-up charge. His real crime was that he had demurred at the idea of getting into bed with her. The fact that the whole story was common knowledge did not suffice to save the young man.

It was essential to arrange Johnny's manumission forthwith. This was no easy matter. First, one obtained the owner's consent. Mrs Godefrooy raised no objection. Next, bail for £200 must be found, in case the child should ever become a charge on the colony. Here, the good lady said flatly that such an undertaking was against her principles and nothing would induce her to do it. No assurance that Stedman would repay her, given time; or that it was a mere formality, since the child would eventually join his father in Europe, made the slightest difference. It was impossible for her to do it, she repeated to the astonished Stedman. All her instincts were against it. But her friend should not be upset. The governor was on his side. In special circumstances, the bail could be waived. He should at once apply in the official manner, 'without which formality, even if I had the bail ready to appear, nothing would be done in the course of business.'

Stedman was quite convinced that the governor would oblige him. How many times had he stood up for His Excellency against

Fourgeoud, even to the detriment of his own future prospects? Why, he and the governor were boon companions. The progress of his *History of Surinam* would never have been so rapid and comprehensive without His Excellency's assistance. Full of joyful expectations, he wrote out his request in the proper form and hurried round to the palace. To his 'inexpressible mortification', the governor put the paper 'in his pocket with one hand, while he gave me a hearty squeeze with the other; and shaking his head told me frankly that he would lay it before the court; but at the same time was perfectly convinced my boy must die a slave, unless I could find the necessary bail, which he was well persuaded very few people would wish to appear for'.

Such were the ups and downs of emancipation. Joanna begged him not to despair. She was quite certain their child would one day be free, she said, though without being able to give reasons for this belief. A couple of months later, events seemed to prove her right. An advertisement appeared urging anyone with objections to young Johnny's freedom to state them at once. Full of delight, Stedman rushed to his nearest friend to celebrate. There, he was laconically informed 'that the above was no more than a form, put in practice on the supposition of my producing the bail required'. Drink was the only answer.

Fourgeoud now felt that for the sake of appearances he should make one last sortie after the rebels. Everyone set out for the stronghold attacked on the previous expedition. The enemy were rumoured to be still cruising about in the vicinity, though some reports said they had fled over the River Maroni into Cayenne, where they could not be pursued. As usual, they discovered nothing, except one very tall old rebel with a white beard, dressed in a sheet who suddenly wandered amongst them, like a ghost, holding a broken cutlass in his hand. On realizing his mistake, he disappeared with amazing swiftness.

They then settled down in a camp on the side of a creek to wait for the reinforcements to arrive from Holland. Stedman was now a major and responsible for the punishment of defaulters, a task for which he felt not the least enthusiasm. The rest of his time he spent drawing and making notes assiduously. It really did seem that his time in Guiana must soon end.

By the first week of January 1777, the new detachments had

arrived by barge from Paramaribo. All the old hands now imagined that they would jump into these same boats and row for civilization. But no. They were to stay and teach the ignorant strangers the routine of the woods: how to get through swamps and thickets; to husband their resources, not so much in case of meeting the enemy as in order to remain alive and on their feet. The lessons were not altogether successful. 'Here one man was to be seen covered over with bloody boils from head to foot; there another led along by two of his comrades in a deep lethargy, who, in spite of pinching and pricking, dozed into eternity; a third swelled by the dropsy.'

At last orders came to leave their new friends to die on the banks of creeks in solitude: for the rebels were going through one of their elusive periods; no drums were heard, no insults shouted from amongst the trees. Yet, Stedman felt a little sad. His life had never been interesting until he came into this country; and it was never to be interesting again. 'Farewell once more ye shady woods, thou pleasing gloomy forest, pregnant with so many wonders and so many plagues, and which, in the opinion of so many sufferers, even surpassed the ten plagues of Egypt.'

As it would be some weeks before the final departure, Stedman hired 'a very neat small house by the water side', at Paramaribo and installed Joanna. They were still perfectly happy together, the only shadow between them being Joanna's inflexible resolve never to leave Surinam if it could be avoided. No more could Stedman cut himself off from Europe and stay in Paramaribo for her sake.

A great round of farewell parties began. 'Feasting and conviviality now prevailed once more at Paramaribo as on our first arrival.' Visitors came at all hours with presents for the voyage home. 'My provisions of live cattle, poultry, wine, rum, etc., etc., were almost sufficient to carry me round the globe.' Even Graman Quacy condescended to call. Invitations arrived from neighbouring plantations. 'Being invited to dine with his excellency the governor, I laid before him my collection of drawings and remarks on the colony of Surinam, which I had the satisfaction to see him honour with the highest approbation.' Seizing the opportunity, Stedman handed him a paper in which he pledged his word of honour – 'being all I possess in the world besides my pay' – that little Johnny would never become a charge on the state, if emancipated. The governor put this petition also into his pocket, squeezed his friend's hand with the greatest cordiality and promised to see to it.

Stedman did not now expect anything, but the governor actually stood by his word a fortnight later: Johnny was emancipated free of charge. It is not recorded whether he was swayed by pure humanitarianism, or by the high opinion he had formed of Stedman's literary powers. 'No man could be more suddenly transported from woe to happiness than I was at this moment, while his poor mother shed tears for joy and gratitude.' Many of his comrades in arms laughed heartily at all this hullaballoo over a slave baby. They did not waste their time or money on such boring subjects. 'Near forty beautiful boys and girls were left to perpetual slavery by their parents of my acquaintance, and many of them without being so much as once enquired after at all.'

At the end of this same month, March 1777, the transports were ready to sail. Everyone prepared to embark. The fatal moment of parting from Joanna had come. Seconded by Mrs Godefrooy and other friends, Stedman made one last effort to induce her to accompany him. But she replied steadily that her position was now such in Surinam that she would rather remain than go to unknown Holland, even though to say goodbye, probably for ever, was the most painful thing in the world. Having made this pronouncement, she fainted. 'At that instant – Heavens! what were my feelings! – Joanna's mother took the infant from her arms, the all-worthy Mrs Godefrooy supporting herself – her brothers and sisters hung around me crying and invoking Heaven aloud for my safety.' Even Fourgeoud, a curious bystander, appeared to be much affected.

All the ships were dressed in flags and all the guns saluted as they weighed and dropped down the river on the tide. On 1st April, 1777, 'with a fresh breeze at E. we put to sea and kept course N. and N.W.' The great adventure was over. Life had nothing much in store for him. 'Motionless and speechless, I hung over the ship's stern till the land quite disappeared.' Even under these terrible circumstances, however, he found it impossible to remain depressed for long. 'By considerable exertions, I got the better of my melancholy though not of my affection, and my mind became once more composed and calm.'

XIX

RETIREMENT

It was a strange sensation to return to Europe after a five years' absence. The cities looked so large and stately as they glided past on the canals. Everyone seemed overdressed in coats, boots and wraps of all sorts. The proletariat, in particular, resembled large bundles of dirty clothes. They stood on the decks gaping, 'nearly the colour of dried parchment by heat and fatigue; and so thin that we looked like moving skeletons'.

At Bois-le-Duc, they disembarked and collected their pay, which many spent on an immediate wild carousal. Those of a more saving nature purchased such small luxuries as cherries and early strawberries. They had often thought of these while starving in the forest of Guiana. But now they tasted insipid beside the memory of tropical fruits. Stedman bought a scarlet coat, a horse and fine livery for Quaco. 'I for the last time entertained my shipmates with whom without exception, I drank an everlasting friendship.' Some did not long survive their homecoming. One morning, soon afterwards, Fourgeoud was 'found dead in his bed, attended only by a negro, and was buried with military honours at The Hague'.

Stedman had great hopes of becoming a famous author if he could address himself to the enormous task of condensing his voluminous notes into a narrative and elaborating the best of his many sketches into pictures suitable for illustrations. The book would be not only the last word on Surinam, but also a monument to the great romance of his life and to the only adventures he had ever had that were worth recording. He still thought of Joanna constantly and wrote by almost every boat. Those days haunted him like a dream so vivid as to be more real than reality. He made a model where eighteen wax figures laboured, danced and sang 'on an island, supported by a crystal mirror and ornamented with gold'. This he presented to the Prince of Orange for his museum.

He preferred to keep those experiences as a golden dream. The

West India Company offered him the assistant governorship of Berbice, but he refused, on the ground that it would only last a few years and there was no pension attached. Berbice was next door to Surinam. He could have arranged for Joanna to join him. He gave away Quaco 'to the Countess of Rosendaal, to whose family I was under very great obligations; and who since, on account of his honesty and sober conduct, not only christened him by the name of Stedman at my desire, but promoted him to be their butler, with a promise to take care of him as long as he lived'.

In 1782, he married a Dutch lady. Wife had been merely a courtesy title for Joanna: it was impossible to enter into such a contract with a slave who had no legal rights and was not even recognized as a human being. 'In the month of August 1783, I received the melancholy tidings' that she had died during the previous November, thus finally sealing the past. Some said she had been deliberately poisoned, but nobody would swear to it. Little Johnny remained alone as a memento. Stedman sent for him and he arrived together with £200, the profits of his mother's business activities.

In 1783, also, the Scots Brigade came to an end. The Dutch were not now the allies of England, having entered the War of Independence on the American side, with France and Spain. It was thought best that the personnel should be incorporated properly into the Dutch army, becoming Dutch subjects. Any officer not wishing to do so was at liberty to retire to England, his pay being guaranteed.

Stedman decided to take this step. He was now a colonel and could sell his commission to a Dutchman for a good sum. Besides, he had always considered himself tremendously English, exactly like his father. The idea of abjuring his allegiance to George III was unthinkable. His brother did not share this prejudice, feeling that since he had lived all his life in Holland, it would be more sensible, as well as agreeable, to continue. Old Mrs Stedman, become very queer in the head, remained at Breda. Though she had welcomed him home with emotion, they soon began to get on each other's nerves as badly as ever. She was essentially a woman to be remembered in absence, rather than encountered in the flesh.

With his wife, baby and Johnny, Stedman removed to Devonshire, where the climate was supposed to be most suited to persons whose health had been undermined by hard service in the tropics. The remaining fourteen years of his life passed quietly. Sometimes the children were ill and he sat up all night with them. At intervals, there were feuds with the neighbours; or Mrs Stedman had hysterics after rows with servant girls; or, in a fit of nostalgia, they toyed with the idea of returning to Holland, though not seriously. Johnny grew up, entered the navy and was unfortunately drowned off Jamaica at the age of seventeen. The anniversary of Joanna's death always brought poignant memories. One of his daughters was named after her. His old enemy, Dr Stedman the philosophic uncle, under whose roof he had disgraced himself so long ago, died without direct heirs and he thus became the owner of a small Scottish property.

His only serious preoccupation during these years was the writing and publishing of his book on Surinam. This would lend his life significance. Those jewelled years, enshrined in print, would give him immortality. All sorts of people who had never met a slave, much less loved and married one, were talking, writing, voting and getting up subscriptions: the movement for the abolition of the slave trade was at its height and might, indeed, have been successful, had not the French Revolution made the words liberty and equality somewhat ambiguous. Stedman himself was against indiscriminate and total emancipation. He thought it would cause anarchy in the West Indies. His opinion had always been that a slave's position under a good master was more secure than that of the free wage earner, liable to be out of work and left to starve, especially in his old age. The proper course was to enact, and enforce, laws obliging owners to behave humanely.

The only way of making these truths self-evident was to write the full story of his experiences in Guiana, not omitting the dark places, endeavouring to convey the nightmare inconsistency of those marvellous days that tinged his thoughts perpetually. He would transmit no hearsay. As a retired person, securely pensioned, he was free to express his real opinion on all subjects. His plan was large and comprehensive. Besides his own adventures, he would include 'the History of that Country and . . . its Productions, Viz. Quadrupedes, Birds, Fishes, Reptiles, Trees, Shrubs,

Fruits and Roots; with an account of the Indians of Guiana and Negroes of Guinea'.

He read all the books then published on the subject in French, English and Dutch. His notes and diaries were voluminous, though not very legible since the day they fell into the River Cottica and were only just fished out in time by an obliging slave who dived after them. He set to work. How often in his early days he had dreamed of devoting himself to the intellectual life and might, indeed, have done so, to a certain extent, but for a fatal instability of mood. Now he had a subject of absorbing interest in itself and also very relevant to the great discussion of the day: were men born free and equal or not? How far did natural rights include black people? Was there anything morally wrong in the fact of slavery, or should one only object from humanitarian principles? Were Negroes actually human beings? Some of the most fervent abolitionists spoke as if they were deserving animals, dumb friends, or something of that sort.

All these considerations impelled Stedman to carry his work through to the end. Like many amateur authors, he found the labour far heavier than he had expected. To arrange the multitudinous events of a five years' expedition into a coherent narrative was difficult enough. To integrate his personal adventures with a careful account of trees, shrubs, reptiles and native customs proved impossible. Only an inexperienced writer would have tried it. Often, he allowed himself to be distracted from the task by trips to London, plays, dances, bawdy houses and ridiculous feuds brought on by the boredom of rural Devonshire.

Yet, he did not give up. Years passed. Johnny grew old enough to become a midshipman. The other children increased to the number of six. It was 1790 before he could negotiate for publication. This, for the eighteenth-century author, was an arduous and long drawn out business. He had personally to find a substantial list of subscribers. Stedman eventually secured 200 and the amount of correspondence involved was enormous. He wrote to every friend and acquaintance he had in England, Holland, Surinam, Demerara and Jamaica, where Johnny had made contacts during his brief naval career. Letters were sent to all well-known people. Some responded, such as Warren Hastings, the Archbishops of Canterbury and York, the Marquis of Bute and the Earl of

Bristol. He obtained permission to dedicate the work to the Prince of Wales.

Then there was the practical matter of seeing the book through the press. '80 elegant Engravings from drawings made by the Author' were to be included. Several engravers were engaged. Some made a hash of it. Others, William Blake for instance, worked superbly but would not answer letters. Stedman became quite friendly with Blake, whom he admired as an artist, and even dined with him, accompanied by his wife. He seems not to have noticed anything very extraordinary about his host on these occasions. Whether this was from inattention, or due to his having met so many queer people in his life, it is difficult to say. He did, however, realize that his drawings came out with a peculiar vigour when engraved by Blake, especially the ones depicting tortures.

The printers were definitely more troublesome than the artists, for they had literary pretensions. The text would be greatly improved, in their opinion, if the villains were made worse and the heroes and heroines more highminded. So they very liberally sprinkled the chapters with 'bawdy oaths, lies and preachings', Stedman furiously noted in his *Journal*. In addition, they toned down the dedication to the Prince of Wales, to make it more in line with certain democratic sentiments imbibed from France. It was May 1796, six years after the first arrangements had been made, before he could say: 'The printer writes me that all, all, all is well and printed to my mind and wishes.'

His health was now precarious. There was war with France again, but he could take no more active part than helping in a recruiting campaign. Joanna, Mrs Godefrooy, the governor, Colonel Fourgeoud and innumerable others, black, white and mulatto, remained as freshly in his thoughts as the day he said goodbye for the last time. He had perpetuated them in two quarto volumes and among the eighty elegant engravings, where they were much admired by many people: the book sold well and even was translated into French and German. The story of Joanna particularly caught the public fancy.

Life felt tame in Devonshire, the surrounding squires un-congenial. He read, with great attention, the voyages of Captain Cook and all his remarkable adventures with the kings and queens of the South Seas. Once, he happened to meet a man who had been present at Cook's murder on Hawaii beach. The captain could have been saved, this person swore, had everyone not panicked, jumped into the boats and left him wounded on the sand.

Though only 52 in 1797, Stedman's time was done. The bondage of Guiana seemed, in retrospect, a wild freedom, once enjoyed, now lost for ever behind the gentle rains and mists of the west country. He determined on one last, futile gesture. In a neighbouring churchyard lay the romantic figure of Bampfylde Moore Carew, a man of respectable parentage who took to the gipsy life, in spite of everything that anyone could say. He became a famous gipsy character, recognized as their king. Books were written, giving a highly coloured account of what must, in reality, have been a harsh and bleak existence. Yet, he had rebelled and never compromised; never retired to a country house with a wife, six children and full servant entourage. He had had the courage to remain outside, or so it seemed to Stedman. He directed that he should be buried next to Moore Carew, preferably at midnight. He died on 5th March, 1797.

BIBLIOGRAPHY

Anderson, M. S. *Europe in the Eighteenth Century*. London, 1961; New York, 1961.

Astley, Thomas. *A General Collection of Voyages and Travels*. London, 1745.

Atkins, John. *A Voyage to Guinea, Brazil and the West Indies*. London, 1737.

Bancroft, Edward. *An Essay on the Natural History of Guiana*. London, 1769.

Bolingbroke, Henry. *A Voyage to the Demerary*. London, 1809.

Boswell, James. *Journal of a Tour to the Hebrides with Samuel Johnson*. London, 1948; New York, 1961.

———. *Life of Dr Johnson*. Oxford, 1953; New York, 1959.

Calderwood, Margaret. *A Journey in England, Holland and the Low Countries*. London, 1756.

Cambridge History of the British Empire, The. 1929.

Cambridge Modern History, The. 1909.

Cayley, Cornelius. *A Tour Through Holland, Flanders and Part of France*. London, 1777.

Chesterfield, Earl of. *Letters to His Son*, ed. Charles Strachey. London, 1924; New York, 1937.

Churchill, A. and J. *A Collection of Voyages and Travels*. London, 1746.

Clarkson, Thomas. *The History of the Abolition of the Slave Trade*. London, 1808.

Collections of the Massachusetts Historical Society. Boston, 1792.

Coupland, R. *The British Anti-slavery Movement*. London, 1933.

Donan, Elizabeth. *Documents Illustrative of the History of the Slave Trade to America*. Carnegie Institute, 1935.

223

Edmundson, George. *The History of Holland.* Cambridge, 1922; New York, 1922.

Fermin, Phillippe. *Description Générale, Historique, Geographique et Physique de la Colonie de Surinam.* Amsterdam, 1769.

Gravesande, Storm van's. *Dispatches,* ed. C. A. Harris and J. A. J. de Villiers. Hakluyt Society, 1911.

Harleian Collection of Voyages and Travels, The. London, 1745.

Harpe, De la. *Abrégé de L'Histoire Générale des Voyages.* Paris, 1780.

Harris, John. *A Complete Collection of Voyages and Travels.* London, 1764.

Hassall, Arthur. *The Balance of Power, 1715–1789.* London, 1905.

Hickey, William. *Memoirs,* ed. Alfred Spencer. London, 1918; New York, 1921-25.

Hiss, Philip Hanson. *A Selective Guide to the English Literature on the Netherlands West Indies.* Netherlands Information Bureau, 1943.

Kallich, Martin, and MacLeish, Andrew (ed.). *The American Revolution Through British Eyes.* New York, 1962.

Lawrence, A. W. *Trade Castles and Forts of West Africa.* London, 1963; Stanford, 1964.

Mannix, Daniel P., and Cowley, Malcolm. *Black Cargoes.* London, 1963; New York, 1962.

Marshall, Dorothy. *English People in the Eighteenth Century.* London, 1956; New York, 1962.

New Cambridge Modern History, The. 1957.

Newton, John. *The Journal of a Slave Trader,* ed. Bernard Martin and Mark Spurrell. London, 1962.

Nicolson, Harold. *The Age of Reason.* London, 1960; New York, 1961.

Nugent, Thomas. *The Grand Tour.* London, 1749.

Owen, Nicholas. *Journal of a Slave-Dealer,* ed. Eveline Martin. London, 1930.

Palgrave, W. G. *Dutch Guiana.* London, 1876.

Palmer, R. R. *The Age of the Democratic Revolution.* Princeton, 1959.

Payne, E. G. (ed.). *Voyages of Elizabethan Seamen to America.* Oxford, 1900.

Pinckard, George. *Notes on the West Indies*. London, 1806.

Pinkerton, John. *A General Collection of the Best and Most Interesting Voyages and Travels*. London, 1813.

Plumb, J. H. *England in the Eighteenth Century*. London, 1963.

Pottle, Frederick A. (ed.). *Boswell in Holland*. London, 1952; New York, 1952.

Robertson, C. G. *England Under the Hanoverians*. London, 1934; New York, 1958.

Rodway, James. *Guiana: British, Dutch and French*. London, 1922; New York, 1922.

————. *The History of British Guiana*. London, 1891.

Stedman, J. G. *Journal*, ed. Stanbury Thompson. London, 1962.

————. *Narrative of a Five Years' Expedition Against the Revolted Negroes of Surinam*. London, 1796.

Stephen, Leslie. *English Thought in the Eighteenth Century*. London, 1881.

Watson, J. Steven. *The Reign of George III, 1760–1815*. Oxford, 1960.

Wesley, John. *Thoughts Upon Slavery*. London, 1774.

Williams, Basil. *The Whig Supremacy, 1714–1760*. Oxford, 1962.

INDEX

Addison, Joseph, 37

Africa, 13, 53; slave trade in, 63 f.; 102, 120, 123, 162 f.

Aix-la-Chapelle, Treaty of, 32

Amazon River, 56

America, North, 14, 26, 49, 63, 83, 99, 118, 168, 196 ff.

America, South, 38, 56

Amsterdam, 13, 20, 21, 43, 99, 119, 126, 166, 185, 189, 198, 210 f.

Amsterdam, Fort, 90, 94, 146

Araby, Captain, 103, 104, 105

Aristotle, 29

Australia, 13

Austria, 14

Austrian Succession, War of, 14, 32, 37

Baltic Sea, 13, 49

Bancroft, Dr Edward, 128, 130, 149 ff., 194

Baptists, 65

Barbados, 39

Barbot, Captain John, 60, 69 ff.

Baron, Captain, 107, 108, 114, 115, 117, 144, 184, 198, 203

Benin, king of, 75 f.

Berbice, 38 ff., 50, 51, 65, 145, 163, 190, 218

Bergen op Zoom, 12, 15, 33, 34, 114, 156

Biscay, Bay of, 52, 53, 55

Blake, William, 221

Boileau, Captain, 72

Bolingbroke, Henry, 89 ff., 101, 110 ff., 121, 125 ff., 139, 149, 195

Bonny, Captain, 203, 204, 207

Boreas, The, 55 ff., 136

Boston, 100, 183

Boston, Captain, 103 ff

Boswell, James, 11, 16, 19, 21, 22, 36, 40, 198

Bougsby, Alderman, 72 f.

Boxmeer, 41 ff.

Brazil, 13, 84, 176

Breda, 37, 48, 218; treaty of, 98

Bristol, 65

Burke, Edmund, 196

Calabar, 79

Calderwood, Mrs Margaret, 18 ff.

Canada, 196

Caramaca, 151, 158

Carew, Bampfylde Moore, 222

Caribbean Sea, 100, 102

Caribs, *see* Indians, American

Catherine, Empress of Russia, 28

Cayenne, 60 f., 88 f., 148, 214

Cayley, Cornelius, 18 ff.

Cery, 117, 146, 216

Ceylon, 13, 45, 174

Charles Edward, Prince, 15 f., 198

Charon, The, 146, 153, 154, 158

Chesterfield, Lord, 11, 23, 29, 30 f., 40

Clarenbeek, 181

227